CONSUMER RIGHTS
Issues and Challenges
Revised Edition

Edited by Yi (Tom) Cai
California State University–Northridge

Bassim Hamadeh, CEO and Publisher
Michael Simpson, Vice President of Acquisitions
Jamie Giganti, Managing Editor
Jess Busch, Graphic Design Supervisor
Marissa Applegate, Acquisitions Editor
Jessica Knott, Project Editor
Luiz Ferreira, Licensing Associate
Mandy Licata, Interior Designer

First published in the United States of America in 2014 by Cognella, Inc.

Trademark Notice: Product or corporate names may be trademarks or registered trademarks, and are used only for identification and explanation without intent to infringe.

Cover image copyright © 2012 by Depositphotos/Olena Vasylkova.
Interior image copyright © 2012 by Bob Hall at http://www.flickr.com/photos/houseofhall/8422489736/

Printed in the United States of America

ISBN: 978-1-62661-796-4 (pbk)/ 978-1-62661-797-1 (br)

www.cognella.com   800-200-3908

CONTENTS

CHAPTER 3: CONSUMER FRAUDS AND PROTECTION

CHAPTER 4: BUDGETING AND CREDIT: MANAGING YOUR MONEY

CHAPTER 5: CONSUMER MAJOR PURCHASES

CHAPTER 6: CONSUMERS IN THE GLOBAL MARKET

CHAPTER 7: SUSTAINABILITY AND CONSUMERS

INTRODUCTION

THE AMERICAN CONSUMER

This course deals with American consumers' economic issues. American consumers suffer from an economic down-turn, never have we seen so many laid-off workers, foreclosed houses, and skyrocketed debts since the Great Depression. In the early 1970's most families owed five percent of their yearly income to consumer debt, now the American family's debt is equal to about a third of their yearly income. Nearly half of the families with credit cards cannot afford even their minimum monthly payment. Fifty million Americans do not have health insurance. The American population in poverty has increased by 24% from 2007 to 2011. Many people criticize the middle class for having "brand-name fever," for shopping on credit cards, and "not living within their means." However, consider a typical Los Angeles family (if there is such a thing!), the husband and wife both work, earning a typical household income of $55,000. If they want to buy a typical house in the local community they would have to pay over half of their disposable income on mortgage related expenses, leaving very few resources for them to allocate to transportation, food, medicine, education, and others. Our desires for brand names and impulse consumption decisions are only a part of the problem. The economic environment in which we live and work, spend and borrow, enjoy and complain, is the other part of the problem. There is no doubt that this environment is very complex, but it is the one we have to face. This course introduces you to the subject of Consumer Economics and shows you how basic economic concepts and analytical tools can help you make sound consumer decisions. This reader is organized around a series of issues which a typical American consumer confronts. Each issue is explored in terms of:

- The research introducing macro-level background of the issue;
- The research exploring consumers' decisions on the issue;
- The choices facing the consumers and the analysis of their choices.

ABOUT MAYA AND JOHN

The packet includes a series of case studies that trace a period in the lives of an ordinary Los Angeles couple, Maya and John Lopez. They are not experts in economics or finance; they have no particular claim to fame or profusion. Rather, they are interested in living their lives and supporting their family. The Lopez's are not necessarily a typical family, but they have traits that are typical, just like us. They go to work; they come home, commuting through the highways each day. Their household income is the median level income. They have one child. They are bilingual. They can be thoughtful or impulsive, selfish or considerate, wise of foolish, serious or glib, efficient or wasteful. Similarly, like us they face the typical questions about allocating their economic resources and making economic decisions: where to live, whether to rent or to buy a house, what kind of cars to buy, how to balance their budget, and how to protect themselves from frauds and scams. Maya and John's experiences may help us see how the economic environment affects real American consumers and how the abstract concepts and principles help us make decisions. Keep in mind that it is not a question of right or wrong decisions as much as understanding how and why we make the decision under certain circumstances.

CHAPTER 1

ECONOMIC FOUNDATION
FOR CONSUMER DECISION

CHAPTER 1 INTRODUCTION

Everyone is a consumer, who has to buy food, clothing, gasoline, and many more scarce commodities in the marketplace. We are all making choices of what to buy, when to buy, how to buy, and from whom to buy, with our limited resources to satisfy our needs and wants. That is a definition of Economics. Understanding of the economic concepts, such as scarcity, demand and supply, and competition, may not be seen as vital as, say, getting a job after graduation or saving money for your first house. However, economics has an impact on every facet of our lives, including what you buy, where you live, and what you do for living. An understanding of economics can help you make better decisions about saving, investing, and consuming. It also helps you open your eyes to consequences of your behavior, make sense of international trades, discover the impacts of government policies on market and yourself, and all in all, become a better consumer. This chapter introduces the basic economic concepts and principles in a non-technical way and invites you to apply them to your everyday life.

THE POWER OF MARKETS

Who Feeds Paris?

Charles Wheelan

In 1989, as the Berlin Wall was toppling, Douglas Ivester, head of Coca-Cola Europe (and later CEO), made a snap decision. He sent his sales force to Berlin and told them to start passing out Coke. Free. In some cases, the Coca-Cola representatives were literally passing bottles of soda through holes in the Wall. He recalls walking around Alexanderplatz in East Berlin at the time of the upheaval, trying to gauge whether there was any recognition of the Coke brand. "Everywhere we went, we asked people what they were drinking, and whether they liked Coca-Cola. But we didn't even have to say the name! We just shaped our hands like the bottle, and people understood. We decided we would move as much Coca-Cola as we could, as fast as we could—even before we knew how we would get paid.'"

Coca-Cola quickly set up business in East Germany, giving free coolers to merchants who began to stock the "real thing." It was a money-losing proposition in the short run; the East German currency was still worthless—scraps of paper to the rest of the world. But it was a brilliant business decision made faster than any government body could ever hope to act. By 1995, per capita consumption of Coca-Cola in the former East Germany had risen to the level in West Germany, which was already a strong market.

In a sense, it was Adam Smith's invisible hand passing Coca-Cola through the Berlin Wall. Coke representatives weren't undertaking any great humanitarian gesture as they passed beverages to the newly liberated East Germans. Nor were they making a bold statement about the future of communism. They were looking after business—expanding their global market, boosting profits, and making shareholders happy. And that is the punch line of capitalism: The market aligns incentives in such a way that individuals working for their own best interest—passing out Coca-Cola, spending years in

Charles Wheelan, "The Power of Markets: Who Feeds Paris?" *Naked Economics: Undressing the Dismal Science*, pp. 3–29. Copyright © 2010 by W. W. Norton & Company, Inc. Reprinted with permission.

graduate school, planting a field of soybeans, designing a radio that will work in the shower—leads to a thriving and ever-improving standard of living for most (though not all) members of society.

Economists sometimes ask, "Who feeds Paris?"—a rhetorical way of drawing attention to the mind-numbing array of things happening every moment of every day to make a modern economy work. Somehow the right amount of fresh tuna makes its way from a fishing fleet in the South Pacific to a restaurant on the Rue de Rivoli. A neighborhood fruit vendor has exactly what his customers want every morning—from coffee to fresh papayas—even though those products may come from ten or fifteen different countries. In short, a complex economy involves billions of transactions every day, the vast majority of which happen without any direct government involvement. And it is not just that things get done; our lives grow steadily better in the process. It is remarkable enough that we can now shop for a television twenty-four hours a day from the comfort of our own homes; it is equally amazing that in 1971 a twenty-five-inch color television set cost an average worker 174 hours of wages. Today, a twenty-five-inch color television set—one that is more dependable, gets more channels, and has better reception—costs the average worker about twenty-three hours of pay.

If you think that a better, cheaper television set is not the best measure of social progress (a reasonable point, I concede), then perhaps you will be moved by the fact that, during the twentieth century, American life expectancy climbed from forty-seven years to seventy-seven, infant mortality plunged by 93 percent, and we wiped out or gained control over diseases such as polio, tuberculosis, typhoid, and whooping cough.[2]

Our market economy deserves a lot of the credit for that progress. There is an old Cold War story about a Soviet official who visits an American pharmacy. The brightly lit aisles are lined with thousands of remedies for every problem from bad breath to toe fungus. "Very impressive," he says. "But how can you make sure that every store stocks all of these items?" The anecdote is interesting because it betrays a total lack of understanding of how a market economy works. In America, there is no central authority that tells stores what items to stock, as there was in the Soviet Union. Stores sell the products that people want to buy, and, in turn, companies produce items that stores want to stock. The Soviet economy failed in large part because government bureaucrats directed everything, from the number of bars of soap produced by a factory in Irktusk to the number of university students studying electrical engineering in Moscow. In the end, the task proved overwhelming.

Of course, those of us accustomed to market economies have an equally poor understanding of communist central planning. I was once part of an Illinois delegation visiting Cuba. Because the visit was licensed by the U.S. government, each member of the delegation was allowed to bring back $100 worth of Cuban merchandise, including cigars. Having been raised in the era of discount stores, we all set out looking for the best price on Cohibas so that we could get the most bang for our $100 allowance. After several fruitless hours, we discovered the whole point of communism: The price of cigars was the same everywhere. There is no competition between stores because there is no profit as we know it. Every store sells cigars—and everything else for that matter—at whatever price Fidel Castro (or his brother Raul) tells them to. And every shopkeeper selling cigars is paid the government wage for selling cigars, which is unrelated to how many cigars he or she sells.

Gary Becker, a University of Chicago economist who won the Nobel Prize in 1992, has noted (borrowing from George Bernard Shaw) that "economy is the art of making the most of life." Economics is the study of how we do that. There is a finite supply of everything worth having: oil, coconut milk, perfect bodies, clean water, people who can fix jammed photocopy machines, etc. How do we allocate these things? Why is it that Bill Gates owns a private jet and you don't? He is rich, you might answer. But why is he rich? Why does he have a larger claim on the world's finite resources than everyone else? At the same time, how is it possible in a country as rich as the United States—a place where Alex Rodriguez can be paid $275 million to play baseball—that one in five children is poor or that some adults are forced to rummage through garbage cans for food? Near my home in Chicago, the Three Dog Bakery sells cakes and pastries *only for dogs.* Wealthy professionals pay $16 for birthday cakes for their pets. Meanwhile, the Chicago Coalition for the Homeless estimates that fifteen thousand people are homeless on any given night in that same city.

These kinds of disparities grow even more pronounced as we look beyond the borders of the United States. Three-quarters of the people in Chad have no access to clean drinking water, let alone pastries for their pets. The World Bank estimates that half of the world's population survives on less than $2 a day. How does it all work—or, in some cases, not work?

Economics starts with one very important assumption: Individuals act to make themselves as well off as possible. To use the jargon of the profession, individuals seek to maximize their own utility, which is a similar concept to happiness, only broader. I derive utility from getting a typhoid immunization and paying taxes. Neither of these things makes me particularly happy, but they do keep me from dying of typhoid or going to jail. That, in the long run, makes me better off. Economists don't particularly care what gives us utility; they simply accept that each of us has his or her own "preferences." I like coffee, old houses, classic films, dogs, bicycling, and many other things. Everyone else in the world has preferences, which may or may not have anything in common with mine.

Indeed, this seemingly simple observation that different individuals have different preferences is sometimes lost on otherwise sophisticated policymakers. For example, rich people have different preferences than poor people do. Similarly, our individual preferences may change over the course of our life cycle as we (we hope) grow wealthier. The phrase "luxury good" actually has a technical meaning to economists; it is a good that we buy in increasing quantities as we grow richer—things like sports cars and French wines. Less obviously, concern for the environment is a luxury good. Wealthy Americans are willing to spend more money to protect the environment *as a fraction of their incomes* than are less wealthy Americans. The same relationship holds true across countries; wealthy nations devote a greater share of their resources to protecting the environment than do poor countries. The reason is simple enough: We care about the fate of the Bengal tiger *because we can.* We have homes and jobs and clean water and birthday cakes for our dogs.

Here is a nettlesome policy question: Is it fair for those of us who live comfortably to impose our preferences on individuals in the developing world? Economists argue that it is not, though we do it all the time. When I read a story in the Sunday *New York Times* about South American villagers cutting down virgin rain forest and destroying rare ecosystems, I nearly knock over my Starbucks latte in surprise and disgust. But I am not they. My children are not starving or at risk of dying from malaria. If they were, and if chopping down a valuable wildlife habitat enabled me to afford to feed my family and buy a mosquito net, then I would sharpen my ax and start chopping. I wouldn't care how many butterflies or spotted weasels I killed. This is not to suggest that the environment in the developing world does not matter. It does. In fact, there are many examples of environmental degradation that will make poor countries even poorer in the long run. Cutting down those forests is bad for the rest of us, too, since deforestation is a major contributor to rising CO_2 emissions. (Economists often argue that rich countries ought to pay poor countries to protect natural resources that have global value.)

Obviously if the developed world were more generous, then Brazilian villagers might not have to decide between destroying the rain forest and buying mosquito nets. For now, the point is more basic: It is simply bad economics to impose our preferences on individuals whose lives are much, much different. This will be an important point later in the book when we turn to globalization and world trade.

Let me make one other important point regarding our individual preferences: Maximizing utility is not synonymous with acting selfishly. In 1999, the *New York Times* published the obituary of Oseola McCarty, a woman who died at the age of ninety-one after spending her life working as a laundress in Hattiesburg, Mississippi. She had lived alone in a small, sparsely furnished house with a black-and-white television that received only one channel. What made Ms. McCarty exceptional is that she was by no means poor. In fact, four years before her death she gave away $150,000 to the University of Southern Mississippi—a school that she had never attended—to endow a scholarship for poor students.

Does Oseola McCarty's behavior turn the field of economics on its head? Are Nobel Prizes being recalled to Stockholm? No. She simply derived more utility from saving her money and eventually giving it away than she would have from spending it on a big-screen TV or a fancy apartment.

Okay, but that was just money. How about Wesley Autrey, a fifty-year-old construction worker in New York City. He was waiting for the subway in Upper Manhattan with his two young daughters in January 2007 when a stranger nearby began having convulsions and then fell on the train tracks. If this wasn't bad enough, the Number 1 train was already visible as it approached the station.

Mr. Autrey jumped on the tracks and shielded the man as five train cars rolled over both of them, close enough that the train left a smudge of grease on Mr. Autrey's hat. When the train came to a stop, he yelled from underneath, "We're O.K. down here, but I've got two daughters up there. Let them know their father's O.K."[3] This was all to help a complete stranger.

We all routinely make altruistic decisions, albeit usually on a smaller scale. We may pay a few cents extra for dolphin-safe tuna, or send money to a favorite charity, or volunteer to serve in the armed forces. All of these things can give us utility; none would be considered selfish. Americans give more than $200 billion to assorted charities every year. We hold doors open for strangers. We practice remarkable acts of bravery and generosity. None of this is incompatible with the basic assumption that individuals seek to make themselves as well off as possible, however they happen to define that. Nor does this assumption imply that we always make perfect—or even good—decisions. We don't. But each of us does try to make the best possible decision given whatever information is available at the time.

So, after only a few pages, we have an answer to a profound, age-old philosophical question: Why did the chicken cross the road? Because it maximized his utility.

Bear in mind that maximizing utility is no simple proposition. Life is complex and uncertain. There are an infinite number of things that we could be doing at any time. Indeed, every decision that we make involves some kind of trade-off. We may trade off utility now against utility in the future. For example, you may derive some satisfaction from whacking your boss on the head with a canoe paddle at the annual company picnic. But that momentary burst of utility would presumably be more than offset by the disutility of spending many years in a federal prison. (But those are just my preferences.) More seriously, many of our important decisions involve balancing the value of consumption now against consumption in the future. We may spend years in graduate school eating ramen noodles because it dramatically boosts our standard of living later in life. Or, conversely, we may use a credit card to purchase a big-screen television today even though the interest on that credit card debt will lessen the amount that we can consume in the future.

Similarly, we balance work and leisure. Grinding away ninety hours a week as an investment banker will generate a lot of income, but it will also leave less time to enjoy the goods that can be purchased with that income. My younger brother began his career as a management consultant with a salary that had at least one more digit than mine has now. On the other hand, he worked long- and sometimes inflexible hours. One fall we both excitedly signed up for an evening film class taught by Roger Ebert. My brother proceeded to miss *every single class for thirteen weeks.*

However large our paychecks, we can spend them on a staggering array of goods and services. When you bought this book, you implicitly decided not to spend that money somewhere else. (Even if you shoplifted the book, you could have stuffed a Stephen King novel in your jacket instead, which is flattering in its own kind of way.) Meanwhile, time is one of our most scarce resources. At the moment, you are reading instead of working, playing with the dog, applying to law school, shopping for groceries, or having sex. Life is about tradeoffs, and so is economics.

In short, getting out of bed in the morning and making breakfast involves more complex decisions than the average game of chess. (Will that fried egg kill me in twenty-eight years?) How do we manage? The answer is that each of us implicitly weighs the costs and benefits of everything he or she does. An economist would say that we attempt to maximize utility given the resources at our disposal; my dad would say that we try to get the most bang for our buck. Bear in mind that the things that give us utility do not have to be material goods. If you are comparing two jobs—teaching junior high school math or marketing Camel cigarettes—the latter job would almost certainly pay more while the former job would offer greater "psychic benefits," which is a fancy way of saying that at the end of the day you would feel better about what you do. That is a perfectly legitimate benefit to be compared against the cost of a smaller paycheck. In the end, some people choose to teach math and some people choose to market cigarettes.

Similarly, the concept of cost is far richer (pardon the pun) than the dollars and cents you hand over at the cash register. The real cost of something is what you must give up in order to get it, which is almost always more than just cash. There is nothing "free" about concert tickets it you have to stand in line in the rain for six hours to get them. Taking the bus for $1.50 may not be cheaper than taking a taxi for $7 if you are running late for a meeting with a peevish client who will pull a $50,000 account if you keep her waiting. Shopping at a discount store saves money but it usually costs time. I am a writer; I get paid based on what I produce. I could drive ninety miles to shop at an outlet in Kenosha, Wisconsin to save $50 on a new pair of dress shoes. Or I could walk into Nordstrom on Michigan Avenue and buy the shoes while I am out for lunch. I generally choose the latter; the total cost is $225, fifteen minutes of my time, and some hectoring from my mother, who will invariably ask, "Why didn't you drive to Kenosha?"

Every aspect of human behavior reacts to cost in some way. When the cost of something falls, it becomes more attractive to us. You can learn that by deriving a demand curve, or you can learn it by shopping the day after Christmas, when people snap up things that they weren't willing to buy for a higher price several days earlier. Conversely, when the cost of something goes up, we use less of it. This is true of everything in life, even cigarettes and crack cocaine. Economists have calculated that a 10 percent decrease in the street price of cocaine eventually causes the number of adult cocaine users to grow by about 10 percent. Similarly, researchers estimated that the first proposed settlement between the tobacco industry and the states (rejected by the U.S. Senate in 1998) would have raised the price of a pack of cigarettes by 34 percent. In turn, that increase would have reduced the number of teenage smokers by a quarter, leading to 1.3 million fewer smoking-related premature deaths among the generation of Americans seventeen or younger at the time.[4] Of course, society has already raised the cost of smoking in ways that have nothing to do with the price of a pack of cigarettes. Standing outside an office building when it is seventeen degrees outside is now part of the cost of smoking at work.

'This broad view of cost can explain some very important social phenomena, one of which is the plummeting birth rate in the developed world. Having a child is more expensive than it was fifty years ago. This is not because it is more expensive to feed and clothe another little urchin around the house. If anything, those kinds of costs have gone down, because we have become far more productive at making basic consumer goods like food and clothing. Rather, the primary cost of raising a child today is the cost of the earnings forgone when a parent, still usually the mother, quits or cuts back on work to look after the child at home. Because women have better professional opportunities than ever before, it has grown more costly for them to leave the workforce. My neighbor was a neurologist until her second child was born, at which point she decided to stay home. *It's expensive to quit being a neurologist.*

Meanwhile, most of the economic benefits of having a large family have disappeared in the developed world. Young children no longer help out on the farm or provide extra income for the family (though they can be taught at a young age to fetch a beer from the refrigerator). We no longer need to have many children in order to ensure that some of them live through childhood or that we have enough dependents to provide for us in retirement. Even the most dour of economists would concede that we derive great pleasure from having children. The point is that it is now more expensive to have eleven of them than it used to be. The data speak to that point: The average American woman had 3.77 children in 1905; she now has 2.07—a 45 percent drop.[5]

There is a second powerful assumption underpinning all of economics: Firms—which can be anything from one guy selling hot dogs to a multinational corporation—attempt to maximize profits (the revenue earned by selling stuff minus the cost of producing it). In short, firms try to make as much money as possible. Hence, we have an answer to another of life's burning questions: Wily did the entrepreneur cross the road? Because be could make more money on the other side.

Firms take inputs—land, steel, knowledge, baseball stadiums, etc.—and combine them in a way that adds value. That process can be as simple as selling cheap umbrellas on a busy corner in New York City when it starts to rain (where do those guys come from?) or as complex as assembling Boeing's 787 Dreamliner (a passenger jet that required 800,000 hours on Cray supercomputers just to design). A profitable firm is like a chef who brings home $30 worth of groceries and creates an $80 meal. She has used her talents to create something that is worth far more than the cost of the inputs. That is not always an easy thing to do. Firms decide what to produce, how and where to produce it, how much to produce, and at what price to sell what they produce—all in the face of the same kinds of uncertainties that consumers deal with.

How? These are massively complex decisions. One powerful feature of a market economy is that it directs resources to their most productive use. Why doesn't Brad Pitt sell automobile insurance? Because it would be an enormous waste of his unique talents. Yes, he is a charismatic guy who could probably sell more insurance policies than the average salesman. But he is also one of a handful of people in the world who can "open" a movie, meaning that millions of people around the world will go to see a film just because Brad Pitt is in it. That is money in the bank in the risky Hollywood movie business, so studios are willing to pay handsomely to put Brad Pitt in a starring role—about $30 million a film. Insurance agencies would also be willing to pay for the Pitt charisma—but more like $30,000. Brad Pitt will go where he is paid the most. And be will be paid the most in Hollywood because that is where he can add the most value.

Prices are like giant neon billboards that flash important information. At the beginning of the chapter, we asked how a restaurant on the Rue de Rivoli in Paris has just the right amount of tuna on most nights. It is all about prices. When patrons start ordering more of the sashimi appetizer, the restaurateur places a larger order with his fish wholesaler. If tuna is growing more popular at other restaurants, too, then the wholesale price will go up, meaning that fishermen somewhere in the Pacific will get paid more for their tuna catch than they used to. Some fishermen, recognizing that tuna now commands a premium over other kinds of fish, will start fishing for tuna instead of salmon. Meanwhile, some tuna fishermen will keep their boats in the water longer or switch to more expensive fishing methods that can now be justified by the higher price their catch will fetch. These guys don't care about upscale diners in Paris. They care about the wholesale price of fish.

Money talks. Why are the pharmaceutical companies scouring the rain forests looking for plants with rare healing properties? Because the blockbuster drugs they may uncover earn staggering amounts of money. Other kinds of entrepreneurial activity take place on a smaller scale but are equally impressive in their own way. For several summers I coached a Little League baseball team near Cabrini Green, which is one of Chicago's rougher neighborhoods. One of our team customs was to go out periodically for pizza, and one of our favorite spots was Chester's, a small shack at the corner of Division and Sedgwick that was a testimony to the resiliency and resourcefulness of entrepreneurs. (It has since been demolished to make way for a new park as part of an aggressive development of Cabrini Green.) Chester's made decent pizza and was always busy. Thus, it was basically an armed robbery waiting to happen. But that did not deter the management at Chester's. They merely installed the same kind of bulletproof glass that one would find at the drive-up window of a bank. The customers placed their money on a small carousel, which was then rotated through a gap in the bulletproof glass. The pizza came out the other direction on the same carousel.

Profit opportunities attract firms like sharks to blood, even when bulletproof glass is required. We look for hold new ways to make money (creating the first reality TV show); failing that, we look to get into a business that is making huge profits for someone else (thereby creating the next twenty increasingly pathetic reality TV shows). All the while, we are using prices to gauge what consumers want. Of course, not every market is easy to enter. When LeBron James signed a three-year $60 million contract with the Cleveland Cavaliers, I thought to myself, "I need to play basketball for the Cleveland Cavaliers." I would have gladly played for $58 million, or, if pressed, for $58,000. Several things precluded me from entering that market, however: (1) I'm five-ten; (2) I'm slow; and (3) when shooting under pressure, I have a tendency to miss the backboard. Why is LeBron James paid $20 million a year? Because nobody else can play like him. His unique talents create a barrier to entry for the rest of us. LeBron James is also the beneficiary of what University of Chicago labor economist Sherwin Rosen dubbed the "superstar" phenomenon. Small differences in talent tend to become magnified into huge differentials in pay as a market becomes very large, such as the audience for professional basketball. One need only be slightly better than the competition in order to gain a large (and profitable) share of that market.

In fact, LeBron's salary is chump change compared to what talk-show host Rush Limbaugh is now paid. He recently signed an eight-year $400 million contract with Clear Channel Communications, the company that syndicates his radio program around the country. Is Rush that much better than other political windbags willing to offer their opinions? He doesn't have to be. He need only be a tiny bit more interesting than the next best radio option at that time of day in order to attract a huge audience—20 million listeners daily. Nobody tunes into their second-favorite radio station, so it's winner-take-all when it comes to listeners and the advertisers willing to pay big bucks to reach them.

Many markets have barriers that prevent new firms from entering, no matter how profitable making widgets may be. Sometimes there are physical or natural barriers. Truffles cost $500 a pound because they cannot be cultivated; they grow only in the wild and must be dug up by truffle-hunting pigs or dogs. Sometimes there are legal barriers to entry. Don't try to sell sildenafil citrate on a street corner or you may end up in jail. This is not a drug that you snort or shoot up, nor is it illegal. It happens to be Viagra, and Pfizer holds the patent, which is a legal monopoly granted by the U.S. government. Economists may quibble over how long a patent should last or what kinds of innovations should be patentable, but most would agree that the entry barrier created by a patent is an important incentive for firms to make the kinds of investments that lead to new products. The political process creates entry barriers for dubious reasons, too. When the U.S. auto industry was facing intense competition from Japanese automakers in the 1980s, the American car companies had two basic options: (1) They could create better, cheaper, more fuel-efficient cars that consumers might want to buy: or (2) they could invest heavily in lobbyists who would persuade Congress to enact tariffs and quotas that would keep Japanese cars out of the market.

Some entry barriers are more subtle. The airline industry is far less competitive than it appears to be. You and some college friends could start a new airline relatively easily; the problem is that you wouldn't be able to land your planes anywhere. There are a limited number of gate spaces available at most airports, and they tend to be controlled by the big guys. At Chicago's O'Hare Airport, one of the world's biggest and busiest airports, American and United control some 80 percent of all the gates.[6] Or consider a different kind of entry barrier that has become highly relevant in the Internet age: network effects. The basic idea of a network effect is that the value of some goods rises with the number of other people using them. I don't think Microsoft Word is particularly impressive software, but I own it anyway because I spend my days e-mailing documents to people who do like Word (or at least they use it). It would be very difficult to introduce a rival word-processing package—no matter how good the features or how low the price—as long as most of the world is using Word.

Meanwhile, firms are not just choosing what goods or services to produce but also how to produce them. I will never forget stepping off a plane in Kathmandu; the first thing I saw was a team of men squatting on their haunches as they cut the airport grass by hand with sickles. Labor is cheap in Nepal; lawn mowers are very expensive. The opposite is true in the United States, which is why we don't see many teams of laborers using sickles. It is also why we have ATMs and self-service gas stations and those terribly annoying phone trees ("If you are now frustrated to the point of violence, please press the pound key"). All are cases where firms have automated jobs that used to be done by living beings. After all, one way to raise profits is by lowering the cost of production. That may mean laying off twenty thousand workers or building a plant in Vietnam instead of Colorado.

Firms, like consumers, face a staggering array of complex choices. Again, the guiding principle is relatively simple: What is going to make the firm the most money in the long run?

All of which brings us to the point where producers meet consumers. How much are you going to pay for that doggie in the window? Introductory economics has a very simple answer: the market price. This is that whole supply and demand thing. The price will settle at the point where the number of dogs for sale exactly matches the number of dogs that consumers want to buy. If there are more potential pet owners than dogs available, then the price of dogs will go up. Some consumers will then decide to buy ferrets instead, and some pet shops will be induced by the prospect of higher profits to offer more dogs for sale. Eventually the supply of dogs will match the demand. Remarkably, some markets actually work this way. If I choose to sell a hundred shares of Microsoft on the NASDAQ, I have no choice but to accept the "market price," which is simply the price at which the number of Microsoft shares for sale on the exchange exactly equals the number of shares that buyers would like to purchase.

Most markets do not look quite so much like the textbooks. There is not a "market price" for Gap sweatshirts that changes by the minute depending on the supply and demand of reasonably priced outerwear. Instead, the Gap, like most other firms, has some degree of market power, which means very simply that the Gap has some control over what it can charge. The Gap could sell sweatshirts for $9.99, eking out a razor-thin profit on each. Or it could sell far fewer sweatshirts for $29.99, but make a hefty profit on each. If you were in the mood to do calculus at the moment, or I had any interest in writing about it, then we would find the profit-maximizing price right now. I'm pretty sure I had to do it on a final exam once. The basic point is that the Gap will attempt to pick a price that leads to the quantity of sales that earn the company the most money. The marketing executives may err either way: they may underprice the items, in which case they will sell out; or they may overprice the items, in which case they will have a warehouse full of sweatshirts.

Actually, there is another option. A firm can attempt to sell the same item to different people at different prices. (The fancy name is "price discrimination.") The next time you are on an airplane, try this experiment: Ask the person next to you how much he or she paid for the ticket, it's probably not what you paid; it may not even be close. You are sitting on the same plane, traveling to the same destination, eating the same peanuts—yet the prices you and your row mate paid for your tickets may not even have the same number of digits.

The basic challenge for the airline industry is to separate business travelers, who are willing to pay a great deal for a ticket, from pleasure travelers, who are on tighter budgets. If an airline sells every ticket at the same price, the company will leave money on the table no matter what price it chooses. A business traveler may he willing to pay $1,800 to fly round trip from Chicago to San Francisco; someone flying to cousin Irv's wedding will shell out no more than $250. If the airline charges the high fare, it will lose all of its pleasure travelers. If it charges the low fare, it will lose all the profits that business travelers would have been willing to pay. What to do? Learn to distinguish business travelers from pleasure travelers and then charge each of them a different late.

The airlines are pretty good at this. Why will your fare drop sharply if you stay over a Saturday night? Because Saturday night is when you are going to be dancing at cousin Irv's wedding. Pleasure travelers usually spend the weekend at their destination, while business travelers almost never do. Buying the ticket two weeks ahead of time will be much, much cheaper than buying it eleven minutes before the flight leaves. Vacationers plan ahead while business travelers tend to buy tickets at the last minute. Airlines are the most obvious example of price discrimination, but look around and you will start to see it everywhere. Al Gore complained during the 2000 presidential campaign that his mother and his dog were taking the same arthritis medication but that his mother paid much more for her prescription. Never mind that he made up the story after reading about the pricing disparity between humans and canines. The example is still perfect. There is nothing surprising about the fact that the same medicine will be sold to dogs and people at different prices. It's airline seats all over again. People will pay more for their own medicine than they will for their pet's. So the profit-maximizing strategy is to charge one price for patients with two legs and another price for patients with four.

Price discrimination will become even more prevalent as technology enables firms to gather more information about their customers. It is now possible, for example, to charge different prices to customers ordering on-line rather than over the phone. Or, a firm can charge different prices to different on-line customers depending on the pattern of their past purchases. The logic behind firms like Priceline (a website where consumers bid for travel services) is that every customer could conceivably pay a different price for an airline ticket or hotel room. In an article entitled "How Technology Tailors Price Tags," the *Wall Street Journal* noted, "Grocery stores appear to be the model of one price for all. But even today, they post one price, charge another to shoppers willing to clip coupons and a third to those with frequent-shopper cards that allow stores to collect detailed data on buying habits."[7]

What can we infer from all of this? Consumers try to make themselves as well off as possible and firms try to maximize profits. Those are seemingly simple concepts, yet they can tell us a tremendous amount about how the world works.

The market economy is a powerful force for making our lives better. The only way firms can make profits is by delivering goods that we want to buy. They create new products—everything from thermal coffee mugs to lifesaving antibiotics. Or they take an existing product and make it cheaper or better. This kind of competition is fabulously good for consumers. In 1900, a three-minute phone call from New York to Chicago cost $5.45, the equivalent of about $140 today. Now the same call is essentially free if you have a mobile phone with unlimited minutes. Profit inspires some of our greatest work, even in areas like higher education, the arts, and medicine. How many world leaders fly to North Korea when they need open-heart surgery?

At the same time, the market is amoral. Not immoral, simply amoral. The market rewards scarcity, which has no inherent relation to value. Diamonds are worth thousands of dollars a carat while water (if you are bold enough to drink it out of the tap) is nearly free. If there were no diamonds on the planet, we would be inconvenienced; if all the water disappeared, we would be dead. The market does not provide goods that we need; it provides goods that *we want to buy*. This is a crucial distinction. Our medical system does not provide health insurance for the poor. Why? Because they can't pay for it. Our most talented doctors do provide breast enhancements and face-lifts for Hollywood stars. Why? Because they can pay for it. Meanwhile, firms can make a lot of money doing nasty things. Why do European crime syndicates kidnap young girls in Eastern Europe and sell them into prostitution in wealthier countries? Because it's profitable.

In fact, criminals are some of the most innovative folks around. Drug traffickers can make huge profits by transporting cocaine from where it is produced (in the jungles of South America) to where it is consumed (in the cities and towns across the United States). This is illegal, of course; U.S. authorities devote a great amount of resources to interdicting the supply of such drugs headed toward potential consumers. As with any other market, drug runners who find clever ways of eluding the authorities are rewarded with huge profits.

Customs officials are pretty good at sniffing out (literally in many cases) large caches of drugs moving across the border, so drug traffickers figured out that it was easier to skip the border crossings and move their contraband across the sea and into the United States using small boats. When the U.S. Coast Guard began tracking fishing boats, drug traffickers invested in "go fast" boats that could outrun the authorities. And when U.S. law enforcement adopted radar and helicopters to hunt down the speedboats, the drug runners innovated yet again, creating the trafficking equivalent of Velcro or the iPhone: homemade submarines. In 2006, the Coast Guard stumbled across a forty-nine-foot submarine—handmade in the jungles of Colombia—that was invisible to radar and equipped to carry four men and three tons of cocaine. In 2000, Colombian police raided a warehouse and discovered a one-hundred-foot submarine under construction that would have been able to carry two hundred tons of cocaine. Coast Guard Rear Admiral Joseph Nimmich told the *New York Times*, "Like any business, if you're losing more and more of your product, you try to find a different way."[8]

The market is like evolution; it is an extraordinarily powerful force that derives its strength from rewarding the swift, the strong, and the smart. That said, it would be wise to remember that two of the most beautifully adapted species on the planet are the rat and the cockroach.

Our system uses prices to allocate scarce resources. Since there is a finite amount of everything worth having, the most basic function of any economic system is to decide who gets what. Who gets tickets to the Super Bowl? The people who are willing to pay the most. Who had the best seats for the Supreme Soviet Bowl in the old USSR (assuming some such event existed)? The individuals chosen by the Communist Party. Prices had nothing to do with it. If a Moscow butcher received a new shipment of pork, he slapped on the official state price for pork. And if that price was low enough that he had more customers than pork chops, he did not raise the price to earn some extra cash. He merely sold the chops to the first people in line. Those at the end of the line were out of luck. Capitalism and communism both ration goods. We do it with prices; the Soviets did it by waiting in line. (Of course, the communists had many black markets; it is quite likely that the butcher sold extra pork chops illegally our the back door of his shop.)

Because we use price to allocate goods, most markets are self-correcting. Periodically the oil ministers from the OPEC nations will meet in an exotic locale and agree to limit the global production of oil. Several things happen shortly thereafter: (1) Oil and gas prices start to go up; and (2) politicians begin falling all over themselves with ideas, mostly bad, for intervening in the oil market. But high prices are like a fever; they are both a symptom and a potential cure. While politicians are puffing away on the House floor, some other crucial things start to happen. We drive less. We get one heating bill and decide to insulate the attic. We go to the Ford showroom and walk past the Expeditions to the Escorts.

When gas prices approached $4 a gallon in 2008, the rapid response of American consumers surprised even economists. Americans began buying smaller cars (SUV sales plunged while subcompact sales rose). We drove fewer total miles (the first monthly drop in 50 years). We climbed on public buses and trains, often for the first time; transit ridership was higher in 2008 than at any time since the creation of the interstate highway system five decades earlier.[9]

Not all such behavioral changes were healthy. Many consumers switched from cars to motorcycles, which are more fuel efficient but also more dangerous. After falling steadily for years, the number of U.S. motorcycle deaths began to rise in the mid-1990s, just as gas prices began to climb. A study in the *American Journal of Public Health* estimated that every $1 increase in the price of gasoline is associated with an additional 1,500 motorcycle deaths annually.[10]

High oil prices cause things to start happening on the supply side, too. Oil producers outside of OPEC start pumping more oil to take advantage of the high price; indeed, the OPEC countries usually begin cheating on their own production quotas. Domestic oil companies begin pumping oil from wells that were not economical when the price of petroleum was low. Meanwhile, a lot of very smart people begin working more seriously on finding and commercializing alternative sources of energy. The price of oil and gasoline begins to drift down as supply rises and demand falls.

If we fix prices in a market system, private firms will find some other way to compete. Consumers often look hack nostalgically at the "early days" of airplane travel, when the food was good, the seats were bigger, and people dressed up when they traveled. This is not just nostalgia speaking; the quality of coach air travel has fallen sharply. But the price of air travel has fallen even faster. Prior to 1978, airline lares were fixed by the government. Every flight from Denver to Chicago cost the same, but American and United were still competing for customers, They used quality to distinguish themselves. When the industry was deregulated, price became the primary margin for competition, presumably because that is what consumers care more about. Since then, everything related to being in or near an airplane has become less pleasant, but the average fare, adjusted for inflation, has fallen by nearly half.

In 1995,1 was traveling-across South Africa, and I was struck by the remarkable service at the gas stations along the way. The attendants, dressed in sharp uniforms, often with bow ties, would scurry out to fill the tank, check the oil, and wipe the windshield. The bathrooms were spotless—a far cry from some of the scary things I've seen driving across the USA. Was there some special service station mentality in South Africa? No. The price of gasoline was fixed by the government. So service stations, which were still private firms, resorted to bow ties and clean bathrooms to attract customers.

Every market transaction makes all parties better off. Firms are acting in their own best interests, and so are consumers. This is a simple idea that has enormous power. Consider an inflammatory example: The problem with Asian sweatshops is that there are not enough of them. Adult workers take jobs in these unpleasant, low-wage manufacturing facilities voluntarily. (I am not writing about forced labor or child labor, both of which are different cases.) So one of two things must be true. Either (1) workers take unpleasant jobs in sweatshops because it is the best employment option they have; or (2) Asian sweatshop workers are persons of weak intellect who have many more attractive job offers but choose to work in sweatshops instead.

Most arguments against globalization implicitly assume number two. The protesters smashing windows in Seattle were trying to make the case that workers in the developing world would be better off if we curtailed international trade, thereby closing down the sweatshops that churn out shoes and handbags for those of us in the developed world. But how exactly does that make workers in poor countries better off? It does not create any new opportunities. The only way it could possibly improve social welfare is if fired sweatshop workers take new, better jobs opportunities they presumably ignored when they went to work in a sweatshop. When was the last time a plant closing in the United States was hailed as good news for its workers?

Sweatshops are nasty places by Western standards. And yes, one might argue that Nike should pay its foreign workers better wages out of sheer altruism. But they are a symptom of poverty, not a cause. Nike pays a typical worker in one of its Vietnamese factories roughly $600 a year. That is a pathetic amount of money. It also happens to be twice an average Vietnamese worker's annual income.[11] Indeed, sweatshops played an important role in the development of countries like South Korea and Taiwan, as we will explore in Chapter 12.

Given that economics is built upon the assumption that humans act consistently in ways that make themselves better off, one might reasonably ask: Are we really that rational? Not always, it turns out. One of the fiercest assaults on the notion of "strict rationality" comes from a seemingly silly observation. Economist Richard Thaler hosted a dinner party years ago at which he served a bowl of cashews before the meal. He noticed that his guests were wolfing down the nuts at such a pace that they would likely spoil their appetite for dinner. So Thaler took the bowl of nuts away, at which point his guests thanked him.[12]

Believe it or not, this little vignette exposes a fault in the basic tenets of microeconomics: In theory, it should never be possible to make rational individuals better off by denying them some option. People who don't want to eat too many cashews should just stop eating cashews. But they don't. And that finding turns out to have implications far beyond salted nuts. For example, if humans lack the self-discipline to do things that they know will make themselves better off in the long run (e.g., lose weight, stop smoking, or save for retirement), then society could conceivably make them better off by helping (or coercing) them to do things they otherwise would not or could not do—the public policy equivalent of taking the cashew bowl away.

The field of behavioral economics has evolved as a marriage between psychology and economics that offers sophisticated insight into how humans really make decisions. Daniel Kahneman, a professor in both psychology and public affairs at Princeton, was awarded the Nobel Prize in Economics in 2002 for his studies of decision making under uncertainty, and, in particular, "how human decisions may systematically depart from those predicted by standard economic theory."[13]

Kahneman and others have advanced the concept of "bounded rationality," which suggests that most of us make decisions using intuition or rules of thumb, kind of like looking at the sky to determine if it will rain, rather than spending hours poring over weather forecasts. Most of the time, this works just fine. Sometimes it doesn't. The behavioral economists study ways in which these rules of thumb may lead us to do things that diminish our utility in the long run.

For example, individuals don't always have a particularly refined sense of risk and probability. This point was brought home to me recently as I admired a large Harley Davidson motorcycle parked on a sidewalk in New Hampshire (a state that does not require motorcycle helmets). The owner ambled up and said, "Do you want to buy it?" I replied that motorcycles are a little too dangerous for me, to which he exclaimed, "You're willing to fly on a plane, aren't you!"

In fact, riding a motorcycle is 2,000 times more dangerous than flying for every kilometer traveled. That's not an entirely fair comparison since motorcycle trips tend to be much shorter. Still, any given motorcycle journey, regardless of length, is 14 times more likely to end in death than any trip by plane. Conventional economics makes clear that some people will ride motorcycles (with or without helmets) because the utility they get from going fast on a two wheeler outweighs the risks they incur in the process. That's perfectly rational. But if the person making that decision doesn't understand the true risk involved, then it may not be a rational trade-off after all.

Behavorial economics has developed a catalog of these kinds of potential errors, many of which are an obvious part of everyday life. Many of us don't have all the self-control that we would like. Eighty percent of American smokers say they want to quit; most of them don't. (Reports from inside the White House suggested that President Obama was still trying to kick the habit even after moving into the Oval Office.) Some very prominent economists, including one Nobel Prize winner, have argued for decades that there is such a thing as "rational addiction," meaning that individuals will take into account the likelihood of addiction and all its future costs when buying that first pack of Camels. MIT economist Jonathan Gruber, who has studied smoking behavior extensively, thinks that is nonsense. He argues that consumers don't rationally weigh the benefits of smoking enjoyment against future health risks and other costs, as the standard economic model assumes. Gruber writes, "The model is predicated on a description of the smoking decision that is at odds with laboratory evidence, the behavior of smokers, econometric [statistical] analysis, and common sense."[14]

We may also lack the basic knowledge necessary to make sensible decisions in some situations. Annamaria Lusardi of Dartmouth College and Olivia Mitchell of the Wharton School at the University of Pennsylvania surveyed a large sample of Americans over the age of fifty to gauge their financial literacy. Only a third could do simple interest rate calculations: most did not understand the concept of investment diversification. (If you don't know what that means either, you will after reading Chapter 7.) Based on her research, Professor Lusardi has concluded that "financial illiteracy" is widespread.[15]

These are not merely esoteric fun facts that pipe-smoking academics like to kick around in the faculty lounge. Bad decisions can have bad outcomes—for all of us. The global financial crisis arguably has its roots in irrational behavior. One of our behavioral "rules of thumb" as humans is to see patterns in what is really randomness; as a result, we assume that whatever is happening now will continue to happen in the future, even when data, probability or basic analysis suggest the contrary. A coin that comes up heads four times in a row is "lucky": a basketball player who has hit three shots in a row has a "hot hand."

A team of cognitive psychologists made one of the enduring contributions to this field by disproving the "hot hand" in basketball using NBA data and by conducting experiments with the Cornell varsity men's and women's basketball teams. (This is the rare academic paper that includes interviews with the Philadelphia 76ers.) Ninety-one percent of basketball fans believe that a player has "a better chance of making a shot after having just made his last two or three shots than he does after having just missed his last two or three shots." In fact, there is no evidence that a player's chances of making a shot are greater after making a previous shot—not with field goals for the 76ers, not with free throws for the Boston Celtics, and not when Cornell players shot baskets as part of a controlled experiment."

Basketball fans are surprised by that—just as many homeowners were surprised in 2006 when real estate prices stopped going up. Lots of people had borrowed a lot of money on the assumption that what goes up must keep going up; the result has been a wave of foreclosures with devastating ripple effects throughout the global economy—which is a heck of a lot more significant than eating too many cashews. Chapter 3 discusses what, if anything, public policy ought to do about our irrational tendencies.

As John F. Kennedy famously remarked, "Life is not fair." Neither is capitalism in some important respects. Is it a good system?

I will argue that a market economy is to economics what democracy is to government: a decent, if flawed, choice among many bad alternatives. Markets are consistent with our views of individual liberty. We may disagree over whether or not the government should compel us to wear motorcycle helmets, but most of us agree that the state should not tell us where to live, what to do for a living, or how to spend our money. True, there is no way to rationalize spending money on a birthday cake for my dog when the same money could have vaccinated several African children. But any system that forces me to spend money on vaccines instead of doggy birthday cakes can only be held together by oppression. The communist governments of the twentieth century controlled their economies by controlling their citizens' lives. They often wrecked both in the process. During the twentieth century, communist governments killed some 100 million of their own people in peacetime, either by repression or by famine.

Markets are consistent with human nature and therefore wildly successful at motivating us to reach our potential. I am writing this book because I love to write. I am writing this book because I believe that economics will be interesting to lay readers. And I am writing this book because I really want a summer home in New Hampshire. We work harder when we benefit directly from our work, and that hard work often yields significant social gains.

Last and most important, we can and should use government to modify markets in all kinds of ways. The economic battle of the twentieth century was between capitalism and communism. Capitalism won. Even my leftist brother-in-law does not believe in collective farming or government-owned steel mills (though he did once say that he would like to see a health care system modeled after the U.S. Post Office). On the other hand, reasonable people can disagree sharply over when and how the government should involve itself in a market economy or what kind of safety net we should offer to those whom capitalism treats badly. The economic battles of the twenty-first century will be over how unfettered our markets should be.

CONSUMER TOPIC 1.1

Competition Counts

Source: "Competition Counts: How Consumers Win When Businesses Compete," http://ftc.gov/bc/edu/pubs/consumer/general/zgen01.pdf, Federal Trade Commission. Copyright in the Public Domain.

THE FTC'S BUREAU OF COMPETITION: PROTECTING FREE ENTERPRISE AND AMERICAN CONSUMERS

What if there were only one grocery store in your community? What if you could buy a camera from only one supplier? What if only one dealer in your area sold cars?

Without competition, the grocer may have no incentive to lower prices. The camera shop may have no reason to offer a range of choices. The car dealer may have no motivation to offer a variety of car models and services.

Competition in America is about price, selection, and service. It benefits consumers by keeping prices low and the quality and choice of goods and services high.

Competition makes our economy work. By enforcing antitrust laws, the Federal Trade Commission helps to ensure that our markets are open and free. The FTC promotes healthy competition and challenges anticompetitive business practices to make sure that consumers have access to quality goods and services, and that businesses can compete on the merits of their work. The FTC does not choose winners and losers—you, as the consumer, do that. Rather, our job is to make sure that businesses are competing fairly within a set of rules.

Through its Bureaus of Competition and Economics, the FTC puts its antitrust resources to work, especially where consumer interest and consumer spending are high: in matters affecting energy, real estate, health care, food, pharmaceuticals, professional services, cable TV, computer technology, video programming, and broadband Internet access.

WHAT IS ANTITRUST?

The word "antitrust" dates from the late 1800s, when powerful companies dominated industries, working together as "trusts" to stifle competition. Thus, laws aimed at protecting competition have long been labeled "antitrust." Fast forward to the 21st century: you hear "antitrust" in news stories about competitors merging or companies conspiring to reduce competition. The FTC enforces antitrust laws by challenging business practices that could hurt consumers by resulting in higher prices, lower quality, or fewer goods or services. We monitor business practices, review potential mergers, and challenge them when appropriate to ensure that the market works according to consumer preferences, not illegal practices.

What kinds of business practices interest the Bureau of Competition? In short, the very practices that affect consumers the most: company mergers, agreements among competitors, restrictive agreements between manufacturers and product dealers, and monopolies. The FTC reviews these and other practices, looking at the likely effects on consumers and competition: Would they lead to higher prices, inferior service, or fewer choices for consumers? Would they make it more difficult for other companies to enter the market?

Here are some business practices the FTC monitors:

Mergers Many mergers benefit consumers by allowing firms to operate more efficiently. Other mergers, however, may result in higher prices, fewer choices, or lesser quality. The challenge for the FTC is to analyze the likely effects of a merger on consumers and competition—a process that can take thousands of hours of investigation and economic analysis. In one FTC case, a major national office supply retailer wanted to buy its closest competitor. Based on evidence that the merger would lead to higher prices for consumers, the FTC went to court and successfully blocked the deal.

Agreements Among Competitors It's illegal for businesses to act together in ways that can limit competition, lead to higher prices, or hinder other businesses from entering the market. In one FTC case, a group of auto dealers threatened to stop advertising in a newspaper if it printed money-saving tips for car shoppers. The FTC's Bureau of Competition challenged the dealers because it is illegal for businesses to act together in ways that can deprive consumers of important information.

Agreements among businesses about price or price-related matters like credit terms are among the most serious business practices the FTC considers. That's because price is usually the principal basis for competition and consumer choice. Price fixing—companies getting together to set prices—is illegal. But that does not mean that all price similarities, or price changes that occur about the same time, are always the result of price fixing. On the contrary, they often result from normal market conditions. For example, prices of commodities such as wheat are often identical because the products are virtually identical, and the prices that farmers charge all rise and fall together without any agreement among them. If a drought causes the supply of wheat to decline, the price to all affected farmers will increase. Uniformly high prices for a product in limited supply also can result from an increase in consumer demand: Just ask any shopper hunting for a "must have" children's toy.

Agreements Between Manufacturers and Product Dealers Many "package deals" create efficiencies that are beneficial to consumers: for example, automobile dealers who sell tires with their cars. You might prefer a different kind of tire, but shipping and selling cars without tires would be silly. On the other hand, some "tie-in" agreements are illegal because they restrict competition without providing benefits to consumers. For example, the antitrust laws likely would not permit a drug manufacturer to require its drug store customers to buy a patient monitoring system they don't want along with the prescription drugs they do want.

Monopoly A monopoly exists when one company controls a product or service in a market. If it's because they offer consumers a better product at a better price, that's not against the law. But a company that creates or maintains a monopoly by unreasonably excluding other companies, or by impairing other companies' ability to compete against them, raises antitrust concerns. For example, a newspaper with a monopoly in a small town could not refuse to run advertisements from businesses that also advertised on a local television station.

Other Anticompetitive Conduct Business strategies that reduce competition may be illegal if they lack a reasonable business justification. For example, a pharmaceutical company's exclusive contracts with suppliers of a key ingredient kept generic drug makers from getting that ingredient. Without competition from generics, the pharmaceutical company was able to raise prices 3,000 percent: a $5 prescription would have cost consumers $150. The FTC, 32 states, and the District of Columbia challenged the contracts, which resulted in a $100 million court settlement for injured consumers.

KEEPING MARKETS COMPETITIVE

By challenging anticompetitive business practices, the FTC helps to ensure that consumers have choices in price, selection, and service. To learn about competition problems, the FTC often receives information from consumers like you. As an informed shopper, you are in the best position to detect an absence of competition for no apparent reason. If you suspect illegal behavior, please notify federal and state antitrust agencies.

CONFIDENTIALITY

The FTC cannot act on behalf of an individual consumer or business, but the information you provide can help expose illegal behavior.

With few exceptions, FTC investigations are not public, and any information you provide or complaint you make will be kept confidential. If you ask us about an investigation, you may be told that we cannot discuss it, or even confirm or deny its existence. But we can receive your information and make sure it gets to appropriate FTC staff. In some cases, a staff person may wish to use the information in court. In that event, you may be asked to provide an affidavit or other statement under oath, or appear as a witness at the trial. These situations are relatively rare, but if those circumstances arise, your identity will have to be disclosed to the lawyers representing the companies or persons under investigation. FTC staff will seek your cooperation before making such disclosures.

HOW YOU CAN HELP

If you have an antitrust problem or complaint, or if you wish to provide information that may be helpful in an investigation, contact the FTC.

E-mail

Antitrust@ftc.gov
If you wish to submit confidential information, send it by mail and mark it "Confidential."

Mail

Federal Trade Commission Bureau of Competition-H374,
Washington, D.C. 20580

Telephone

1–877–FTC–HELP
(1–877–382–4357)

CONSUMER TOPIC 1.2

Concentration Ratio

A concentration ratio is an economic measure of the proportion of total output produced in an industry by a given number of firms in the industry. Concentration ratios are usually used to show the extent of market control of the largest firms in the industry and indicate the degree of competition. The following table shows some examples of concentration ratios in selected industry in the U.S.

Table 1.1: Percentage of industry output produced by the four leading firms in that industry.

INDUSTRY	PERCENT OF INDUSTRY: 4 LARGEST FIRMS
Cigarettes	95
Household laundry equipment	93
Greeting cards	91
Breweries	90
Electric Lamps	89
Battery	87
National commercial banks	56

Source: U.S. Census Bureau (2007). Concentration ratios. Retrieved from: http://www.census.gov/econ/concentration.html

CASE STUDY

Maya and John are a couple that have been married for three years, they have been living in an apartment for the past four years in Encino. In an ordinary sunny morning, Maya finds a flat tire on her Corolla. Panicked, she wake up John and takes the key of his Jeep; her work schedule is not flexible at all!

John could easily feel that his boss was not happy when he called for an absence. Frustration aside, he needs to get the flat tire repaired. John doesn't want to call the towing truck and he knows how expensive that could be. However, replacing the flat tire with the spare is no small task given John's subpar mechanic skills and the fact that his mind is full of a recent case he has been dealing with at work. Two and half hours after he started, the spare is successfully on the car as John collapses in a heap in their living room. As he is useless for another half an hour, John searches online and finds a good deal of tires in a nearby tire shop. He ends up spending the whole day to take care of the tire problem for Maya.

Maya is happy to see her newly equipped Corolla when coming home. As she is joking about the car wash not even letting John's Jeep in, Maya seriously complains that she spent almost $85 to fill up the tank. John admits that he might have some mud on his car but comments she will always see a highway congested of cars and SUVs in L.A. no matter how high the gas price would be. Maya doesn't argue with John considering it took her almost two hours on the highway in this morning. However, she starts thinking seriously about how to reduce their budget on gasoline.

Use the economic concepts to analyze the case:

What do you think about John's decision to save money by fixing the car by himself?

What do you think about John's comment on gasoline price?

What do you think about Maya's plan to reduce their budget on gasoline?

CONSUMER RESOURCES:

U.S. Census Bureau Economic Statistics: http://www.census.gov/econ/

Federal Trade Commission Bureau of Economics: http://www.ftc.gov/be/index.shtml

CIA The World Factbook: https://www.cia.gov/library/publications/the-world-factbook/

Resources for Economists on the Internet: http://rfe.org/

CHAPTER 2

CONSUMER INFORMATION AND DECISION-MAKING

CHAPTER 2 INTRODUCTION

You want to know the MPG, the engine, and the safety features of a car before you buy it; you want to know how other students say about the professor before you register for a class. Information plays an important role in our decision making. Thanks to the Internet, consumers have more ways than ever to get information about almost anything. Do we then make more informed and less impulse purchases online than in the traditional market? What are the similarities and differences between online and traditional media as consumer information environments; and what do they mean to consumers? You may get some insights from this chapter.

IMPULSE BUYING

A Literature Review

Supriya M. Kalla and A.P. Arora

ABSTRACT

This article reviews extant literature in the field of impulse buying. This review has been undertaken with a specific focus on understanding the phenomenon of 'impulse buying' and the factors that work towards motivating impulsive action in perspective of buying. Starting with a historical overview that provides genesis of this thought, the review moves into analysis of current definitions of 'impulse buying'. After providing a thorough picture of this phenomenon, the article deals with internal and external motivators of impulse buying. At various points in the article and at the end, future research directions that follow the relevant sections are discussed as propositions.

Design/methodology/approach: The existing body of academic literature in the area under consideration is reviewed and an attempt has been made to provide an integrated portrayal of current level of knowledge in this field. In addition, this literature review comprises contributions from different and yet relevant fields of knowledge, in order to present a holistic perspective of impulse buying phenomenon. This article covers thoughts on the subject from domain of marketing and for developing a deeper understanding of consumer with respect to the phenomenon of 'impulse buying'; this review looks into disciplines of psychology and social psychology. Academic papers, books and other electronic sources that were used for this purpose were then chronologically placed from 1959–2009. Research papers and books from this time period have been selected basis their relevance to topic of this review. As a first step, the keywords used in electronic journal databases were 'impulse' and 'impulse buying'. As a second step, contributions that concentrate on previously

Supriya M. Kalla and A.P. Arora, "Impulse Buying: A Literature Review," *Global Business Review*, vol. 12, no. 1, pp. 145–157. Copyright © 2011 by International Management Institute. Reprinted with permission.

suggested scope of review were selected. References from these studies were examined to identify further contributions from additional sources.

Originality/value: This study critically reviews the current state of research and knowledge across related disciplines. From an academic perspective, it may serve as a starting point for a future research agenda that addresses current knowledge gaps in this field of 'impulse buying'. From a practitioner's perspective, it is helpful for understanding relevant influence factors and for developing appropriate selling strategies.

> We go through life like a person riding a horse; the horse is 95% and we are just 5%. The horse is our subconscious mind and we are the rider. In many situations, we the rider is not in control of the horse. Buyer's remorse is but one of the many things we do to justify what our horse made us do.—Phillip Hesketh in his book titled 'Life is a game so fix all the odds'.

INTRODUCTION

The fact that shopping can be done for so many reasons other than need for product or service (Tauber, 1972), opens way for a deeper exploration into behaviour that is different from that of an 'economic man'.[1]

Impulse buying behaviour has remained an enigma in marketing world for long. It is a behaviour which literature states as the darker side of consumer behaviour (Wansink, 1994) and which is considered normatively wrong. Yet it accounts for a substantial volume of goods sold every year (Bellenger et al., 1978; Clover, 1950; Cobb and Hoyer, 1986; Kollat and Willet, 1967). Impulse buying becomes a manifestation of a person's wish to indulge. Therefore, in many studies, it has been approached with a perspective of behaviour that is driven by hedonistic (Kivetz and Simonson, 2002) or pleasure seeking goals that may cause a person to experience desires for related objects or products (Ramanathan and Menon, 2006). In today's marketing context characterized by growing aspiration levels, a willingness to spend and visible eagerness to use consumption as an expression is becoming a way of life. This is further fueled by the availability of products and newer retail formats like supermarkets and hypermarkets that provide much higher impetus to impulse buying.

All the preceding reasons ensure that marketers and retailers have several reasons to understand and many opportunities to cash in on impulse buying.

This review discusses existing literature from two perspectives. First, it draws from literature the necessary elements to develop a thorough understanding of what impulse buying is about. Second, the review discusses some of the inconsistencies in literature and identifies literature gaps in the research area under review.

IMPULSE: THE PHENOMENON

The core meaning of impulse is 'akrasia' or 'weakness of will'. Akrasia is 'free, intentional action contrary to the agent's better judgment' (Audi, 1989; Mele, 1987). This stance on 'impulse' is supported by rich philosophical literature, beginning with Plato and Aristotle.

Psychological Impulses

The notion of psychological impulse persists to this day, in both lay understanding and psychological theorizing. James (1890) (cited in Rook 1987) defined impulse as ephemeral thoughts usually tied to forceful urges. Wolman (1973) (cited in Rook 1987) discussed the nature of impulse as it being biochemically and psychologically stimulated. The biochemical aspect of it functions neurophysiologically as waves of active change that continue along a nerve fiber and trigger a particular somatic or mental response. The psychological aspect of impulse functions as stimulating and motivating agents those originate from both conscious and unconscious activity.

In the more contemporary psychology literature, Goldenson (1984) described impulse as a strong, sometimes irresistible, urge—a sudden inclination to act without deliberation. In psychoanalysis, impulse denotes the psychological aspect of instinctual drive, such as sex, hostility and hunger. For Freud (1911), impulses are manifestations of 'id' that conscious censorship could not suppress. The 'id' cannot tolerate any delay in gratification and is regulated by the pleasure principle, which demands immediate tension reduction; in other words, instant pleasure and no pain. The priorities of 'id' are well captured by the phrase 'I want what I want—and I want it NOW!' In contrast to id's pleasure principle, the ego is governed by the reality principle, which postpones the discharge of energy until an appropriate situation in the real world appears. The ego temporarily suspends pleasure for the sake of realistic constraints. Work on psychological impulses indicates that a ban impulse has a sense of immediacy, spontaneity, urgency and intensity to respond quickly (Liebert and Liebert, 1998).

At the onset, an impulse is very action-oriented and kinetic due to immediate response to the stimuli. It is seen as directly stimulus evoked, and thus reactive. Once triggered, an impulse encourages a tendency to gratify one's immediate pleasures without considering its consequences. An impulse is also characterized as uncontrollable and overpowering, so it leads to a feeling of being out of control or helplessness and it accompanies emotional arousal or reactivity (Zuckerman, 1994).

Earlier research in this direction has described the nature of psychological impulses as highly emotional and very low on thoughtfulness of the act. As discussed in a later part of this article, this stance of researchers on psychological impulses has a direct implication for the impulse buying phenomenon.

IMPULSE BUYING: DEFINITIONAL ARGUMENT

Initial definitions of 'impulse buying' have described the phenomenon as generally synonymous with unplanned buying: any purchase that a shopper makes and has not been planned in advance (Bellenger et al., 1978; Stern, 1962).

However, later studies regarding 'unplanned v/s impulse' aspect of buying indicate that describing an impulse buy as 'unplanned' where the decision is made only within the confines of the store, is incomplete. In addition, prior studies in respect to this approach have been criticized. Research done by Rook (1987) suggests that not all unplanned purchases are impulsively decided. It is possible for a purchase to involve high degrees of planning and still be highly impulsive; and some unplanned purchases may be quite rational. This argument over unplanned versus impulse gained clarity with Iyer's (1989) work, which suggested that all impulse buying is at least unplanned, but all unplanned purchases are not necessarily decided impulsively.

Behavioural dimensions of impulse buying are another focus area and many researchers agree that impulse buying involves a hedonistic (Park et al., 2006) or affective component (Piron, 1991; Shiv and Fedorikhin, 1999; Weinberg and Gottwald, 1982). For instance, Rook (1987) reports accounts by consumers who felt the product 'calling' them, almost demanding they purchase it. This emphasis on behavioural elements of impulse buying led to definitions which took into account hedonically complex nature of impulses and the fact that impulses can lead to emotional conflict which is likely to stimulate an action.

This phase of work on impulse buying has been followed by research to understand nature of 'impulse buying' with respect to the product purchased. In this direction, seminal works by Rook (1987) and Stephen and Loewenstein (1991) suggest that it is people and not the product that experience the urge to consume on impulse. With the emphasis coming on to people, later research work discussed the importance of internal motivators leading to the act of impulse buying and defined impulse buying as an interplay of internal and external motivators. External motivators refer to marketer controlled or sensory stimuli emanating from the marketing system e.g., the product itself or atmospherics, while internal motivators refer to cravings, overwhelming desires to buy, and internal thoughts (Hoch and Loewenstein, 1991).

Hence, with time, various dimensions have been added to the definitions of impulse buying. However, this divergence in definitions of 'impulse buying' evokes the necessity for a closer examination of the concept of impulse buying.

MOTIVATORS OF IMPULSE BUYING

Hoch and Loewenstein (1991), talked about impulse buying being a reactive purchase in the context of strong enough stimulation and motivation that can override restraints. The reactive nature of the phenomenon of impulse, as discussed, calls for a thorough exploration of various motivators of impulse buying. Therefore, the next part of the review deals with various motivators of impulse purchase.

On the basis of literature, the motives of impulse purchase are divided into two kinds—internal motivators of shopper and external motivators in shopping environment. For the purpose of this review, these are called shopper related factors and shop related factors, respectively.

INTERNAL MOTIVATORS OF IMPULSE BUYING (SHOPPER RELATED FACTORS)

This set of factors is based on premise that impulse buying can be instigated by internal motivators like a sudden desire to buy something without apparent external visual encouragement. These can also be categorized as factors that relate to internal thought processes of the shopper. People can suddenly experience the urge to go out and buy something, with no direct visual confrontation (Shapiro, 1992). This sudden urge to buy something can emanate from various thoughts such as self-discrepancy, defined as a difference between actual self and ideal self. This has been studied by various researchers in context of an urge for symbolic self-completion (Wicklund and Gollwitzer, 1981) that may result in impulse buying. Dittmar (2005) found that excessive shoppers differed from ordinary consumers in a number of ways: they were more motivated to buy in order to bolster their self-image and they reported greater 'gaps' between how they see themselves (actual self) and how they wish to be seen (ideal self). They held stronger materialistic values, believing that acquiring material goods is a major route towards success, identity and happiness. They did more impulse buying and they regretted it more. This suggests that there is a continuum from ordinary to excessive impulse buying, with need to bolster self-image being one of the major underlying motivators of this behaviour.

O'Guinn and Faber (1989) have studied self-esteem in context of impulse buying and found it negatively related to compulsive buying behaviour. Verplanken et al. (2005) suggest that low self-esteem is likely to be a particularly powerful source of the types of negative psychological state that result in use of impulse buying as a means of psychological relief. In continuation to above argument, existing research on this phenomenon also shows that low self-esteem is generally associated with increased susceptibility to influence from others (Cox, 1964). In marketing literature, the need to maintain or augment self-esteem has been associated with materialism and with purchases in some specific esteem-enhancing product categories such as those that enhance physical appearance (Arndt et al., 2004). However, Arndt et al. (2004) discussed only physical appearance but other related factors can also be looked at from the proposed perspective.

People buy products not only for what they can do but also for what they mean (Levy, 1959). This aspect of considering products as 'symbols' of being and consumption as an indicator of being, took on a new facet wherein researchers started studying 'hedonic consumption'. This is defined as those facets of consumer behaviour that relate to multi-sensory, fantasy and emotive aspects of one's experience with products. Past research suggests that individuals (Hirschman and Holbrook, 1982) respond to multi-sensory impressions from external stimuli (such as a perfume) by encoding these sensory inputs. In addition, they also react by generating multi-sensory images within themselves, all of which is also experienced. These internal multi-sensory images can be of two types: first, historic imagery, that involves recalling an event that actually did occur. Second, fantasy imagery, that consumer responds by producing a multi-sensory image not drawn directly from a prior experience. Instead of replaying a historic sequence, consumer constructs an imaginary one. Hence, it could be said that the hedonic consumption is tied to imaginative constructs of reality (Singer, 1966). Thus hedonic consumption acts are not based on what consumers know to be real but rather on what they desire reality to be. This can possibly be linked with the concept of self-discrepancy (Dittmar, 1992; Lunt and Livingstone, 1992). This discrepancy between real and desired could play a role in invoking impulse—an impulse to travel the psychological distance between real and desired and an act of buying on impulse could possibly help in this journey. The above link between hedonic consumption, self-discrepancy, and impulse is a derived link and has not been researched. Further research in this direction can provide more clarity on the topic.

Interestingly, as a type of internal stimuli, Piron (1989, 1991) recognized the role and importance of autistic stimuli in motivating impulse purchases. Emphasis on autistic or self-generated stimuli in consumer behaviour emerged from Hirschman's (1985) study on cognitive processes (Malter, 1996) that are involved in experiential consumption. Autistic thought is generated in response to internal impulses and is self-contained and self-serving. Such mental activity frequently occurs as a response to unattainable or forbidden objectives, which can only be obtained vicariously via fantasy. Autistic thoughts do not follow logic or rationality and are frequently associated with emotion and sensuality. Therefore, autistic thoughts can possess great evocative power (Hirschman, 1985) and can possibly lead to impulse buying. Another factor that has been found to influence impulse buying is 'affect' (Silvera et al., 2008). When asked to name the single mood that most often preceded an impulse purchase, respondents most frequently mentioned 'pleasure' followed by 'carefree' and 'excited' (Hirschman, 1985). In particular, people who feel happy may be disposed to reward themselves generously and to feel as if they have freedom to act (Rook and Gardner, 1993). Some people indulge in impulse purchase as a way to relieve unpleasant mood (Elliott, 1994). It can also be seen as behaviour often motivated by attempts to cheer up self or be nice to oneself (Mick and DeMoss, 1990).

Self-regulatory resource availability is considered an important element in determining when and why people engage in impulsive spending. Self-regulatory resources (Muraven et al., 1998) are conceptualized as a generalized pool of energy that allows people to overcome incipient urges and substitute a desirable behaviour for an undesired one (Baumeister and Vohs, 2004). This pool of resources is global, and essentially self-regulated behaviours across a variety of situations pull from this resource. However, this resource is finite—meaning that behaviours or responses in one domain that draw upon this resource cause all other subsequent self-control (Tice et al., 2001) endeavours to be less successful. This point has been discussed in connection with temporal dimensions and Baumeister (2002) has suggested that people's ability to resist temptation is at its lowest level at the end of the day as the self's resources become progressively depleted during the day. Therefore, people are more vulnerable to buying on impulse towards evening and end of the day. Day part analysis of impulse proneness of consumers may have implications for the sales promotion activities (Liao et al., 2009) that can be explored in detail.

Positive and negative feeling states have been discussed in a study by Youn and Faber (2000) and they suggest that both positive and negative feeling states are potential motivators for impulse buying. Their study specifically discussed the impact of 'positive feelings', 'depressed feelings', 'feeling flat' and 'painful feelings'.

Verplanken et al. (2005) propose that negative rather than positive affect is a driving force behind chronic impulse buying: impulse buying for escaping (Youn and Faber, 2000) the negative psychological states. Their study finds negative affect to be partially positively related to cognitive impulse buying tendency and positively related to affective impulse buying tendency. Along with studies of extreme moods, the study done by Tauber (1972) discusses mental diversion from boredom as a motivation for an unplanned shopping trip. In all this, personality played no role in unplanned buying (Kollat and Willet, 1967).

IMPULSE BUYING BECAUSE OF NEGATIVE AFFECT

Sneath et al. (2009) have explored another area, which has a bearing on impulse buying tendency. They state that impulse buying can also be induced because of depression. These authors have discussed the context of Hurricane Katrina disaster victims, who engaged in distinct purchasing behaviours to manage emotional states, recoup losses and restore their sense of self. In the aftermath of a traumatic event, impulsive buying appears to be a rational and beneficial behaviour (Sneath et al., 2009). This relieving effect of 'impulse buying' links with cathartic effect of the same (Rook and Gardner, 1993).

This negative association between impulse buying tendency and subjective wellbeing (Dittmar, 2008) needs to be explored further.

EXTERNAL MOTIVATORS OF IMPULSE BUYING (SHOP RELATED FACTORS)

External motivators are specific prompts associated with shopping set-up. Buying impulses can be set off when a consumer incidentally encounters a relevant visual stimulus in the retail environment, usually the product (Liang and Meng, 2008) itself or some promotional stimuli (Piron, 1991). Here, buying impulses begin with a consumer's sensation and perception driven by the environmental stimulus, and are followed by a sudden urge to acquire it (I see I want to buy) (Rook and Hoch, 1985). A strong perceptual attraction to stimulus obviates the need or ability to consider analytic evaluation or ordinary restrictions. Such a powerful attraction arises quickly, immediately, and on the spot. Thus, this 'rapidity' characteristic of 'buying impulse' offers compelling evidence that the reactive impulse buying leads to action immediately at the moment of being exposed to triggering stimuli.

Many authors have discussed the importance of visual stimuli in initiating impulse in buying scenario. There have been specific references to shopping malls (Bloch et al., 1994, Lehtonen and Maenpaa, 1997) that are characterized by collection of stores with wide variety of products, opportunities for social bonding and norming of tastes. In the context of malls, another factor that was linked with impulse buying is self-service environment (Lehtonen and Maenpaa, 1997; Stern, 1962). In addition, shopping pleasure gets further enhanced with a shopper being free and unobserved to try on new things and styles and fantasize, wrapped in the anonymity of a self-service environment.

In past research on 'impulse buying', 'encounter with the object' was considered a very powerful trigger to the act of impulse buying. As the research by Rook (1987) suggests, consumers have the most difficult time resisting the urge in the moments following their encounter with the object. Physical proximity can stimulate sensory inputs that affect desire. Touching products in a store, tasting free samples of food, sniffing enticing aromas, or test-driving a luxury automobile can enhance desire to purchase a good (Vohs and Faber, 2007). A recent research by Peck and Childers (2006), studied the relationship between impulse purchase and the individual difference in autotelic NFT (need for touch), as well as an environmental encouragement to touch and concluded that individuals higher in autotelic NFT purchased more impulsively than their lower autotelic NFT counterparts. NFT and autotelic NFT seem to be a potential explanation of many a phenomenon happening in the market place, however, this topic needs to be explored in detail and is likely to differ by cultural contexts.

Another factor that has been strongly linked with enhanced urges to buy is in-store browsing. It is seen as producing encounters with desirable products (Jones et al., 2003) that may produce an urge to buy. This urge becomes difficult to resist due to physical proximity of the product. These initial attempts to understand external motivators of impulse buying have streamed in a huge list of 'things to focus on' for malls and department stores. These also include specific roles played by different forms of in-store signage, which effectively increase unit sales of products (Woodside and Waddle, 1975; Abratt and Goodey, 1990). On similar lines, it was found that visual merchandising is another driver of impulse purchase, wherein 'looked good on shelf' was one of the key reasons which made people decide to buy impulsively (Rostocks, 2003). On similar lines, Cox (1970) discussed a positive relationship between the amount of shelf space given to an impulse product that has high consumer acceptance and total unit sales of that brand. 'Stimulating store environment' has been studied in association with impulse buying. This was found to lead to a momentary loss of self-control, thus enhancing the likelihood of impulse purchase (Mattila and Wirtz, 2008). This finding has been consistent with the research in psychology, which suggests that high arousal or over-stimulation lessens people's self-regulation (Baumeister et al., 1998) and is seen as playing a crucial role in creating an environment for impulse buying (Wirtz et al., 2007).

They found that highly stimulating and pleasant store environments lead to enhanced impulse buying. Certain ambient factors like fast tempo and high volume music (Holbrook and Anand, 1990), ambient scents (Mattila and Wirtz, 2001) and colours (Valdez and Mehrabian, 1994) were studied in relation to in-store stimulation levels. These were found to have a bearing on in-store stimulation levels and impulse buying tendency. All these findings further support the understanding of 'recreational shopper' (Bellenger and Korgaonkar, 1980), who goes for shopping with a latent desire for recreation. The above quoted researches suggest that exciting and stimulating store environments are likely to enhance levels of impulse purchases. However, there seems to be a dearth of research in obtaining a holistic understanding of nature of stimulation, its impact on mood of the shopper and its relationship with impulse buying tendency.

Mattila and Wirtz (2008) also found that social factors influence impulse buying. Social factors include two types: store employees and other customers. Previous research findings suggest that employee behaviours predict customer evaluations (Bittner, 1990). Prior work also indicates that helpfulness of salespeople in assisting customers influences his willingness to buy (Baker et al., 1994). While exploring the role of social factors in impulse buying, it is important to consider the work done by Rook and Fisher (1995) who, on the contrary suggested that anonymity might encourage impulse purchasing. Shoppers tend to try on new things, styles and fantasize, wrapped in the anonymity of a self-service environment. This contradiction may merit further exploration in order to understand their impact on impulse buying by the shoppers. Research on 'perceived crowding' (Machleit et al., 2000) postulates that human density is negatively correlated with satisfaction (Dion, 2004) and number of purchases (Grossbart et al., 1990). However, Biyani (2005) discusses that crowding and not so orderly display of goods can make the buyer feel at ease and so can lead to impulse buying. Hence, there is a need for further exploration (possibly culture specific) of the impact of crowding and perceived crowding on impulse buying.

Expanding further on 'rapidity' that is characteristic of impulse purchase, the research by Bernthal et al. (2005) observed that the people who possess credit cards are more likely to purchase impulsively. The act of spending through credit cards frees the spender of psychological implications of spending, as the card involved acts as a temporary shield. Further the incidence of gifting and self-gifts gets a further propulsion through credit cards. All this goes a step further in explaining the role that credit cards play in acting as catalysts of impulse purchase. Research done in the same direction (Pirog and Roberts, 2007) has emphasized the role of personality in credit card usage. Four elemental personality traits—emotional instability, introversion, materialism and the need for arousal—are found to be positively associated with credit card misuse. The research that is linking impulse buying and credit cards is limited to specific purchases, such as gifting for others and self-gifting. The role of credit cards (and other forms of credit), in catalyzing other forms of impulse purchases, is yet to be explored.

Further, Hoch and Loewenstein (1991) suggest that buying may beget more buying, having 'fallen off the wagon'. This suggests a form of momentum in which additional urges are acted upon more quickly than previous urges. The shopping formats are likely to play a big role in utilizing this trigger. Malls and large-scale department stores are more likely to initiate this momentum of buying and the reason for the same could possibly be attributed to much higher levels of exposure and facilitated visual contact with an array of attractively displayed products. In addition, 'fallen off the wagon' is an interesting concept and needs to be checked further in context of discount stores, large-scale department stores and possibly even fairs and exhibitions.

SUMMARY

In earlier sections, an attempt was made to present a review of research work done to explore the phenomenon of 'impulse buying'. Along with this, the review also looks into a clarification of underpinnings of this phenomenon. It starts with the various definitions of 'impulse buying'. Their relation with unplanned buying, behavioural dimension, internal and external motivators is explored at length. In sum, the study reviews existing literature on the impulse buying phenomenon while Table 1 gives a gist of various motivators explored in this review article.

Table 1.

INTERNAL MOTIVATORS	EXTERNAL MOTIVATORS
Self-discrepancy	Visual stimulus
Hedonic needs	Shopping format
Mood states	Self-service
Self regulatory resource availability	Store environment
Autistic stimuli	Discounts
Social status	Display
Subjective well-being (or lack of it)	Shelf space
	Ambient factors
	Social factors
	Perceived crowding
	Ownership of credit card

LITERATURE GAPS

Based on the literature review given in previous sections, it can be concluded that though large numbers of studies have been carried out in the past in this field, however, some of the facets of this phenomenon have remained unexplored:

- Current theories in economics (e.g., discounting models), marketing (e.g., information-processing models) and psychology (e.g., addiction models) do not fully explain underlying reasons for impulse buying.
- 'Impulse buying' as a buying format has gained momentum in India post the emergence of modern day retail formats, the existing studies on impulse are mostly restricted to the West. The Indian scenario has remained largely unexplored until recently (Kaur and Singh, 2007).

NOTE

1. Imaginary 'perfectly rational' person who, by always thinking marginally, maximizes his or her economic welfare and achieves consumer equilibrium.

REFERENCES

Abratt, R., & Goodey, S.D. (1990). Unplanned buying and in-store stimuli in supermarkets. *Managerial and Decision Economics*, 11 (2), 111–121.

Arndt, J., Sheldon, S., Tim, K., & Sheldon, K.M. (2004). The urge to splurge: A terror management account of materialism and consumer behaviour. *Journal of Consumer Psychology*, 14(3), 198–212.

Audi, R. (1989). Practical reasoning. New York: Routledge, Chapman & Hall.

Baker, J., Grewal, D., & Parasuraman, A. (1994). The influence of store environment on quality inferences and store image. *Journal of Academy of Marketing Science*, 22(4), 328–339.

Bloch, P.H., Ridgway, N.M., & Dawson, S.A. (1994). The shopping mall as consumer habitat. *Journal of Retailing*, 70(1).

Baumeister, R., Bratslavsky, E., Muraven, M., & Tice, D. (1998). Ego depletion: Is the active self a limited resource. *Journal of Personality & Social Psychology*, 74(5), 1252–1265.

Baumeister, R.F. (2002).Yielding to temptation: Self-control failure, impulsive purchasing, and consumer behaviour. *Journal of Consumer Research*, 28(4), 670–676.

Baumeister, R.F., & Vohs, K.D. (2004). *Handbook of self regulation: Research, theory and applications*. New York: Guilford Press.

Bellenger, D.N., Robertson, D., & Hirschman, E. (1978). Impulse buying varies by product. *Journal of Advertising Research*, 18(6), 15–18.

Bellenger, D.N., & Korgaonkar, P.K. (1980). Profile the recreational shopper. *Journal of Retailing*, 56(3), 77–92.

Bernthal, M.J., Crockett, D., & Rose, R.L. (2005). Credit cards as lifestyle facilitators. *Journal of Consumer Research*, 32(1), 130–145.

Bittner, M.J. (1990). Evaluating service encounters: The effects of physical surroundings and employee responses. *Journal of Marketing*, 54(2), 69–82.

Biyani, K. (2005). *It happened in India*. New Delhi: Rupa & Co.

Clover, V.T. (1950). Relative importance of impulse buying in retail stores. *Journal of Marketing*, 25(2), July, 66–70.

Cobb, C.J., & Hoyer, W.D. (1986). Planned versus impulse purchase behaviour. *Journal of Retailing*, 62(4), 384–409.

Cox, K. (1964). The responsiveness of food sales to shelf space changes in supermarkets. *Journal of Marketing Research*, 1(2), 63–67.

_____. (1970). The effect of shelf space on sales of branded products. *Journal of Marketing Research*, 7(1), 55–58.

Dion, D. (2004). Personal control and coping with retail crowding. *International Journal of Service Industry Management*, 15(3), 250–263.

Dittmar, H. (1992). The social psychology of material possessions: To have is to be. New York & Hemel Hempstead: St Martin Press and Harvester Wheatsheaf.

_____. (2005). Compulsive buying—A growing concern? An examination of gender, age, and endorsement of materialistic values as predictors. *British Journal of Psychology*, 96(4), 467–491.

_____. (2008). *Consumer society, identity, and well-being: The search for the 'Good Life' and the 'Body Perfect'. European monographs in Social Psychology Series* (edited by Rupert Brown). London and New York: Psychology Press.

Elliott, R. (1994). Addictive consumption: Function and fragmentation in post modernity. *Journal of Consumer Policy*, 17(2), 159–179.

Freud, S. (1911/1956). Formulations of the two principles of mental functioning. In J. Strachey and A. Freud (Eds), *The standard edition of the complete psychological works of Sigmund Freud*, Vol.12., London: Hogarth.

Goldenson, R.M. (1984). *Longman dictionary of Psychology and Psychiatry*. New York: Longman.

Grossbart, S., Hampton, R., Rammohan, B., & Lapidus, R.S. (1990). Environmental dispositions and customer responses to store atmospherics. *Journal of Business Research*, 21(3), 225–241.

Hoch, S.J., & Loewenstein, G.F. (1991). Time inconsistent preferences and consumer self-control. *Journal of Consumer Research*, 17(4), 492–507.

Hirschman, E.C., & Holbrook, M.B. (1982). Hedonic consumption: emerging concepts, methods and propositions. *Journal of Marketing*, 46(3), 92–101.

Hirschman, E.C. (1985). Cognitive processes in experiential consumer behaviour. In Jagdish N. Sheth (Ed.), *Research in consumer behavior*, Vol. 1 (pp. 31–42). Greenwich: Jai Press, Inc.

Holbrook, M.B., & Anand, P. (1990). Effects of tempo and situational arousal on the listener's perceptual & affective responses to music. *Psychology of Music*, 18(2), 150–162.

Iyer, E.S. (1989). Unplanned purchasing: Knowledge of shopping environment and time pressure. *Journal of Retailing*, 65(1), 40–57.

Jones, M., Reynolds, K., Weun, S., & Beatty, S. (2003). The product specific nature of impulse buying tendency. *Journal of Business Research*, 56(7), 505–511.

Kaur, P., & Singh, R. (2007). Uncovering retail shopping motives of Indian youth. *Young Consumers*, 8(2), 128–138.

Kivetz, R. & Simonson, I. (2002). Earning the right to indulge: Effort as a determinant of customer preferences toward frequency program rewards. *Journal of Marketing Research,* 39(2), 155–170.

Kollat, D.T., & Willet, R.P. (1967). Is impulse purchasing really a useful concept for marketing decisions? *Journal of Marketing,* 33(1), 79–83.

Lehtonen,T., & Maenpaa, P. (1997). Shopping in the East Centre Mall. In P. Falk, & C. Campbell (Eds), *The shopping experience* (pp. 136–165). London: SAGE.

Levy (1959). Symbols for sale. *Harvard Business Review,* 37(4), 117–124.

Liao, Shu-Ling, Yung-Cheng Chu, & Chia-Hsien (2009). The effects of sales promotion strategy, product appeal and consumer traits on reminder impulse buying behaviour. *International Journal of Consumer Studies,* 33(3), 278–284.

Liang, Guo, & Xiangyu Meng (2008). Consumer knowledge and its consequences: An international comparison. *International Journal of Consumer Studies,* 32(3), 260–268.

Liebert, R.M., & Liebert, L.L. (1998). *Liebert & Spiegler's personality: Strategies and issues.* Pacific Grove, CA: Brooks/Cole.

Lunt, P.K., & Livingstone, S. M. (1992). *Mass consumption and personal identity.* Milton Keynes: Open University Press.

Machleit, K.A., Eroglu, S.A., & Mantel, S.P. (2000). Perceived retail crowding and shopping satisfaction: What modifies the relationship. *Journal of Consumer Psychology,* 9(1), 29–42.

Malter, A.J. (1996). An introduction to embodied cognition: Implications for consumer research. *Advances in Consumer Research,* 23(1), 272–276.

Mattila, A.S., & Wirtz, J. (2001). Congruency of scent and music as a driver of in-store evaluations and behavior. *Journal of Retailing,* 77(2), 273–289.

_____. (2008). The role of store environmental stimulation and social factors on impulse purchasing. *Journal of Services Marketing,* 22(7), 562–567.

Mele, A.R. (1987). Irrationality: An essay on Akrasia, self-deception, and self-control. *US: Oxford University Press.*

Mick, D.G., & DeMoss, M. (1990). Self gifts: Phenomenological insights from four contexts. *Journal of Consumer Research,* 17(3), 322–332.

Muraven, M., Tice, D., & Baumeister, R. (1998). Self-control as limited resource: Regulatory depletion patterns. *Journal of Personality and Social Psychology,* 74(3), 774–789.

O'Guinn, T.C., & Faber, R.J. (1989). Classifying compulsive consumers: Advances in the development of a diagnostic tool. *Advances in Consumer Research,* 16, 738–744.

Park, E.J., Kim, E.Y., & Forney, J. (2006). A structural model of fashion-oriented impulse buying behaviour. *Journal of Fashion Marketing and Management,* 10(4), 433–446.

Peck, J., & Childers, T.L. (2006). If I touch it I have to have it: Individual and environmental influences on impulse purchasing. *Journal of Business Research,* 59(6), 765–769.

Piron, F. (1989). *A definition and empirical investigation of impulse purchasing.* Unpublished Dissertation, The University of South Carolina, Columbia.

_____. (1991). Defining impulse purchasing. *Advances in Consumer Research,* 18, 509–514.

Pirog, S.F., & Roberts, J.A. (2007). Personality and credit card misuse among college students: The mediating role of impulsiveness. *Journal of Marketing Theory and Practice,* 15(1), 365–378.

Ramanathan, S., & Menon, G. (2006). Time-varying effects of chronic Hedonic goals on impulsive behaviour. *Journal of Marketing Research,* 43(4), 628–641.

Rook, D.W. (1987). The buying impulse. *Journal of Consumer Research, 14*(2), 189–199.

Rook, D.W., & Gardner, M.P. (1993). In the mood: Impulse buying's affective antecedents. *Research in Consumer Behavior, 6,* 1–28.

Rook, D.W., & Hoch, S.J. (1985). Consuming Impulses. In Morris Holbrook & Elizabeth Hirschman (Eds), *Advances in Consumer Research,* 12 (pp. 23–27). Provo, UT: Association for Consumer Research.

Rook, D.W., & Fisher, R.J. (1995). Normative influences on impulse buying behaviour. *Journal of Consumer Research, 22*(3), 305–313.

Rostocks, L. (2003). Tapping into the shopper impulse. *Canadian Grocer, 117*(8).

Shapiro, J.M. (1992). Impulse buying: A new framework. *Developments in Marketing Science, 15,* 57–80.

Silvera, D.H., Lavack, A.M., & Kropp, F. (2008). Impulse buying: The role of affect, social influence and well-being. *Journal of Consumer Marketing, 25*(1), 23–33.

Singer, J.L. (1966). Daydreaming: An introduction to the experimental study of inner experience. *New York: Random House.*

Shiv, B., & Fedorikhin, A. (1999). Heart and mind in conflict: The interplay of affect and cognition in consumer decision making. *Journal of Consumer Research, 26*(3), 278–292.

Sneath, J.Z., Lacey, R., & Kennett-Hensel, P.A. (2009). Coping with a natural disaster: Losses, emotions, and impulsive and compulsive buying. *Marketing Letters, 20*(1), 45–60.

Stephen J.H. & Loewenstein, G.F. (1991). Time-inconsistent preferences and consumer self-control. *The Journal of Conusmer Research, 17*(4), 492–507.

Stern, H. (1962). The significance of impulse buying today. *Journal of Marketing, 26*(2), 59–62.

Tauber, E.M. (1972). Why do people shop? *Journal of Marketing, 36*(4), 46–59.

Tice, D., Bratslavsky, E., & Baumeister, R. (2001). Emotional distress regulation takes precedence over impulse control: If you feel bad, do it! *Journal of Personality and Social Psychology, 80*(1), 53–67.

Valdez, P., & Mehrabian, H. (1994). Effects of color on emotions. *Journal of Experimental Psychology: General. 123*(4), 394–409.

Verplanken, B., Herabadi, A.G., Perry, J.A., & Silvera, D.H. (2005). Consumer style and health: The role of impulsive buying in unhealthy eating. *Psychology and Health, 20*(4), 429–441.

Vohs, K.D., & Faber, R.J. (2007). Spent resources: Self regulatory resource availability affects impulse buying. *Journal of Consumer Research, 33*(4), 537–547.

Wansink, B. (1994). The dark side of consumer behaviour: Empirical examinations of impulsive and compulsive consumption. *Advances in Consumer Research, 21,* 508.

Weinberg, P., & Gottwald, W. (1982). Impulsive consumer buying as a result of emotions. *Journal of Business Research, 10*(1), 43–57.

Wicklund, R.A., & Gollwitzer, P.M. (1981). Symbolic self-completion, attempted influence, and self-deprecation. *Basic and Applied Social Psychology, 2*(2), 89–114.

Wirtz, J., Mattila, A.D., & Tan, R.L.P. (2007). The role of desired arousal in influencing consumer's satisfaction evaluations and in-store behaviors. *International Journal of Service Industry Management, 18*(1), 23–50.

Woodside, A.G., & Waddle, G.L. (1975). Sales effects of in-store-advertising. *Journal of Advertising Research, 15*(3), 29–33.

Youn, S., & Faber, R.J. (2000). Impulse buying: Its relation to personality traits and cues. *Advances in Consumer Research, 27,* 179–185.

Zuckerman, M. (1994). *Behavioural expressions and biosocial bases of sensation seeking.* Cambridge: Cambridge University Press.

ADVERTISING AND THE CONSUMER INFORMATION ENVIRONMENT ONLINE

Ronald J. Faber, Mira Lee, and Xiaoli Nan

The Internet has apparently become an important source of information for consumers and partly because of this trend, the Internet now presents a huge opportunity for advertisers who seek effective communication with their target markets. The purpose of this article is to provide an understanding of the qualities and potentials of the Internet as an advertising medium. First, an overview of the various forms of Internet advertising is provided, as well as a review of existing literature regarding the effectiveness of each form. The article next compares the Internet with traditional mass media from the perspective of the consumer information environment and shows how unique characteristics of the Internet may alter consumer experience and decision making. The article concludes with a discussion of the needs and challenges facing the field.

According to E-Marketer (2003), there were 153 million Internet users in the United States at the end of 2002, and an estimated 10 million more were expected to come online in 2003. Internet users engage in all kinds of activities online. Among the most common are searching for information, communicating, seeking entertainment, and shopping (Korgaonkar & Wolin, 1999; S. Rodgers & Sheldon, 2002). The Internet has become an important source for consumer information both through advertising and other product-related sites. According to recent estimates, Internet advertising revenue in the United States totaled U.S.$5.95 billion in 2002 (Interactive Advertising Bureau, 2003).

The continuing growth of Internet users and the development of the Internet advertising industry have prompted considerable research interest in this form of advertising. A recent editor's column in the *Journal of Advertising* listed Internet advertising as one of the three fastest growing areas of

Ronald J. Faber, Mira Lee, and Xiaoli Nan, "Advertising and the Consumer Information Environment Online," *American Behavioral Scientist*, vol. 48, no. 4, pp. 447–466. Copyright © 2004 by Sage Publications. Reprinted with permission.

research in advertising during the past few years (Faber, 2002). Another growth trend cited by Faber (2002) was research examining content areas that were not traditionally viewed as advertising. These include things such as sponsorship, nonpaid promotional communication, and brand placements.

These two trends are not completely independent. One of the outcomes of increased product promotions on the Internet has been a rapid development of more alternative delivery forms and less clear-cut distinctions between advertising, other forms of brand promotion and information dissemination, and other types of brand and product information. For example, we traditionally think of advertising as a paid-for message appearing in some type of media or in a place that can attract large numbers of consumers (e.g., billboards on the highway or posters on buses). The Internet contains some forms of advertising that would match this description. However, on the Internet, advertisers also have their own home pages. Here they may sell goods, provide information about their products, and offer additional benefits to consumers. This begins to blur the role of advertising and other marketing functions. Other sites may sell multiple brands much like brick and mortar stores. Such sites may provide information about many brands or provide brand reviews. It is not always clear if such information is independently determined or a form of paid promotion by a particular brand. Again, the clarity between advertising and independent information on the Internet becomes less clear. This has led to a growing need to better define what is considered advertising and to reconsider many assumptions about how advertising works.

This article begins with a review of the various formats that advertising can take on the Internet. These include forms resembling more traditional advertising formats as well as more unique and emerging formats. A brief review of the existing literature regarding each form is also given. Following this, an effort is made to delineate the unique qualities of the Internet and how they may alter the consumer experience and brand decision making. Of particular concern here is how these unique features of Internet advertising may alter important outcome variables in advertising, such as brand memory, attitudes, intentions, and decision-making strategies. Finally, we hope to present a clearer view of the change the Internet has created in the broader perspective of the consumer information environment. Advertising research is often approached from the perspective of the advertiser and examines how he or she can influence the consumer's attitude or preference for a given brand. A more critical perspective may be from the view of the consumer and how he or she navigates through the vast amount of often conflicting and occasionally irrelevant information found in the broad consumer environment. We believe it is this broader approach that will be the most important for understanding the role of Internet communication regarding products and services. We conclude with a discussion of the future needs and challenges facing the field.

FORMS OF NEW MEDIA ADVERTISING

In an article on Interactive advertising, S. Rodgers and Thorson (2000) identified five types of ad formats found on the Internet. These were banners, interstitials and pop-ups, sponsorships, hypertext links,[1] and Web sites. As new media continue to develop, a few additional formats have begun to emerge and others are likely in the future. The following section identifies and describes these formats and provides a brief review of findings regarding each of them.

Banner ads. Banner ads are graphic images (usually 468 x 60 pixels) displayed on an HTML page used as an ad (Interactive Advertising Bureau, 2002). They typically appear as rectangular-shaped boxes located at the top, sides, or bottom of the page. Banner ads are primarily used to build Web traffic by allowing consumers to click them to be hyperlinked to advertised Web sites for more information. Banner ads are the predominant form of new media advertising, representing 55% of all online ads (Interactive Advertising Bureau, 1999) and 32% of all new media advertising revenue (Interactive Advertising Bureau, 2002). However, the average click-through rate has been continuously declining and now runs at about 0.3% (Nielsen/Netratings, 2000). Efforts to trick people into clicking on these ads through misleading messages have also led to consumer dislike for this format. Due mainly to the very low click-through rate, some researchers have expressed skepticism about the effectiveness of banner ads (Cross, 1999).

Some authors, however, have argued that the effectiveness of banner ads should not be judged solely by their click-through rates (Briggs & Hollis, 1997). Instead, banner ads may also function much like billboards in more traditional media environments. Although the banner can contain only a limited amount of information, usually just the brand name and a brief slogan, it can serve to increase brand awareness and as a reminder to existing brand users. Using an experimental study, Briggs and Hollis (1997) showed that exposures to standard static banner ads enhanced brand awareness, brand strength, and consumer loyalty even when click-throughs did not occur.

A number of researchers have examined potential strategies to enhance the effectiveness of banner ads. Just as with traditional ads, size and motion increase performance. Large, animated banner ads have been shown to result in quicker response, to be better recalled, and to trigger more click-throughs than small, nonanimated banner ads (Li & Bukovac, 1999). Brown (2002) found that banner ads containing pull-down menus generated higher attention, liking, persuasion, and click-throughs than standard static banner ads. He argued that these favorable findings might be due to the fact that consumers liked the increased quality of information made available to them by the pull-down menus.

Another strategy for attracting consumers is to personalize the ad message. G. Nowak, Shamp, Hollander, and Cameron (1999) found that personalization increased the likelihood that consumers would click the banner ad and appeared to enhance attitudes toward the Web sites and their sponsors. A newer form of banner advertising is the smart banner. This is a keyword-activated banner that appears on a search engine Web page when consumers enter relevant keywords into a search engine. Dou, Linn, and Yang (2001) argued that if keyword-activated banners are "smart" enough to provide exact matches, they have the potential to enhance the effectiveness of banner ads by displaying them at the right point of a consumer's specific interests and needs. Thus, the future of banner ads may rely on their ability to successfully target consumers and appear at the time when information is desired. Beyond that, it may serve a reminder function for frequently purchased consumer brands.

Pop-up ads. According to Nielsen/NetRatings, during the first seven months of 2002, advertisers purchased and launched more than 11.3 billion pop-up ad impressions on the Internet (Martin & Ryan, 2002). Pop-ups are ads that appear in a separate window on top of the content a user is viewing. The pop-up window will not go away until the user actively closes it.

Cho, Lee, and Tharp (2001) reported that pop-up ads yielded more click-throughs, more favorable attitude toward the ad and the brand, and higher purchase intention than standard banner ads. However, a more recent study found that pop-up ads were perceived as irritating and annoying

(Edwards, Li, & Lee, 2002). Negative sentiments about pop-up ads occur because they interrupt the activity that people are engaged in on the Web. An industry consumer survey conducted by GartnerG2 (2002) show that compared to other forms of new media advertising, pop-up ads were considered most irritating. From an advertiser's perspective, however, irritating ads may not always be bad. Some have argued that irritating ads help consumers remember the brand name and may even increase sales (Robertson, Zielinski, & Ward, 1984). Some Internet advertisers use pop-up ads because of the "in your face" impact they have (Dillabough, 2002). However, major online content/service providers such as EarthLink and America Online have recently responded to consumers' complaints about pop-ups by employing new software that allows users to block pop-up ads ("America Online," 2003).

Some advertisers are also attempting to make pop-up ads less annoying. One strategy is to use them in situations where users are likely to be online for diversion or to avoid boredom rather than where they are focused on a specific goal. Another strategy to reduce annoyance may be to increase the value of pop-up ads. Edwards et al. (2002) found that when pop-up ads provided value to consumers, they were perceived as less irritating.

Commercial Web sites. Whether commercial Web sites should be considered as media advertising has been an issue of much debate (Berthon, Pitt, & Watson, 1996; Choi, Miracle, & Biocca, 2001; Ducoffe 1996; Hwang, McMillan, & Lee, 2003; Singh & Dalal, 1999). Currently, however, there appears to be a growing consensus that they should. For example, Singh and Dalal (1999) argued that home pages resemble ads in physical appearance and perform the same basic functions—to inform and to persuade—as other advertising messages. Recently, Hwang et al. (2003) content analyzed home pages of 160 corporate Web sites and concluded that the entire corporate Web site was an extension of traditional corporate advertising.

However, unlike other advertising formats, Web sites require active effort to achieve exposure (Chatterjee, 1996). That is, although consumers usually come across banner ads and/or pop-ups incidentally, they must make an effort to access commercial Web sites. Thus, consumers control exposure to this form of promotional material. This should enhance their attitude toward this form of advertising and guarantee that it is used when the information will be most useful and desired. Although most forms of advertising can be seen as typically involving low involvement processing, Web sites may be processed more centrally. Here, the actual information on the site may be considered and evaluated. This works well for both the consumer and the advertiser because Web sites can provide almost unlimited amounts of information and the user can select those bits that are most relevant to their concerns.

Although cognitive processing may play an important role, this is not to say that emotional and/or aesthetic content on a Web site will not matter. Most assuredly they do. Researchers examining commercial Web sites as advertising have examined specific features available on these sites (Choi et al., 2001; Coyle & Thorson, 2001; Ghose & Dou, 1998; Li, Daugherty, & Biocca, 2001, 2002). They have found that interactivity in commercial Web sites appears to enhance perceptions of telepresence (Coyle & Thorson, 2001). In turn, these perceptions of telepresence positively influence various advertising effectiveness measures. For example, Choi et al. (2001) found that the use of an anthropomorphic agent (a computer-generated entity that is endowed with a human form) on a commercial Web site increases a sense of social presence and telepresence, which subsequently influences attitudes toward the site and the brand, purchase intention, and intention to revisit the site.

Presentation modes on Web sites can also enhance their use as an information agent. For example, three-dimensional product presentations allow consumers to zoom in and out a certain part of a product, view visual details of the product by using a 360° rotation function, and even customize their future product to fit their own lifestyle. Li et al. (2001, 2002) found that when examining three-dimensional products, consumers are active information processors, are more likely to feel presence with a product, and are more likely to feel pleasure or enjoyment of interacting with the product. In addition, three-dimensional product presentations have been found to yield higher consumer learning, brand attitude, and purchase intentions than flat, static two-dimensional photo images of products (Li et al., 2002).

Finally, company Web sites can enhance the opportunity for trial and actual purchase of a product. Clothing sites such as Land's End allow consumers to provide physical information about themselves and use this to see an image of how an item would actually look on them (see the My Virtual Model feature on http://www.landsend.com). Similarly, music, movie, and game sites allow consumers to sample the content prior to purchasing. This form of trial decreases perceived risk for the consumer and enhances the likelihood of purchasing. In addition, Web sites often combine information about the brand with an immediate opportunity to purchase the item. This greatly alters the traditional advertising situation where ad processing and brand information retrieval occur at separate points in time (Baker & Lutz, 2000).

Internet sponsorships. One of the least understood but commonly used forms of new media advertising is Internet sponsorship (Interactive Advertising Bureau, 2002). For the past 6 years, Internet sponsorships have represented from 24% to 37% of all new media advertising revenue (Interactive Advertising Bureau, 2002). Internet sponsorships use an association with a Web site or a specific content section of a Web site to give an advertiser visibility for marketing purposes (Interactive Advertising Bureau, 2002; S. Rodgers & Thorson, 2000). Like sponsorships in traditional media channels, Internet sponsorships are often called advertising fragments—messages that are restricted to the brand name or to a few words that summarize the brand's unique selling propositions (Pham & Vanhuele, 1997; S. Rodgers & Thorson, 2000). For example, Macy's and Pfizer's logos appear on the American Heart Association's (n.d.) official Web site along with the text message "Macy's and Pfizer are proud national sponsors of the American Heart Association's Go Red For Woman Campaign." In a study examining the effects of Internet sponsorships, S. Rodgers (2003) found that the perceived link between the sponsor and sponsee is important in that relevant sponsors tend to elicit greater recall, better brand evaluations, and higher purchase intent than irrelevant sponsors. Despite the popularity of Internet sponsorships in practice, academic research on Internet sponsorships have been sparse. More research is needed to advance our knowledge about this form of new media advertising.

Paid keyword search listing. Surveys have found that approximately half of all Web users report using search engines (London, 2000; Overture, 2003). As a result, a growing number of advertisers have begun using paid search listings as a form of advertising to get their site noticed when consumers use search engines.

To ensure marketing message placement and ranking in listings in the search results, advertisers usually select keywords that are relevant to their business and then purchase those keywords from paid listing providers. When a consumer enters specific words into a search engine (e.g., Google, Yahoo Search, or Ask Jeeves), the search engine checks with the paid listing provider's database and provides a list of Web sites related to keywords (Overture, 2003). These paid listings are often placed at the top or side of a search results page and known to consumers as sponsored links. According to the Interactive Advertising Bureau (2002), keyword searches accounted for 9% of the total new media advertising revenues in the second quarter of 2002.

Paid keyword search listings are believed to offer several benefits as an advertising tool. Like smart banners, they effectively target consumers at the right point in time. Moreover, because a consumer is highly motivated to process information when he or she uses keyword searches, advertisers' search listings may not only get click-throughs but also have the potential to increase conversion rates after click-throughs (Greenberg, 2000). Despite these perceived benefits of paid keyword search listings as an advertising tool, assumptions about their effectiveness appear to be based primarily on anecdotal rather than empirical evidence. Future research is clearly needed here.

Advergames. Playing computer games is an entertainment activity enjoyed by many consumers (Interactive Digital Software Association, 2000). In 2001, U.S. sales of game hardware and software rose 43% to hit U.S.$9.4 billion. This exceeds the revenues from Hollywood's box office receipts (A. Rodgers, 2002). As playing games has become a major part of many consumers' recreational life, advertisers have begun incorporating brand messages into this medium. Web-based computer games that incorporate advertising messages are referred to as advergames. Currently, most advergames are placed either on major gaming Web sites (e.g., http://www.zone.msn.com) where companies pay for the privilege of having them available along with other online games or on the corporate Web sites of the products and services they are advertising. For example, an online snowmobile racing game for the Nabisco products can be found on a Nabisco Web site (http://www.nabiscoworld.com). Using a computer keyboard's directional buttons, consumers drive a snowmobile through a track, competing with other snowmobiles. The snowmobile has numerous decals with Nabisco brand names and logos, and advertisements seen along the track's billboards are for Nabisco products.

As an advertising tool, advergames have several unique benefits. First of all, they can enhance brand awareness. A survey of game players at MSN Gaming Zone taken before Toyota's Adrenaline game went online found that Toyota's brand awareness ranked 6th among major car companies. A second survey of game players, taken 3 months after the game went online, found that Toyota's brand awareness had risen to 2nd (Marriott, 2001).

In addition to increasing brand awareness, positive attitudes toward an advergame may lead to favorable attitudes toward the promoted brand and the game sponsor (Ward & Hill, 1991). Data from college advergame players show that attitudes toward advergames are positively associated with attitudes toward the Web site on which the game is placed and relationship building with the Web site (Youn & Lee, in press). Finally, because players are often required to register to play advergames or to be eligible for prizes, advergames can be a big asset for advertisers eager to capture useful customer relationship management data (Chen & Ringel, 2001).

Mobile advertising. The forms of new media advertising mentioned so far are primarily designed to be used with the Internet. A different form of new media communications is intended to take advantage of the on-the-go nature of modern consumers and is referred to as mobile advertising (Senn 2000; Stafford, in press). This technology uses wireless communication to reach consumers via cell phones, pages, and personal digital assistants. In some countries such as Japan and Finland, these devices have already become important forms of new media communication. Although their use for promotion has been slower in the United States, the diffusion of mobile devices has already begun to surpass the Internet (Perlado & Barwise, in press). Thus, the use and importance of mobile advertising is likely to grow in the future.

It is unlikely that mobile technology will be rich enough to support the amount of content or the quality of visual we associate with print or electronic media advertising. More likely, it will take the form of short text messages intended to inform, remind, or notify consumers. Thus, it can best be used to support relationships with existing customers rather than to be used to attempt to acquire new consumers (Perlado & Barwise, in press). For example, mobile advertising may help to remind consumers to make a purchase or to provide information for immediate consumer decisions.

Perhaps the major advantage of mobile advertising is that it is able to reach people at exactly the moment they are making purchase decisions. For example, it can be used to provide information about sales promotions at the time of purchase to help sway consumer choices for parity products.

By using global satellite positioning, or identifying the closest cell tower, mobile devices can help consumers find nearby establishments that will meet their immediate needs. For example, portals or sites for downtown areas can provide opportunities for consumers to check on the location and operating hours of stores or find out about the specials offered at local restaurants, where different bands are playing, or the time and location of a desired movie. In addition, mobile devices can be used to deliver promotional messages as consumers pass by or stop at specific displays or stores transmitting a signal (Stafford, in press).

A crucial drawback to the use of mobile advertising may be annoyance and clutter. The customer must have an intrinsic desire for the message or it will be perceived as irritating and intrusive. The widespread public support for a do-not-call list for telephones suggests that people will not put up with uninvited cell phone calls or text messages. Thus, prior relationships and permission to contact the consumer are likely to be critical in the future success of mobile advertising (Perlado & Barwise, in press).

One possibility is to put the control of such advertising in the hands of the consumer. For example, rather than having the advertiser push the message to the consumer, potential customers will need to initiate the contact with an advertiser or portal to get information and messages relevant for a purchase choice.

Alternatively, advertisers may need to compensate consumers for receiving their message. Existing advertising pays a middleman to help get the message to the consumers. Magazines or television stations receive money for allowing advertisers to use their programming to attract consumers to their message. With mobile advertising, advertisers may try to pay people directly to receive their message. The potential of such a format has already been shown to be successful (Barwise & Strong, 2002). In this study, young urban adults (aged 16 to 30) in the United Kingdom were paid for agreeing to receive up to three text messages per day during a 6-week period. More than three quarters of the participants said they read most of the messages sent to them and approximately 20% said they responded to at least one message for a product or service. Satisfaction with this form of communication was surprisingly high. In the future, people may be offered free or reduced-cost cell phones or personal digital assistants in exchange for accepting some ads. This will necessitate sending any one consumer only a very limited number of messages, but the targeting and timing of such messages can potentially make them very effective.

COMPARING THE INTERNET AND TRADITIONAL MASS MEDIA

Coupey (1999) suggested that to achieve efficiency in research effort, it is necessary to recognize the ways in which new media and traditional media are similar and how they differ. To the degree they are similar, findings from research with traditional media can be generalized to the Internet. The places where they differ, however, require new theories and exploration. Thus, from a theoretical perspective, it is critical to recognize the ways in which new media alter the consumers' information environment.

The consumer information environment denotes the entire array of product-related data available to the consumer (Bettman, 1975). Some important characteristics of this information environment are type of information available, amount of information available, modes of presentation, and modes of information organization.

In terms of the types of information available, the Internet does not seem to differ substantially from traditional mass media. Both the Internet and traditional mass media provide consumers with physical and functional information regarding a brand, insights regarding brand users, brand reliability and efficacy, and brand image (Jones & Slater, 2003). However, the sheer amount of product information available online is unparalleled by that in any traditional medium. There is now not only a huge amount of free product information provided by marketers on corporate home pages but also unlimited amounts of information available on online outlets such as consumer forums. However, to be meaningful, consumers must want and use such a wide array of information.

For the most part, the Internet replicates the modalities of existing media. Although it is capable of combining the attributes of television, print, and radio into a single presentation of video, text, and sound (Coupey, 1999), such efforts are still limited by speed and bandwidth. However, the not-too-distant future is likely to see an increasingly common combination of multiple modalities that can lead to vivid online experiences sometimes referred to as telepresence. Steuer (1992) defined *telepresence* as the mediated perception of an environment. Coyle and Thorson (2001) defined *presence* as the direct experience of reality and noted that telepresence is the simulated perception of direct experience. This has important implications for consumer decision making. The most important information in consumers' brand choices comes from direct experience (Schudson, 1984). In the absence of direct experience, consumers rely on interpersonal communication and lacking that, use mass media advertising (Arndt & May, 1981). Through telepresence, the Internet may be able to simulate direct experience, making this a particularly important and useful form of information for consumers.

Another important characteristic of the consumer information environment is how information is organized. In traditional mass media, product information is typically organized by brand. For example, traditional advertisements usually discuss one brand at a time and present only a favorable subset of the available information about that brand. Additional information about other brands or alternative attributes must typically be acquired at different times, when other advertisements or alternative sources of information are encountered (Bettman, Johnson, & Payne, 1991). This makes it difficult for consumers to use compensatory decision-making rules where high scores on some attributes outweigh low scores on other attributes.

In traditional media, there are occasional situations that facilitate compensatory decision making by providing comparative information on several brands across a number of attributes. Perhaps the best example of this is *Consumer Reports*; they provide matrix tables showing how different brands perform on each of several attributes. Such information displays have become much more common on the Internet in product reviews on individual's Web sites and as an added value on sites for online retailers. Some sites even allow consumers to specify desired values on particular attributes and receive a listing of brands that meet these criteria. The greater availability of such information displays will allow consumers to more easily use compensatory decision-making strategies if they so desire.

In addition to the previously discussed characteristics, the Internet may differ from traditional mass media sources on two other dimensions. These can be labeled information flexibility and information accessibility. *Information flexibility* refers to the ability to tailor the information to the needs and desires of the receiver. Flexibility can be achieved through actions of either the sender or the receiver. Online marketers are able to gather information about specific customers and use this information to customize their message. For example, an advertiser can use cookies to determine where the audience member has been on the Internet and infer from that what information they may desire. In addition, they can ask consumers to register to use a Web site and from this information, create a database to profile each consumer. By knowing this information, the advertiser can tailor the message sent to best meet the interests and concerns of each consumer. In this way, Internet communication more closely resembles interpersonal rather than mass communication. Researchers have long viewed the ability to tailor messages to the needs and concerns of the receiver to be a central advantage of interpersonal communication over mass communication (Arndt & May, 1981; McGuire, 1969).

Consumers are also able to create flexibility in the information reaching them. Given the far greater capacity to transmit and store information via the Internet relative to other forms of product information, a company can produce a vast array of information and allow the consumer to select just those pieces they are most concerned with. This allows each receiver, with just a few clicks, to select what he or she wants to know about and ignore less relevant information.

The Internet's high information flexibility is made possible by one of its most salient features—interactivity. Most researchers seem to agree that interactivity is the fundamental feature that makes the Internet different from traditional mass media. Unfortunately, however, there is little agreement on how to define this term. For example, Steuer (1992) defined *interactivity* as the extent to which users can participate in modifying the form and content of a mediated environment in real time. Ha and James (1998) defined *interactivity* as the extent to which the communicator and the audience respond to, or are willing to facilitate, each other's communication needs. The differences in definitions may be due to the different focus authors adopt (McMillan & Hwang, 2002). Some define *interactivity* as a process, stressing terms such as *interchangeable* and *responsive.* Others define *interactivity* in terms of features such as user control and two-way communication. Still others view interactivity subjectively from the perspective of consumers' perceptions. Although much disagreement regarding this concept remains, three elements of interactivity commonly appear in definitions of this term: (a) two-way communication, (b) user control, and (c) speed of response (McMillan & Hwang, 2002). It is hoped that future researchers can build on these commonalities to develop a clearer and more consistent definition.

The final characteristic of the consumer information environment that may distinguish Internet information from more traditional sources is information accessibility. *Accessibility* refers to the user's ability to control when and where information is available. With the Internet and wireless technology, brand and product information can be accessed from almost any location on the earth and at any time. Other forms of new media can use satellite tracking and cell phone or Wi-Fi technology to provide consumers with information about the closest location to purchase a brand or provide a list of possible alternative consumption choices. For example, a hungry traveler can use a cell phone or other handheld device to request a listing of Italian restaurants within a 1 mile radius of where he or she is standing that are medium priced and take a specific credit card. Such technological possibilities change the role advertising needs to play in fostering top-of-mind awareness and may well change the way people make decisions.

THE ONLINE INFORMATION ENVIRONMENT AND CONSUMER BEHAVIOR

The previous section shows that the Internet differs from traditional mass media in terms of amount of information available, modes of presentation, modes of information organization, information flexibility, and information accessibility. These differences arise from the Internet's unique features such as interactivity, multimodality, and the capability of storing and providing a vast amount of information. This leads to the question of whether, and how, these unique characteristics will alter consumer behavior. To answer this question, we look at several outcome variables commonly assessed in consumer behavior research. These include brand memory, attitudes, intention, and choice as well as information processing strategies.

Brand memory, attitude, intention, and choice. To examine potential effects of new media, many researchers have compared the impact of an ad presented on the Internet with the same message presented in a traditional media format. For example, Gallagher, Foster, and Parsons (2001a) investigated consumer responses to identical advertisements and promotional articles presented in print and Web formats. In the print format, advertisements were inserted in an article in a promotional brochure. In the Web format, the identical advertisements were hyperlinked to texts within the same promotional article appearing on a computer screen. Thus, advertisements presented in the Web format possessed the unique feature of interactivity (in this case, it simply means viewers had control over which ads they viewed and in what order). They found that format did not significantly affect total recall or recognition measures. In a replication using adult Web users, Gallagher, Parsons, and Foster (2001b) again found that the medium made no difference in consumers' memory for advertisements. In both Gallagher et al. studies, the same advertisements presented in different media (i.e., print vs. Web) did not engender differences in attitude toward the ad, brand, or brand choice. Other researchers using similar research strategies have occasionally found differences, but these have not been consistent (e.g., Bezjian-Avery, Calder, & Iacobucci, 1998; Sundar, Narayan, Obregon, & Uppal, 1998).

It is not surprising to find no differences in advertising effects resulting from pure medium difference given how many of these studies are designed. Researchers frequently have tried to make the stimuli in different media as comparable as possible to exclude confounding variables (Bezjian-Avery et al., 1998; Gallagher et al., 2001a, 2001b; Sundar et al., 1998). However, this research strategy also tends to exclude meaningful differences between the media that should lead to real differences in advertising effects. For example, in the studies by Gallagher et al. (2001a, 2001b), the difference between print and Internet conditions is the fact that subjects get to click on the five ads in the

Internet version. Thus, the only difference is in selecting the order to view the ads and in not viewing one or more if the subject did not want to. In an experimental setting, it is hard to imagine that such a difference would lead to meaningful affects on brand attitude or preference. Interactivity may be important only when the consumer has a great deal of choices to select from and time is an issue. In studies that have taken important aspects of the Internet into account in designing media differences (e.g., personalization and consumer control), significant differences are typically found. For example, Nowak et al. (1999) found that perceived personalization of banner ads was positively related to attitude toward the commercial Web sites and attitude toward the Web sponsors. Hence, when examining media differences in advertising effects, researchers need to focus on the meaningful ways in which each medium differs and theorize on the basis of these underlying differences.

One must also be careful in generalizing from findings with an emerging medium like the Internet. It is difficult to determine if an effect is simply due to novelty or substance. We may initially be influenced by a novel format or strategy that is entertaining and enjoyable. However, with time, as this strategy becomes more commonplace, it can lose its impact and even become tedious and annoying. Thus, we need to distinguish between novelty effects and those that are truly due to a particular medium or technique.

Online consumer information processing. The information processing perspective of consumer behavior is grounded in a general model (see Bettman, 1979) that depicts people as limited information processors and describes the cognitive components, systems, and operating principles that are presumed to be involved in how people process information (Meyers-Levy & Malaviya, 1999). Consumer information processing is often intertwined with information search and decision making.

Information search is composed of internal information search (i.e., search information from one's memory) and external information search (i.e., search information from sources other than one's memory). External information search can be further divided into (a) goal-directed search (i.e., purposeful information search before purchase) and (b) general search (i.e., nonpurposeful, hedonic information search). Peterson and Merino (2003) argued that because of the relatively low cost of information search on the Internet and the entertainment value of the Internet, consumers will engage in more general information search online than they will offline. This suggests consumers will be more knowledgeable when the time comes for them to make brand decisions. In addition, because information search over the Internet is often times aided by search tools such as search engines and intelligent agents, it can be more structured and systematic than offline information search (Peterson & Merino, 2003; Rowley 2000).

The typical consumer decision-making scenario consists of a set of alternatives (brands), each described by several attributes (Bettman et al., 1991). Bettman and Kakkar (1977) argued that consumers process information in the fashion that is easiest given the way the information is displayed. They found that when information was organized by brand, brand processing was generally used, whereas attribute formats led to more attribute processing. As previously discussed, in traditional mass media advertising, product information is typically organized by brand. However, in an online environment, it is common to see product information organized by attribute or presented in the form of brand by attribute matrices. This difference in information organization may lead consumers to engage in more attribute-based, rather than brand-based, processing. Attribute-based information presentation may enhance the ability of consumers to engage in more compensatory and more complex decision-making strategies.

In making decisions, consumers can use information retrieved from memory, information obtained from the environment, or both (Lynch & Srull, 1982). In a physical store, when making decisions about which brand to choose, consumers are typically aided by information available from the retail display (brand names, package information, etc.) but also retrieve brand and attribute information from memory. In making a selection, consumers usually form a consideration set which includes only a few brand alternatives. In this way, consumers save cognitive effort but run the risk of overlooking the "best" alternative. In contrast, the Internet provides not only a vast amount of brand and attribute information but also search tools that help screen brand alternatives for consumers and generate a consideration set that contains the best alternatives. Thus, in the online information environment, the consumers can benefit from getting a higher quality consideration set. Because this consideration set is often constructed by using a search tool rather than being retrieved from memory, this decision process can best be termed as stimulus based rather than memory based (Peterson & Merino, 2003).

CONCLUSIONS

Any discussion of the role of new media in consumer decisions is clearly complex. There is no one form of advertising or consumer communications. Media planners in advertising have long recognized that different media have various strengths and weaknesses and are good for different objectives (Sissors & Bumba, 1990). Although many people talk about Internet advertising as if it were a single category, in reality, the Internet provides analogies to all forms of traditional media. Banner ads are similar to billboards in that they can carry only a minimum amount of information and they are located in high traffic areas.

Many Web ads such as pop-ups are similar to print ads found in magazines or newspapers. Web pages may be more similar to in-store brochures and retail displays. Although for the most part underused to date, because of limited bandwidth, commercials similar to radio and television ads are likely to be a common format as Internet connections change. Other forms of strategic communications such as product placements and sports sponsorships are mirrored on the Internet in advergames and content sponsors. Thus, we cannot meaningfully talk about Internet advertising but must instead talk about types of Internet advertising.

We have provided a brief review of research on the effectiveness of different types of Internet advertising (e.g., banner ads, pop-up ads, commercial Web sites). However, it is interesting to note that most studies have limited their focus to only a single type of Internet advertising. Rarely investigated is the relative effectiveness of different types of Internet ads for different functions or for different types of people. Traditional media research finds that individual difference variables such as demographics and psychographics can provide valuable insights into how and when advertising works. Future research might profitably explore similar individual differences in relation to specific types of new media advertising.

Such research with new media advertising may become particularly valuable given that unobtrusive methods of measuring behaviors exist for many of these forms of promotion. This will make collecting such data easier than with more traditional media and less dependent on audience self-reporting of their behavior. Perhaps the most frequently used measure of online ad effectiveness is the click-through. *Click-through* refers to the average number of times a Web user clicked on a banner ad (or pop-up ad) and was then exposed to the target Web site (Novak & Hoffman, 1997). Click-throughs can be recorded and used to indicate that a user has attended to both the banner ad (or pop-up ad) and the target Web site. Another measure to gauge effectiveness of online advertising is *pages accessed*. Currently, advertisers can track both numbers of pages and types of pages accessed by consumers. Tracking data regarding how many and which pages consumers accessed not only guarantee ad exposures but also offer insights into consumers' navigation patterns through the site. Finally, *time spent on a site* is also used to measure online advertising effectiveness. Time spent on a site (sometimes referred to as *stickiness)* can indicate depth of processing or involvement (for a more detailed discussion of Web advertising measures, see Bhat, Bevan, & Sengupta, in press).

Although future research comparing the effectiveness of various forms of new media advertising with each other and with more traditional media messages is needed, research must exert great care in carrying out such studies. Many studies attempt to look at differences in traditional and new media by replicating the two forms as exactly as possible. In the process, much of the uniqueness of the new media gets ignored. Not surprisingly, there will be little difference between the formats when this occurs. Instead, we need to build comparisons that allow for the uniqueness of each medium to emerge. Even print ads in the Internet can combine motion, sound, and interactivity. More important, they may differ in the ability to deliver a well-targeted audience, the size of audience, and the degree of skepticism the audience brings to the message. Study designs must incorporate these real life differences to be meaningful.

A big difference in media may be the degree to which an ad is seen as intrusive or under the control of the audience member. One of the major complaints about Internet ads these days is their intrusiveness, especially for pop-up ads. These occur without warning and often interfere with the focus of the user. Frequently, they are for a product that the user is uninterested in. It is not surprising users have strong negative attitudes toward this type of advertising.

Alternative delivery approaches could drastically change consumers' perceptions of control and their attitudes toward advertising information. One alternative is to use tracking information regarding where the consumer has been and the type of Web sites visited to help advertisers better target consumers to match their interests and desires. Although consumers are very wary of this type of data gathering on their behavior, it has the ability to reduce the annoyance of exposure to unwanted products and brands. Another alternative relies on software programs to select ads for brands related to the topics consumers are searching or surfing on the Internet. These ads are kept in a file and allow the user to access this information when and if they want. This provides the user with a sense of control and makes the advertising far more appreciated and useful. A third approach does not use technology but rather, offers consumers the opportunity to sign up to receive future ads. Several popular service Web sites currently use this approach. For example, airlines or travel sites let consumers choose to receive e-mail notices about special fares or offers. Products and services with loyalty programs and frequent special offers may benefit greatly from this approach. Overall, the more the user feels in control of the information, the more influential it is likely to be in making consumer decisions.

Finally, the Internet may be changing the form of consumer decision making and where information comes from. In traditional situations, most mass mediated consumer information is under the control of the manufacturer. They produce ads and press releases to inform people about their brands. With the Internet, however, far more opportunities exist for "third parties" to influence a wide range of consumers. Web sites devoted to a specific product category may carry comparative information about a range of brands. Fans, self-proclaimed experts, and interested organizations may all develop sites that discuss different brands. Retail sites also provide brand comparisons for their customers. These sites allow people to process more complex and complete information and arrive at decisions based on an effort to maximize desired attributes. This may alter the way many consumer decisions are made.

However, it should be remembered than no matter how easy search engines and decision tools become, they will still require more of an effort than most people want to invest for many consumer decisions. People will continue to base many of their choices on habit, prior experience, or impulse. Thus, the ability to help remind and reinforce brand decisions will still be an important goal for advertisers. The Internet may play a role here as well, albeit through different techniques and formats. In these less involving decisions, linking positive feelings with a brand and enhancing recall and recognition via repetition will be important. Activities such as advergames, sponsorship, and value-added tools on one's Web site are likely to be valuable ways of achieving these outcomes. Consumers are likely to find that the Internet offers a vast array of consumer-related information in a variety of formats that may affect their brand choices in the future.

NOTE

1. Although S. Rodgers and Thorson (2000) identified hypertext links as one form of new media advertising, most researchers view hypertext links as one of the features that can be found on a Web site rather than a distinct form of advertising (Ha & James, 1998). Thus, in this article we do not include a discussion of hypertext links.

REFERENCES

American Heart Association. (n.d.) [Home page]. Retrieved from www.americanheart.org

America Online (Internet service launches new software that enables users to block pop-up ads). (2003). *Mediaweek,* 13(11), 5.

Arndt, J., & May, F. D. (1981). The hypothesis of a dominance hierarchy of information sources. *Journal of the Academy of Marketing Science, 9,* 337–351.

Baker, W. E., & Lutz, R. J. (2000). An empirical test of an updated relevance-accessibility model of advertising effectiveness. *Journal of Advertising,* 29(1), 1–13.

Barwise, P., & Strong, C. (2002). Permission based mobile advertising. *Journal of Interactive Marketing,* 16(1), 14–24.

Berthon, P., Pitt, L. E., & Watson, R. T. (1996). The World Wide Web as an advertising medium: Toward an understanding of conversion efficiency. *Journal of Advertising Research,* 36(1), 43–54.

Bettman, J. R. (1975, December). Issues in designing consumer information environment. *Journal of Consumer Research, 2,* 169–177.

Bettman, J. R. (1979). *An information processing theory of consumer choice.* Reading, MA: Addison-Wesley.

Bettman, J. R., Johnson, E. J., & Payne, J. W. (1991). Consumer decision making. In T. S. Robertson & H. H. Kassarjian (Eds.), *Handbook of consumer behavior* (pp. 50–84). Englewood Cliffs, NJ: Prentice Hall.

Bettman, J. R., & Kakkar, P. (1977). Effects of information presentation format on consumer information acquisition strategies. *Journal of Consumer Research, 3*(4), 233–240.

Bezjian-Avery, A., Calder, B., & Iacobucci, D. (1998). New media interactive advertising vs. traditional advertising. *Journal of Advertising Research,* 38(4), 23–32.

Bhat, S., Bevans, M., &Sengupta, S. (in press). Survey of measures evaluating advertising effectiveness based on users'Web activity. In M. R. Stafford &R. J. Faber (Eds.), *Advertising, promotion, and new media.* Armonk, NY: M. E. Sharpe.

Briggs, R., & Hollis, N. (1997). Advertising on the Web: Is there response before click-through? *Journal of Advertising Research,* 37(2), 33–45.

Brown, M. (2002). The use of banner advertisements with pull-down menus: A copy testing *approach.* Journal of Interactive Advertising, *2(2). Available from* http://www.jiad.org/

Chatterjee, P. (1996). *Modeling consumer network navigation in World Wide Websites: Implications for advertising.* Unpublished dissertation proposal, Vanderbilt University, Nashville, TN.

Chen, J., & Ringel, M. (2001). *Can advergaming be the future of interactive advertising?* Retrieved from http://www.locz.com.br/loczgames/advergames.pdf

Cho, C. H., Lee, J. G., & Tharp, M. (2001). Different forced-exposure levels to banner advertisements. *Journal of Advertising Research,* 41(4), 45–56.

Choi, Y. K., Miracle, G. E., & Biocca, F. (2001). The effects of anthropomorphic agents on advertising effectiveness and the mediating role of presence. *Journal of Interactive Advertising, 2*(1). Available from http://www.jiad.org/

Coupey, E. (1999). Advertising in an interactive environment: A research agenda. In D. W. Schumann & E. Thorson (Eds.), *Advertising and the World Wide Web* (pp. 197–215). Mahwah, NJ: Lawrence Erlbaum.

Coyle, J. R., & Thorson, E. (2001). The effects of progressive levels of interactivity and vividness in Web marketing sites. *Journal of Advertising,* 30(3), 65–78.

Cross, K. (1999). *Whither the banner.* Retrieved from http://www.business2.com/b2/web/articles/0,17863,527540,00.html

Dillabough, C. (2002). *Industry must unite to stop growth of pop-up plague.* Retrieved from http://www.dealgroupmedia.com.au/news28.cfm

Dou, W., Linn, R., & Yang, S. (2001). How smart are "smart banners"? *Journal of Advertising Research,* 41(4), 31–43.

Ducoffe, R. H. (1996). Advertising value and advertising on the Web. *Journal of Advertising Research,* 26(5), 21–35.

Edwards, S. M., Li, H., &Lee, J. H. (2002). Forced exposure and psychological reactance: Antecedents and consequences of the perceived intrusiveness of pop-up ads. *Journal of Advertising, 31*(3), 83–96.

E-Marketer. (2003). *North America online: Demographics and usage.* Retrieved from http://www.emarketer.com/ReportList.aspx?pageNum=2&channelID=7

Faber, R. (2002). From the editor: A glance backward and the view ahead. *Journal of Advertising, 31*(4), 1–3.

Gallagher, K., Foster, K. D., & Parsons, J. (2001a). The medium is not the message: Advertising effectiveness and content evaluation in print and on the Web. *Journal of Advertising Research, 41*(4), 57–70.

Gallagher, K., Parsons, J., & Foster, K. D. (2001b). A tale of two studies: Replicating advertising effectiveness and content evaluation in print and on the Web. *Journal of Advertising Research, 41*(4), 71–81.

GartnerG2. (2002). *Unpopular pop-ups won't stop.* Retrieved from http://www.gartnerg2.com/site/default.asp

Ghose, S., & Dou, W. (1998). Interactive functions and their impacts on the appeal of Internet presence sites. *Journal of Advertising Research,* 38(2), 29–43.

Greenberg, K. (2000). Search patterns. *Mediaweek,* 10(35), 72.

Ha, L., & James, E. L. (1998). Interactivity reexamined: A baseline analysis of early business Websites. *Journal of Broadcasting & Electronic Media,* 42(4), 457–474.

Hwang, J. S., McMillan, S. J., & Lee, G. (2003). Corporate Web sites as advertising: An analysis of function, audience, and message strategy. *Journal of Interactive Advertising, 3*(2). Available from http://www.jiad.org/

Interactive Advertising Bureau. (1999). *IAB Internet advertising revenue report.* Retrieved from http://www.iab.net/resources/adrevenue/archive_1999.asp#

Interactive Advertising Bureau. (2002). *Internet ad revenue report.* Available from http://www. iab.net

Interactive Advertising Bureau. (2003). 4Q 2002 total $1.5 billion—2.3% increase over 3Q 2002 full-year revenue totals slightly under $6 billion. *Retrieved from* http://www.iab.net/news/pr_2003_4_9.asp

Interactive Digital Software Association. (2000). *Sixty percent of all Americans play video games, contributing to the fourth straight year of double-digit growth for the interactive entertainment industry.* Retrieved from http://www.theesa.com/pressroom.html

Jones, J. P., & Slater, J. S. (2003). *What's in a name: Advertising and the concept of brands.* Armonk, NY: M. E. Sharpe.

Korgaonkar, P. L., & Wolin, L. D. (1999, March/April). A multivariate analysis of Web usage. *Journal of Advertising Research, 39,* 53–68.

Li, H., & Bukovac, J. L. (1999). Cognitive impact of banner ad characteristics: An experimental study. *Journalism and Mass Communication Quarterly,* 76(2), 341–353.

Li, H., Daugherty, T., & Biocca, F. (2001). Characteristics of virtual experience in electronic commerce: A protocol analysis. *Journal of Interactive Marketing,* 15(3), 13–30.

Li, H., Daugherty, T., & Biocca, F. (2002). Impact of 3-D advertising on product knowledge, brand attitude, and purchase intention: The mediating role of presence. *Journal of Advertising, 31*(3), 43–58.

London, D. (2000). Solving the search riddle: The path to search engine optimization becomes a more complicated route as the Web grows. *B to B, 85,* 20.

Lynch, J. G., & Srull, T. K. (1982, June). Memory and attentional factors in consumer choice: Concepts and research methods. *Journal of Consumer Research, 9,* 18–37.

Marriott, M. (2001, July 5). Untangling the online gaming web. *The New York Times,* p. G1.

Martin, D., & Ryan, M. (2002). Pop-ups abound, but most advertisers remain inline. Retrieved from http://www.adrelevance.com/intelligence/intel_snapshot.jsp?pr=020829

McGuire, W. J. (1969). The nature of attitudes and attitude change. In G. Lindzey & E. Aronson (Eds.), *The handbook of social psychology* (Vol. 3, 2nd ed., pp. 136–314). Reading, MA: Addison-Wesley.

McMillan, S. J., & Hwang, J.-S. (2002). Measures of perceived interactivity: An exploration of the role of direction of communication, user control, and time in shaping perceptions of interactivity. *Journal of Advertising, 31*(3), 29–42.

Meyers-Levy, J., & Malaviya, P. (1999). Consumer processing of persuasive advertisements: An integrative framework of persuasion theories. *Journal of Marketing, 63,* 45–60.

Nielsen/Netratings. (2000, December 1). *Nielsen/Netratings reporter.* Retrieved from http://209.249.142.22/weekly.asp#uages

Nowak, G. J., Shamp, S., Hollander, B., & Cameron, G. T. (1999). Interactive media: A means for more meaningful advertising? In D. W. Schumann & E. Thorson (Eds.), *Advertising and the World Wide Web* (pp. 197–215). Mahwah, NJ: Lawrence Erlbaum.

Novak, T. P., & Hoffman, D. L. (1997). New metrics for mew media: Toward the development of Web measurement standards. *World Wide Web Journal, 2*(1), 213–246.

Overture. (2003). *History & evolution of search marketing.* Available from http://adage.com

Perlado, V. R., & Barwise, P. (in press). Mobile advertising: A research agenda. In M. R. Stafford & R. J. Faber (Eds.), *Advertising, promotion, and new media.* Armonk, NY: M. E. Sharpe.

Peterson, R. A., & Merino, M. C. (2003). Consumer information search behavior and the Internet. *Psychology and Marketing, 20*(2), 99–121.

Pham, M. T., & Vanhuele, M. (1997). Analyzing the memory impact of advertising fragments. *Marketing Letters, 8*(4), 407–417.

Robertson, T. S., Zielinski, J., & Ward, S. (1984). *Consumer behavior.* Glenview, IL: Scott, Foresman.

Rodgers, A. L. (2002). *Game theory.* Retrieved from http://pf.fastcompany.com/build/build_feature/yaya.html.

Rodgers, S. (2003). The effects of sponsor relevance on consumer reactions to Internet sponsorships. *Journal of Advertising, 32(4),* 67–76.

Rodgers, S., & Sheldon, K. M. (2002). An improved way to characterize Internet users. *Journal of Advertising Research, 42*(5), 85–94.

Rodgers, S., & Thorson, E. (2000). The interactive advertising model: How users perceive and process online ads. *Journal of Interactive Advertising, 1*(1). Available from http://www.jiad.org/

Rowley, J. (2000). Product search in e-shopping: A review and research propositions. *Journal of Consumer Marketing, 17*(1), 20–35.

Schudson, M. (1984). *Advertising, the uneasy persuasion: Its dubious impact on American society.* New York: Basic Books.

Senn, J. A. (2000). The emergence of m-commerce. *Computer, 33*(12), 148–151.

Singh, S. N., & Dalal, N. P. (1999). Web home pages as advertisements. *Communications of the ACM, 42*(8), 91–98.

Sissors, J. Z., & Bumba, L. (1990). *Advertising media planning.* Lincolnwood, IL: NTC Business Books.

Stafford, T. F. (in press). Mobile promotional communication and machine persuasion: A new paradigm for source effects? In M. R. Stafford & R. J. Faber (Eds.), *Advertising, promotion, and new media.* Armonk, NY: M. E. Sharpe.

Steuer, J. (1992). Defining virtual reality: Dimensions determining telepresence. *Journal of Communication, 42,* 73–93.

Sundar, S. S., Narayan, S., Obregon, R., & Uppal, C. (1999). Does Web advertising work? Memory for print vs. online media. *Journalism and Mass Communication Quarterly, 75*(4), 822–835.

Ward, J. C., & Hill, R. P. (1991). Designing effective promotional games: Opportunities and problems. *Journal of Advertising,* 20(3), 69–81.

Youn, S., &Lee, M. (in press). Advergame playing motivation and effectiveness: A "uses and gratifications" perspective. In M. R. Stafford & R. J. Faber (Eds.), *Advertising, promotion, and new media.* Armonk, NY: M. E. Sharpe.

RONALD J. FABER is professor of mass communication and director of graduate studies in the School of Journalism and Mass Communication at the University of Minnesota. He is a former editor of the *Journal of Advertising* and coeditor, with M. R. Stafford, of *Advertising, Promotion, and the New Media* (M. E. Sharpe, in press). He has published widely in the areas of advertising, marketing, communication, psychology, and psychiatry.

MIRA LEE is an assistant professor in the Department of Advertising at Michigan State University. Her main research interest is new media and interactive advertising effectiveness. The focus of most of her recent scholarly activity has been the strategic use of advergames—Web-based entertainment games that incorporate advertising messages—as promotional communications tools. She received her M.A. and Ph.D. from the University of Minnesota and her B.A. from KyungPook National University in Korea.

XIAOLI NAN is a Ph.D. candidate in the School of Journalism and Mass communication at the University of Minnesota. Her current research focuses on the effects of persuasive messages in both traditional and emerging media. In particular, she is interested in understanding the psychological processes that underlie the persuasive effects of advertising messages, health communications, and political campaigns. Her work has appeared in *Marketing Theory* and a number of national/international conference proceedings. She holds an M.A. in mass communication from the University of Minnesota and a B.A. in advertising from Beijing University.

CONSUMERS' ADOPTION OF ONLINE SHOPPING

Yi Cai, California State University Northridge, USA
Brenda J. Cude, University of Georgia, USA

ABSTRACT

Online shopping is a broadly defined activity that includes searching for product information, buying products or services, and communicating with retailers and other consumers. It has been described as a "flow experience:" consumers' goal-directed as well as experiential activities on the Internet. Four factors, namely consumer characteristics, consumer perceptions, e-tailer attributes, and product characteristics, have been identified as the determinants of consumers' adoption of online shopping. Researchers have developed and applied several theories and models, such as diffusion of innovation, theory of reasoned action, theory of planned behavior, and technology acceptance model, to explain why and how consumers shop online.

INTRODUCTION

Nowadays the Internet plays a critical role in a large and ever-growing array of activities such as communicating, information searching, entertaining, shopping, and social networking. Asia was the leading geographic region in terms of Internet users in 2009, reaching approximately 740 million, followed by Europe with approximately 420 million (MarketResearch.com, 2010). The U.S. remains the leading country in terms of Internet penetration rate. According to a Pew Internet and American Life Project (2010) survey, 79% of American adults use the Internet, and many Internet users shop online, a broadly defined activity that includes searching for product information (78% of Internet users),

Yi Cai and Brenda J. Cude, "Consumers' Adoption of Online Shopping," *Encyclopedia of Cyber Behavior*, ed. Zheng Yan, pp. 466–476. Copyright © 2012 by IGI Global. Reprinted with permission.

buying products or services (66%), and communicating with retailers and other consumers, for example, about rating products or services (32%).

This chapter reviews important research related to consumer adoption of online shopping. It begins with an overview of the pioneering scholars' research about the characteristics of the Internet as a shopping channel for consumers and the "digital divide" among consumers. The next section reviews the theories and models proposed by leading researchers with respect to consumer online shopping adoption. The final section introduces future research directions.

OVERVIEW

Internet as a Shopping Channel: Online Flow Experience

D. L. Hoffman and T. P. Novak from the University of California at Davis are pioneering scholars who introduced the "online flow experience" to describe the characteristics of the Internet as a shopping channel for consumers. Originally, "flow" was described by Nakamura and Csikszentmihalyi (2009) as an experience of complete absorption in the present moment. The experience was characterized as an integration of the constructs of perceived challenges or opportunities, clear goals, feedbacks, focus, control, and the autotelic (*auto* = self; *telos* = goal) nature of activities. Hoffman and Novak (1996, 2009) introduced and validated a conceptual model of flow in a computer-mediated environment, which is characterized by interactivity, intrinsic enjoyment, and loss of self-consciousness and self-reinforcement. The framework provides insight into understanding consumers' goal-directed as well as experiential activities on the Internet. Specifically, the model describes 1) the factors that create compelling online experiences (i.e., the antecedents; e.g., skills, interactivity, motivation, and vividness); 2) the nature of a compelling flow experience (e.g., involvement, attention, and flow); and 3) outcomes of the flow experience (e.g., increased learning and exploratory mindset).

Many studies have been built upon this conceptual model of online flow experience. Novak, Hoffman, and Yung (2000) demonstrated that the constructs underlying the model could be measured and their research validated empirically most of the relationships in the model. Other studies also have established and tested the role of flow in predicting consumer online behavior (Korzaan, 2003; Sanchez-Franco, 2006; Skadberg & Kimmel, 2004). Other researchers also extended the model by incorporating constructs such as ease of use, perceived usefulness, and further antecedents of flow including novelty, personal innovativeness, attractiveness, and playfulness (Agarwal & Karahanna, 2000; Choi, Kim, & Kim, 2007; Hsu & Lu, 2003; Huang, 2003). The most recent applications of the flow experience to cyber consumer behavior have been investigations of simulated shopping experience involving virtual (e.g., visual and functional) control of products online (Jiang & Benbasat, 2005; Suh & Chang, 2006). The researchers showed through virtual reality simulations that the flow experience can enhance consumers' product knowledge and decrease their perceptions of risk (Suh & Chang, 2006).

Digital Divide

J. Van Dijk from the University of Twente, Netherland is a pioneering scholar focusing on the "digital divide" among consumers, which is a delay in the introduction of information technology to some ethnic and social groups. An outcome is that information equipment is less available to some and those individuals have a different ability to access the Internet. With the evolution and advancement in information technology, discussions of solutions to the "digital divide" have shifted from technical and physical barriers to social barriers. Van dijk (1997, 2006) developed a comprehensive model (Van Dijk, 2006) that incorporates different types of access such as motivational, material, skills, and usage access into a process rather than a single event of obtaining a particular technology. In light of this comprehensive model, the factors explaining information technology accessibility and its specific implication (e.g., who does and does not shop online) can be physical, psychological, emotional, and social or cultural in nature.

Furthermore, organizations such as the International Telecommunication Union (2010), the World Economic Forum (2010), and the United Nations Educational, Scientific and Cultural Organization (2010) have looked more broadly at the role of the Internet in the global society. The efforts of those organizations to redefine the concept include categorizing dimensions of the "digital divide" such as opportunity, infrastructure, and utilization; analyzing a variety of reasons such as economic, social, cultural, and content-related issues; and developing numerical e-opportunity indices such as the Network Readiness Index (World Economic Forum, 2010) and the Digital Opportunity Index (International Telecommunication Union, 2010).

CONSUMERS' ADOPTION OF ONLINE SHOPPING — DETERMINANT FACTORS AND THEORIES

Factors Influencing Online Shopping Acceptance

The current leading researchers in online shopping adoption include F. Davis from the University of Arkansas and V. Venkatech from the University of Maryland (Venkatech & Bala, 2008; Venkatesh & Davis, 2000; Venkatesh, Morris, Davis, & Davis, 2003), and S. Shim from the University of Arizona (Shim & Drake, 1990; Shim, Eastlick, Lotz, & Warrington, 2001). One theme in online-shopping-adoption research that has received wide attention is the factors that influence consumers to shop online. Researchers have identified four determinants of consumers' adoption of online shopping, namely consumer characteristics, consumer perceptions, e-tailer attributes, and product characteristics (Lian & Lin, 2008). Numerous empirical studies have indicated that consumer characteristics are influential in the acceptance of online shopping. Researchers in the United States and other countries have found consistently that demographics and socioeconomic status such as age, gender, education level, and income influence consumers' acceptance of online shopping (Brashear, Kashyap, Musante, & Donthu, 2009; Hashim, Ghani, & Said, 2009; Swinyard & Smith, 2003). Other factors belonging to this category include consumers' value orientation (Jayawardhena, 2004; Wu, Cai, & Liu, 2011), personality traits (Huang & Yang, 2010), and consumer self-efficacy and anxiety (O'Cass & French, 2003; Yao & Li, 2009).

A second category of determinants of adoption of online shopping is consumer perception. Variables in the dimension include perceived convenience (Gupta & Kim, 2007; Pechtl, 2003); perceived usefulness and ease-of-use (Ha & Stoel, 2009; Kim, Fiore, & Lee, 2007; Shih, 2004); perceived benefits (Eastin, 2002); perceived enjoyment (Kim et al., 2007); and perceived risk (Lee & Huddleston, 2010; Shih, 2004).

A third category is e-tailer attributes. Previous studies have found the following e-tailer attributes are important when examining consumer online shopping acceptance: web design and web quality (Hausman & Siekpe, 2009; Poddar, Donthu, & Wei, 2009); e-tailer reputation (Eastlick, Lotz, & Warrington, 2006; Goode & Harris, 2007); and security and privacy (Goode & Harris, 2007); Mukherjee & Nath, 2007; Shih, 2004; Youn & Lee, 2009).

A fourth category of factors affecting consumer adoption of online shopping is product characteristics. Researchers have examined the following variables as they relate to consumer online shopping acceptance: product type (Moon, Chadee, & Tikoo, 2008; Roman, 2010); cost (Alba et al., 1997; Moon et al., 2008); and online product suitability characteristics such as tactility, importance of customization, shipping cost, importance of instant satisfaction, and information intensity Rosen & Howard, 2000).

Theories and Models Explaining Consumer Cyber Behavior

Several theories and models that incorporated a variety of determinant factors for online shopping adoption have been employed to explain why and how consumers shop online. The following theories and models serve as major conceptual and theoretical frameworks in the current research on consumers' adoption of online shopping.

Diffusion of Innovation

According to Rogers (2003), diffusion is a process indicating how innovations (ideas or practices that individuals perceive as being new) are communicated to individuals within a society over time and how consumers adopt or reject the innovations. Rogers identified five stages that consumers experience when deciding to adopt or reject and innovation: 1) knowledge (awareness of an innovation); 2) persuasion (attitude toward the innovation); 3) decision (adoption or rejection of the innovation); 4) implementation (commitment to the innovation); and 5) confirmation (evaluation of the decision results). Rogers also postulated that the five characteristics of innovations, relative advantages, compatibility, complexity, trialability, and observability, influence the consumer decision to adopt or reject an innovation. Researchers employed the theory in the context of online shopping and demonstrated the diffusion process for consumers' online shopping behavior (Lennon, Kim, Johnson, Jolly, Damhorst, & Jasper, 2007; Wu et al., 2011); other researchers also showed that the characteristics of innovations positively influenced consumers' adoption of online shopping (Verhoef & Langerak, 2001).

Theory of Reasoned Action and Theory of Planned Behavior

Derived from the social psychology setting, the Theory of Reasoned Action (TRA) was proposed by Ajzen and Fishbein (Ajzen & Fishbein, 1980; Fishbein & Ajzen, 1975). The components of TRA are three general constructs: behavioral intention, attitude, and subjective norm. TRA suggests that a person's behavioral intention depends on the person's attitude about the behavior and subjective norms. Also, a person's behavioral intention leads to his/her actual behavior. Ajen (1985) extended the TRA by adding a new component, "perceived behavior control," to address volitional (under a person's control) or non-volitional behaviors for predicting behavioral intention and actual behavior. According to the extended theory, and Theory of Planned Behavior (TPB), "attitude toward the behavior," "subjective norm," and "perceived behavioral control" lead to the formation of a "behavioral intention." Furthermore, "perceived behavioral control" is presumed to not only affect actual behavior directly, but also to affect it indirectly through behavioral intention.

TRA and TPB have been applied extensively in the context of consumers' information technology adoption. Hansen (2008) suggested that the theories are particularly suitable for the purpose of investigating consumer online shopping behavior for the following reasons: 1) consumers may perceive both difficulties and risks when considering online shopping; their cognitive resources can be used to form beliefs and in turn result in the development of attitudes toward the behaviors in question; 2) Internet shopping requires skills, opportunities, and resources, and thus perceived behavioral control is a relevant concept; and 3) consumers may seek normative guidance (subjective norm) from relevant sources when trying to reduce risk and difficulties related to online shopping.

A number of researchers have applied the TRA and TPB in their empirical studies of consumer online shopping behavior. Researchers who have applied TPB confirmed that consumer online shopping behavior is influenced by individuals' attitudes toward the shopping channel, the subjective norm, and the amount of control perceived during the purchasing process (Fitzgerald & Kiel, 2001; Keen, Wetzels, De Ruyter, & Feinberg, 2004; Shim et al., 2001).

Other researchers who employed the TRA and TPB as the theoretical framework incorporated a variety of factors into the investigation of consumer online shopping behavior. For example, George (2002) found that consumers' experiences, their concerns about privacy, and their perceptions of the trustworthiness of the Internet were associated with their Internet shopping behaviors. Hsu, Yen, Chiu, and Chang (2006) reported that consumers' disconfirmation and satisfaction play a role in their continuance intention in the online shopping context. In Childers, Carr, Peck, and Carson's (2001) research, hedonic aspects of online shopping behaviors, such as perceived enjoyment and flexibility in navigation, played a role equal to the influence of utilitarian aspects of online shopping behaviors.

Technology Acceptance Model

The Technology Acceptance Model (TAM) is one of the most influential extensions of the TRA. The TAM proposed by Davis (1989) is intended to explain technological usage by examining the effect of perceived ease of use (PEOU) and perceived usefulness (PU) on individuals' intention to use the technology and actual usage behavior. The PEOU refers to the perception that use of a technology does not require additional effort, while the PU reflects the degree to which a user considers that such usage improves his or her task performance (Davis, 1989). The model was later expanded to TAM 2 (Venkatesh & Davis, 2000) and TAM 3 (Venkatesh & Bala, 2008). The first expansion included additional determinants of TAM's PU by incorporating theoretical constructs spanning social influence processes (subjective norm, voluntariness, and image) and cognitive instrumental processes (job relevance, output quality, result demonstrability, and perceived ease of use). Individuals' intention to use is also affected directly by the subjective norm; however, this relationship is mediated by experience and voluntariness. The latter expansion of the TAM further incorporated determinants of TAM's PEOU, namely, computer self-efficacy, perception of external control, computer anxiety, computer playfulness, perceived enjoyment, and objective usability. The PEOU also remains as a direct determinant of PU and individuals' intention to use the technology. Another expansion of the TAM is the Unified Theory of Acceptance and Use of Technology (UTAUT) (Venkatesh et al., 2003). The UTAUT formulated four constructs, namely performance expectancy, effort expectancy, social influence, and facilitating conditions, as determinants of individuals' intention to use the technology; also four major factors, gender, age, experience, and voluntariness, were introduced as key moderators of the relationship between the determinants and individuals' intention to use the technology.

The TAM and its expansions have been tested within a wide variety of computer settings and has been shown to be a robust predictor of consumers' adoption and use of technology in a variety of contexts, including online banking (Chau & Lai, 2003), online game playing (Hsu & Lu, 2003), and online shopping (Ha & Stoel, 2009). Researchers have argued, however, that the original TAM variables may not adequately capture key factors influencing consumers' use of online shopping, a situation involving users' voluntary choices rather than unavoidable use of technology (Vijayasarathy, 2004). Therefore, in explaining consumers' online shopping behavior, researchers have added factors to the model including consumers' socioeconomic characteristics (Hernandez, Jimenez, & Martin, 2011), online shopping quality (Ha & Stoel, 2009), self-efficacy (Hernandez et al., 2011; Vijayasarathy, 2004), security and privacy (Vijayasarathy, 2004), and trust (Ha & Stoel, 2009).

FUTURE RESEARCH DIRECTIONS

In recent years, the phenomenal growth in the number of mobile phone users has resulted in an unprecedented growth in mobile commerce. Researchers have identified the advantageous features of mobile phone as a shopping channel for meeting people's needs in all areas of their life (Lai, Lai, & Jordan, 2010): 1) as mature and efficient as desktop computer applications, the touch interface of mobile devices introduced a new and friendly experience (e.g., touch-based interface) to users and improved the perceived ease of use of mobile applications; and 2) the sophisticated and ubiquitous communication capabilities enable users to shop anywhere at any time. However, challenges, such as security, privacy, social concerns, and situational concerns, also arise considering the large amount of private information the mobile devices carry.

It is essential to explore, identify, and analyze the important factors that affect consumer acceptance and predict further adoption of mobile commerce. The theories employed in the e-commerce research, such as Diffusion of Innovation, TRA, TPB, and TAM, also have been widely used as theoretical frameworks in mobile commerce studies. Researchers have argued, however, that most of those theories were conceived in an organizational environment and their root constructs are basically utilitarian: performance expectancy, effort expectancy, social influence, and facilitating conditions (Aldas-Manzano, Ruiz-Mafe, & Sanz-Blas, 2009). As its personal nature and ubiquitous communication are both features of mobile commerce, both intrinsic and extrinsic factors should play important role in determining consumers' acceptance. In future studies, the theoretical frameworks should be extended to include not only utilitarian factors but also individual factors (e.g., intrinsic motivation, cultural orientation, and personality) and situational factors (e.g., situational or environmental concerns, location and time sensitive, security and privacy concerns).

REFERENCES

Agarwal, R., & Karahanna, E. (2000). Time flies when you're having fun: Cognitive absorption and beliefs about information technology usage. *Management Information Systems Quarterly, 24*(4), 665–694. doi: 10.2307/3250951

Ajzen, I. (1985). From intentions to actions: A theory of planned behavior. In Kuhl, J., & Beckmann, J. (Eds.), *Action control: From cognition to behavior* (pp. 11–39). New York, NY: Springer-Verlag. doi: 10.1007/978-3-642-69746-3_2

Ajzen, I., & Fishbein, M. (1980). *Understanding attitudes and predicting social behavior.* Englewood Cliffs, NJ: Prentice-Hall.

Alba, J., Lynch, J., Weitz, B., Janiszewski, C., Lutz, R., Sawyer, A., & Wood, S. (1997). Interactive home shopping: Consumer, retailer, and manufacturer incentives to participate in electronic marketplaces. *Journal of Marketing, 61*, 38–53. doi: 10.2307/1251788

Aldas-Manzano, J., Ruiz-Mafe, C., & Sanz-Blas, S. (2009). Exploring individual personality factors as drivers of m-shopping acceptance. *Industrial Management & Data Systems, 109*(6), 739–757. doi:10.1108/02635570910968018

Brashear, T. G., Kashyap, V., Musante, M. D., & Donthu, N. (2009). A profile of the Internet shopper: Evidence from six countries. *Journal of Marketing Theory and Practice, 17*(3), 267–282. doi:10.2753/MTP1069-6679170305

Chau, P. K., & Lai, V. S. (2003). An empirical investigation of the determinants of user acceptance of Internet banking. *Journal of Organizational Computing and Electronic Commerce, 13*(2), 123–145. doi:10.1207/S15327744JOCE1302 3

Childers, T. L., Carr, C. L., Peck, J., & Carson, S. (2001). Hedonic and utilitarian motivations for online retail shopping behavior. *Journal of Retailing, 77*(3), 511-535. doi:10.1016/S0022-4359(01)00056-2

Choi, D. H., Kim, J., & Kim, S. H. (2007). ERP training with a web-based electronic learning system: The flow theory perspective. *International Journal of Human-Computer Studies, 65*(3), 223–243. doi:10.1016/j.ijhcs.2006.10.002

Davis, F. D. (1989). Perceived usefulness, perceived ease of use and user acceptance of Information Technology. *Management Information Systems Quarterly, 13*(3), 319–339. doi :10.2307/249008

Eastin, M. S. (2002). Diffusion of e-commerce: An analysis of the adoption of four e-commerce activities. *Telematics and Informatics, 19*(3), 251–267. doi:10.1016/S0736-5853(01)00005-3

Eastlick, M. A., Lotz, S. L., & Warrington, P. (2006). Understanding online B-to-C relationship: An integrated model of privacy concerns, trust, and commitment. *Journal of Business Research, 59*(8), 877–886. doi:10.1016/j.jbusres.2006.02.006

Fishbein, M., & Ajzen, I. (1975). *Belief, attitude, intention, and behavior: An introduction to theory and research.* Reading, MA: Addison-Wesley.

Fitzgerald, L. M., & Kiel, G. C. (2001). Applying a consumer acceptance of technology model to examine adoption of online purchasing. *Proceedings of the Australian and New Zealand Marketing Academy Conference.* Auckland, New Zealand: ANZMAC.

George, J. F. (2002). Influences on the intent to make Internet purchases. *Internet Research: Electronic Networking Applications and Policy, 12*(2), 165–180. doi:10.1108/10662240210422521

Goode, M. H., & Harris, L. C. (2007). Online behavioral intentions: An empirical investigation of antecedents and moderators. *European Journal of Marketing, 41(5)*, 512–536. doi: 10.1108/03090560710737589

Gupta, S., & Kim, H. W. (2007). The moderation effect of transaction experience on the decision calculus in online repurchase. *International Journal of Electronic Commerce, 12*(1), 127–158. doi:10.2753/JEC1086-4415120105

Ha, S., & Stoel, L. (2009). Consumer e-shopping acceptance: Antecedents in a technology acceptance model. *Journal of Business Research, 62*(5), 565–571. doi:10.1016/j.jbusres.2008.06.016

Hansen, T. (2008). Consumer values, the theory of planned behavior and online grocery shopping. *International Journal of Consumer Studies, 32*(2), 128–137. doi:10.1111/j.1470-6431.2007.00655.x

Hashim, A., Ghani, E. K., & Said, J. (2009). Does consumers' demographic profile influence online shopping? *Canadian Social Science, 5*(6), 19–31.

Hausman, A. V., & Siekpe, J. S. (2009). The effect of Web interface features on consumer online purchase intentions. *Journal of Business Research, 62*(1), 5–13. doi:10.1016/j.jbusres.2008.01.018

Hernandez, B., Jimenez, J., & Martin, M. J. (2011). Age, gender and income: Do they really moderate online shopping behavior? *Online Information Review, 35*(1), 113–133. doi:10.1108/14684521111113614

Hoffman, D. L., & Novak, T. P. (1996). Marketing in hypermedia computer-mediated environment: Conceptual foundations. *Journal of Marketing, 60*(3), 50–68. doi:10.2307/1251841

Hoffman, D. L., & Novak, T. P. (2009). Flow online: Lessons learned and future prospects. *Journal of Interactive Marketing, 23*(1), 23–34. doi:10.1016/j.intmar.2008.10.003

Hsu, C., & Lu, H. (2003). Why do people play online games? An extended TAM with social influences and flow experiences. *Information & Management, 41*(7), 853–868. doi:10.1016/j.im.2003.08.014

Hsu, M.-H., Yen, C.-H., Chiu, C.-M., & Chang, C.-M. (2006). A longitudinal investigation of continued online shopping behavior: An extension of the theory of planned behavior. *International Journal of Human-Computer Studies, 64*(9), 889–904. doi:10.1016/j.ijhcs.2006.04.004

Huang, J., & Yang, Y. (2010). The relationship between personality traits and online shopping motivations. *Social Behavior and Personality, 38*(5), 673–680. doi:10.2224/sbp.2010.38.5.673

Huang, M. (2003). Designing website attributes to induce experiential encounters. *Computers in Human Behavior, 19*(4), 425–442. doi: 10.1016/S0747-5632(02)00080-8

International Telecommunication Union. (2010). *Digital opportunity index.* Retrieved from http://www.itu.int/ITU-D/ict/doi/index.html

Jayawardhena, C. (2004). Personal value influence on e-shopping attitude and behavior. *Internet Research, 14*(2), 127–138. doi :10.1108/10662240410530844

Jiang, Z., & Benbasat, I. (2005). Virtual product experience: Effects of visual and functional control of product on perceived diagnosticity and flow in electronic shopping. *Journal of Management Information Systems, 21*(3), 111–147.

Keen, C., Wetzels, M., De Ruyter, K., & Feinberg, R. (2004). E-tailers versus retailers: Which factors determine consumer preferences? *Journal of Business Research, 57*(7), 685–695. doi:10.1016/S0148-2963(02)00360-0

Kim, J., Fiore, A. M., & Lee, H. (2007). Influences of online store perception, shopping enjoyment, and shopping involvement on consumer patronage behavior towards an online retailer. *Journal of Retailing and Consumer Services, 14*(2), 95–107. doi :10.1016/j.jretconser.2006.05.001

Korzaan, M. L. (2003). Going with the flow: Predicting online purchase intentions. *Journal of Computer Information Systems, 43*(4), 25–31.

Lai, C. F., Lai, K. W., & Jordan, E. (2010). A model for the study of user adoption behaviours of mobile commerce. *International Journal of Enterprise Network Management, 4*(1), 16–25. doi:10.1504/IJENM.2010.034473

Lee, H., & Huddleston, P. T. (2010). An investigation of the relationships among domain innovativeness, overall perceived risk and online purchase behavior. *International Journal of Internet Marketing and Retailing, 3*(1), 1–4. doi:10.1504/IJEMR.2010.030504

Lennon, S. J., Kim, M., Johnson, K. K., Jolly, L. D., Damhorst, M. L., & Jasper, C. R. (2007). A longitudinal look at rural consumer adoption of online shopping. *Psychology and Marketing, 24*(4), 375–401. doi:10.1002/mar.20165

Lian, J., & Lin, J. (2008). Effects of consumer characteristics on their acceptance of online shopping: Comparisons among different product types. *Computers in Human Behavior, 24*(1), 48–65. doi:10.1016/j.chb.2007.01.002

MarketResearch.com . (2010). *Global B2C e-commerce report 2010.* Retrieved from http://www.marketresearch.com/product/display.asp?productid=2657232&SID=16107898-500875505-489621899

Moon, J., Chadee, D., & Tikoo, S. (2008). Culture, product type, and price influences on consumer purchase intention to buy personalized products online. *Journal of Business Research, 61*(1), 31–39. doi:10.1016/j.jbusres.2006.05.012

Mukherjee, A., & Nath, P. (2007). Role of electronic trust in online retailing: A re-examination of the commitment-trust theory. *European Journal of Marketing, 41*(9), 1173–1202. doi:10.1108/03090560710773390

Nakamura, J., & Csikszentmihalyi, M. (2009). Flow theory and research. In Snyder, C. R., & Lopez, S. J. (Eds.), *Oxford handbook of positive psychology* (pp. 195–206). New York, N Y: Oxford University Press.

Novak, T. P., Hoffman, D. L., & Yung, Y. (2000). Measuring the customer experience in online environment: A structural modeling approach. *Marketing Science, 19*(1), 22–42. doi:10.1287/mksc.19.1.22.15184

O'Cass, A., & French, T. (2003). Web retailing adoption: Exploring the nature of Internet users' Web retailing behavior. *Journal of Retailing and Consumer Services, 10*(2), 81–94. doi:10.1016/S0969-6989(02)00004-8

Pechtl, H. (2003). Adoption of online shopping by German grocery shoppers. *The International Journal of Retail. Distribution and Consumer Research, 13*(2), 145–159. doi:10.1080/0959396032000099088

Pew Internet and American Life Project. (2010). *Online activities.* Retrieved from http://www.pewinternet.org/Static-Pages/Trend-Data/Online-Activities-Daily.aspx

Poddar, A., Donthu, N., & Wei, Y. (2009). Web site customer orientations, web site quality, and purchase intentions: The role of web site personalities. *Journal of Business Research, 62*(4), 441–450. doi:10.1016/j.jbusres.2008.01.036

Rogers, E. M. (2003). *Diffusion of innovations* (5th ed.). New York, NY: Free Press.

Roman, S. (2010). Relational consequences of perceived deception in online shopping: The moderation roles of type of products, consumer's attitude toward the Internet and consumer's demographics. *Journal of Business Ethics, 95*(3), 373–391. doi:10.1007/s10551-010-0365-9

Rosen, K. T., & Howard, A. L. (2000). E-retail: Gold rush or fool's gold? *California Management Review, 42*(3), 72–100.

Sanchez-Franco, M. J. (2006). Exploring the influence of gender on Web usage via partial least squares. *Behaviour & Information Technology, 25*(1), 19–36. doi:10.1080/01449290500124536

Shih, P. (2004). An empirical study on predicting user acceptance of e-shopping on the Web. *Information & Management, 41*(3), 351–368. doi:10.1016/S0378-7206(03)00079-X

Shim, S., & Drake, M. F. (1990). Consumer intention to utilize electronic shopping: The Fishbein behavioral intention model. *Journal of Direct Marketing, 4*(3), 22–33. doi:10.1002/dir.4000040305

Shim, S., Eastlick, M. A., Lotz, S. L., & Warrington, P. (2001). An online prepurchase intentions model: The role of intention to search. *Journal of Retailing, 77*(3), 397–416. doi: 10.1016/S0022-4359(01)00051-3

Skadberg, Y. X., & Kimmel, J. R. (2004). Visitors' flow experience while browsing a web site: Its measurement, contributing factors and consequences. *Computers in Human Behavior, 20*(3), 403–422. doi :10.1016/S0747-5632(03)00050-5

Suh, K., & Chang, S. (2006). User interfaces and consumer perceptions of online stores: The role of telepresence. *Behaviour & Information Technology, 25*(2), 99–113. doi: 10.1080/01449290500330398

Swinyard, W. R., & Smith, S. M. (2003). Why people (don't) shop online: A lifestyle study of the Internet consumer. *Psychology and Marketing, 20*(7), 567–597. doi:10.1002/mar.10087

United Nations Educational, Scientific and Cultural Organization. (2010). *Information society policies: Annual world report 2009.* Retrieved from http://www.unesco.org/pv_obj_cache/pv_obj_id_EA2014ECE492323A92A2B334275F85D5 F-7B20A00/filename/ifap_world_report_2009.pdf

Van Dijk, J. (1997). The reality of virtual community. *Trends in Communication, 1*(1), 39–63.

Van Dijk, J. (2006). Digital divide research, achievements and shortcomings. *Poetics, 34,* 221–235. doi:10.1016/j.poetic.2006.05.004

Venkatesh, V., & Bala, H. (2008). Technology acceptance model 3 and a research agenda on interventions. *Decision Sciences, 39*(2), 273–315. doi:10.1111/j.1540-5915.2008.00192.x

Venkatesh, V., & Davis, F. D. (2000). A theoretical extension of the technology acceptance model: Four longitudinal field studies. *Management Science, 46*(2), 186–204. doi:10.1287/mnsc.46.2.186.11926

Venkatesh, V., Morris, M. G., Davis, G. B., & Davis, F. D. (2003). User acceptance of Information Technology: Toward a unified view. *Management Information Systems Quarterly, 27*(3), 425–478.

Verhoef, P. C., & Langerak, F. (2001). Possible determinants of consumers' adoption of electronic grocery shopping in the Netherlands. *Journal of Retailing and Consumer Services, 8*(5), 275–285. doi: 10.1016/S0969-6989(00)00033-3

Vijayasarathy, L. R. (2004). Predicting consumer intentions to use on-line shopping: The case for an augmented technology acceptance model. *Information & Management, 41*(6), 747–762. doi:10.1016/j.im.2003.08.011

World Economic Forum. (2010). *Global Information Technology report 2009-1010.* Retrieved from http://www.weforum.org/issues/global-information-technology

Wu, L., Cai, Y., & Liu, D. (2011). Internet usage and online shopping among Chinese consumers: An investigation of demographics and value orientations. *International Journal of Consumer Studies, 35*(4). doi:10.1111/j.1470-6431.2010.00982.x

Yao, G., & Li, Q. (2009). *The effects of online shopping familiarity and Internet self-efficacy on the formation of trust toward online shopping.* International Conference on E-Business and Information System Security, 2009 May 23–24, Wuhan, China.

Youn, S., & Lee, M. (2009). The determinants of online security concerns and their influence on e-transactions. *International Journal of Internet Marketing and Advertising, 5*(3), 194–222. doi:10.1504/IJIMA.2009.026370

CONSUMER TOPIC 2.1

FTC Fighting Against Misleading Information

Source: Federal Trade Commission (October, 2012). FTC acts to halt medical plan scheme that targeted vulnerable consumers. Retrieved from: http://www.ftc.gov/opa/2012/10/iab.shtm

The Federal Trade Commission charged a telemarketing operation with bilking millions of dollars from thousands of consumers by tricking them into buying what they believed was comprehensive health insurance, when in fact they had paid for something decidedly less. At the FTC's request, a federal court stopped the defendants from marketing or selling any products or services related to medical discount plans or health-related insured benefits, pending resolution of the case.

"The FTC is committed to cracking down on those who prey on vulnerable consumers, including the unemployed, uninsured, and consumers with pre-existing medical conditions, by falsely claiming to offer coverage that is generally accepted by medical providers across the nation," said David Vladeck, Director of the FTC's Bureau of Consumer Protection.

According to the FTC's complaint, the defendants contacted consumers who had submitted their contact information to websites that purported to offer quotes and plan information from health insurance companies. They charged consumers an initial fee ranging from $50 to several hundred dollars, and a monthly fee ranging from $40 to $1,000. But instead of providing comprehensive health insurance, the defendants sold consumers membership in an obscure "trade association" called Independent Association of Businesses or IAB, that provides purported discounts on services, including golf, travel, and limited health care services, and some type of insurance benefits, such as hospitalization and disability insurance.

In recent instances, the defendants behind the telemarketing scheme allegedly falsely stated that their medical benefits plan is affiliated with state-sanctioned healthcare programs, or that it is a qualified health insurance plan under the Patient Protection and Affordable Care Act.

Excerpt from: "FTC Acts to Halt Medical Plan Scheme that Targeted Vulnerable Consumers," http://www.ftc.gov/opa/2012/10/iab.shtm. Federal Trade Commission, 2012. Copyright in the Public Domain.

The FTC complaint alleged that the defendants' telemarketers called hundreds of thousands of telephone numbers on the National Do Not Call Registry and did not pay the required fee for access to numbers listed on the Registry. They also allegedly failed to promptly connect consumers to a sales representative and delivered prerecorded messages to consumers who had not agreed in writing to receive such calls. The telemarketers also failed to clearly disclose the seller's identity or inform consumers that they were selling association memberships, and repeatedly called consumers who had told them to stop calling, according to the complaint.

CONSUMER TOPIC 2.2

Do Not Call Goes to Mobile

Ami Rop

**NATIONAL
DO NOT CALL
REGISTRY**

As businesses know, prospective customers have gone mobile. That's why the FTC's Do Not Call Registry services are now even more accessible to consumers. The Registry website has been updated to be PDA-friendly. Consumers can go to www.donotcall.gov from their mobile devices and register a phone number, verify their registration, or file a complaint. Consumers are already taking advantage of this new way of keeping their Registry information up to date.

The Registry's mobile move also serves as a reminder to telemarketers or businesses that use telemarketing services that Do Not Call remains a popular and consumer-driven program. So compliance is more important than ever. Over 204 million consumer numbers are on the Registry and more people add their lines every day.

Ami Rop, "Do Not Call Goes Mobile," http://business.ftc.gov/blog/2011/03/do-not-call-goes-mobile. Federal Trade Commission, 2011. Copyright in the Public Domain.

CONSUMER TOPIC 2.3

Advertising Practices to Watch Out For

Source: California Department of Consumer Affairs (2012). Don't be swayed: Savvy shoppers guide to advertising. Retrieved from: http://www.dca.ca.gov/publications/savvy_shopper.shtml

Merchants use advertisements to attract consumers and sell their products. Consumers use advertisements to compare products and make informed choices. Both groups should know that State and Federal laws require all advertising to be fair and accurate.

Determining if an ad is false or inaccurate is sometimes tricky. Even an ad that's legally true can be misleading. Here are some advertising practices to watch out for.

Advertised But Sold Out

The store must have enough of the advertised item on hand to meet a reasonably expectable demand, unless the advertisement states "limited to stock on hand" or has similar wording. A store that is out of an item may offer you a "rain check," so you can buy the item later at the sale price. A rain check is a store courtesy, not a legal requirement. Even with a rain check, the store is not excused from having enough supply of the advertised item in stock to meet reasonably expectable demand.

Assembly Required

If a children's toy is sold unassembled, the outside of the package must clearly state that the product is unassembled.

Bait and Switch

A product is advertised at a low price to draw shoppers to the store (that's the "bait"). Once there, a salesperson tells shoppers that the advertised product is of poor quality and steers them to a high-priced item (that's the "switch"). A merchant cannot advertise a product that he or she doesn't really intend to sell.

Going Out of Business Sale

If a company advertises that it is going out of business, liquidating, or quitting, the statement must be true.

Limits on the Quantity Sold

Stores cannot limit how many of an advertised item a shopper can buy unless the ad states "limited to one per customer" or has similar wording.

Low-price Claims

If a retail store, or even a car dealer, claims to have the lowest prices in town, he or she must be able to support that claim. A more general claim, such as "low, low prices" does not have to be proven.

Misleading Pictures

The item sold in the store must be the same one pictured in the ad.

Package Prices

The store must tell you if you have to buy more than one of an item to get a discount. For example, an ad cannot say "Batteries: 10 cents each" if the batteries are sold only in packages of 10. However, the ad could say "Batteries: 10 cents each, sold only in packages of 10 for $1 per package."

Regular Price or Sale Price?

To be on "sale," the item must have been offered for purchase at a higher "regular" price within the previous three months. Watch out for a "regular" price that's inflated just to make the sale price look more appealing.

True But Misleading

If an advertisement says an item is "available through Sunday at only $5.99," but the item can be purchased after Sunday at $5.99, the ad is misleading, even though it is literally true.

Used, Defective, Irregular, or Refurbished

If an advertised item is used, defective, irregular, or refurbished, the ad must say so clearly.

CASE STUDY

On a usual busy Friday, Maya's boss gives her a bonus check and lets her get off from work early. Being in a good mood and $1,000 richer, she steps in a mall and is dragged to a store by its gigantic "Today Only" sign. While Maya is waiting in the line to check out a hand bag, she engages in this multi-self conversation:

Frugal Maya: Don't do it, this thing costs $850, and it's not even leather! It's more than a month's grocery budget. Don't you remember last time when you bought a luxury handbag, you and John ate ramen for a month?

Critical Maya: Calm down. Think over. Do you really NEED it? Do you have a better use of that bonus check? What about the maintenance you planned next month for the two cars?

Closed Maya: Come on, it's a good deal, marked down from $1,050! It's going to be shining in the party this weekend. I'd regret forever if I miss it today. Plus, I'm using the bonus money, it's meant to be spent on these kinds of things.

You would like to help Maya make a rational decision. Read the following note before making your recommendations:

INFORMATION SEARCH AND DECISION MAKING

A traditional model of consumer decision making involves several steps in a buying process. The first one is *problem recognition*—you realize a problem or a need. Perhaps, for example, Maya does not have enough handbags for her stuff or their cars are getting more difficult to start and are not accelerating well. She certainly will try to solve the problem or fulfill the need. The second step is *information search*—when trying to solve a problem, a consumer is likely to search for more information. She/he may pay more attention to advertisement or similar items purchased by friends. She/he may actively search for information by visiting stores, checking newspapers and magazines, talking to friends, or even recalling his/her own purchase experiences. After getting the information, a set of alternatives becomes candidates to buy. The third step involves *evaluation of alternatives.* To evaluate the available alternatives, there is no single evaluation process applied by all consumers or by one consumer in all buying situations. However, three essential concepts can be taken into consideration when making the evaluation: value (knowing what are important for you), goal setting (knowing your purpose), and cost/benefit analysis (obtaining the highest net benefit). The next step is *purchase decision,* where we decide to buy or not to buy, where to buy, when to buy, and how to buy. The final step is *post-purchase evaluation*. This evaluation may result in a satisfaction or dissatisfaction, which leads to high or low probability of repurchases.

Now what is your recommendation to Maya? Would you be able to recommend to Maya a comparison shopping plan following the information searching and decision process?

(continued)

CONSUMER RESOURCES

Accuracy in Media: http://www.aim.org

Consumer Union: http://www.consumerreports.org

Consumer World: http://www.consumerworld.org

Federal Trade Commission Bureau of Consumer Protection: http://www.ftc.gov/bcp/index.shtml

More resource from FTC for consumers: http://www.consumer.gov

CHAPTER 3

CONSUMER FRAUDS AND PROTECTION

CHAPTER 3 INTRODUCTION

Consider the following scene: you received a phone call from John Smith working at the Bank of Y. From his enthusiastic voice you learned that you have been chosen to get a fantastic new credit card even you do not have any credit history. What you need to do is to provide your social security number to him to start the process. Feeling skeptical, the other day you received an email from the Bank of Y, telling you that they were concerned about your financial privacy and security, and asking you to click a hyper-link to verify your information for the protection purposes. What should you do? There are many faces of consumer frauds and they are everywhere. Read the chapter and learn how to protect ourselves.

THE US CONSUMER MOVEMENT

A New Era Amid Old Challenges

Robert N. Mayer

According to social science theory, the US consumer movement should either never have existed or ceased to exist by now. During the 1960s, Olson (1965) explained in his book *The Logic of Collective Action* why the efforts to provide pure public goods for a large constituency (in this case, consumer advocacy and policies that, if provided at all, are available to everyone) was doomed by the free rider problem. In 1972, economist Anthony Downs described how issues such as environmentalism and consumerism had short shelf lives (Downs 1972). After a period of initial public enthusiasm, people, he believed, would lose interest in these issues as they learned about the high costs of addressing them. In 1981, marketing professors Paul Bloom and Stephen Greyser compared the consumer movement to a product or service in the declining stages of its life cycle. Bloom and Greyser (1981) painted a picture of consumer organizations competing with each other in an intense struggle for survival.

A 50TH ANNIVERSARY

Despite the theoretical reasons why the US consumer movement should not exist, here we are celebrating the 50th anniversary of President Kennedy's Message to Congress on Protecting the Consumer Interest (Kennedy 1962). In a speech that is often used to mark the beginning of the third wave of the consumer movement, Kennedy laid out four consumer rights: (1) the right to safety, (2) the right to be informed (and protected from fraudulent practices), (3) the right to choose among a variety of products and services at competitive prices and (4) the right to be heard in the formulation of government policy.

Robert N. Mayer, "The US Consumer Movement: A New Era Amid Old Challenges," *The Journal of Consumer Affairs*, vol. 46, issue 2, pp. 171–189. Copyright © 2012 by John Wiley & Sons, Inc. Reprinted with permission.

What is perhaps less well known is that President Kennedy also created, within his Council of Economic Advisors, a Consumers' Advisory Council "to examine and provide advice to the government on issues of broad economic policy, on governmental programs protecting consumer needs, and on needed improvements." The twelve appointees to the Consumers' Advisory Council were a "who's who" of the consumer leaders of the time (Consumer Reports 1962). One of these members was Dr. Colston E. Warne, president of the country's preeminent consumer organization, Consumers Union (CU) and an ACCI Distinguished Fellow. The Council also contained two other future ACCI Fellows—Helen Nelson and Richard L.D. Morse.

President Kennedy convened the first Council meeting in July 1962. At the meeting, the President told the Council members that he wanted them to "come forward with as many important decisions and proposals as you can, and bring them to my attention." Kennedy told the Council that they were not "window dressing" and that he hoped, well beyond his administration, that the Council would be "a definite part of our governmental structure." After Kennedy's assassination, President Lyndon Johnson took the bold step of establishing the first White House Special Assistant for Consumer Affairs. Johnson chose Esther Peterson, after whom another distinguished lectureship at this conference is named. The Consumers' Advisory Council was folded into a new entity, the President's Committee on Consumer Interests. The Committee reported to the new Special Assistant but never became as influential as perhaps President Kennedy had hoped. ACCI members, however, were willing and active participants in the consumer movement of the 1960s.

ADDITIONAL CONSUMER RIGHTS AND SIGNS OF MOVEMENT STRENGTH

Building on the platform erected by President Kennedy, consumer organizations have expanded and reordered the list of consumer rights. The list used today by Consumers International and consumer groups around the world begins with the right to satisfaction of basic needs such as food, shelter and, lest we think this right is only relevant in less developed countries, health care. The list also includes the rights to redress, consumer education and a healthy environment.

Momentum is currently strong for adding a ninth consumer right—the right to privacy. In February 2012, President Obama introduced a blueprint for a "Consumer Privacy Bill of Rights" (Obama 2012). Using the 50th anniversary of Kennedy's message as a springboard, Senator Richard Blumenthal (D-CT) recently argued for a new consumer right to privacy (Blumenthal 2012). On that same day, CU's President Jim Guest made the same proposal at the annual assembly of the Consumer Federation of America (CFA), and Helen McCallum, Director General of Consumers International, made a call for a consumer right to privacy as part of the celebration of World Consumer Rights Day (Guest 2012; McCallum 2012).

Beyond pressing for an additional consumer right, there are other indicators of the health of the US consumer movement. There are at least eight consumer organizations with annual revenues of $2 million or more. The big boy is, of course, CU with an annual budget of around a quarter of a billion dollars. Three other organizations—Public Citizen, the National Consumer Law Center (NCLC) and the Center for Responsible Lending (CRL)—have annual budgets of $8 million or more. Four others have annual revenues of between two and three million dollars: National Consumers League, US Public Interest Research Group (US PIRG),[1] the CFA and Consumers Action.

Like any healthy ecosystem, the leading consumer organizations are diverse in geographical location and revenue sources (Mayer 2005). Although four of the eight leading consumer organizations are based in Washington, DC, others are headquartered in New York, Massachusetts, North Carolina and California. CU raises the bulk of its money via subscriptions to its product testing magazine, whereas NCL relies heavily on money it earns from projects conducted with businesses. NCLC derives critical support from *cy pres* awards (funds from lawsuits where victim compensation is not feasible) and CRL has been nourished by foundation funding. So much for the cut-throat competition that Bloom and Greyser foresaw.

A SIGNAL ACHIEVEMENT

An organization's revenues and expenditures are really just inputs. An advocacy organization's outputs should be measured, for example, in terms of consumers educated (and scams avoided), statutes and regulations successfully lobbied for (and bad ones fended off) or lawsuits won. I would argue that the consumer movement's most important such output during the last thirty years was the successful lobbying campaign in support of creating the Consumer Financial Protection Bureau (CFPB). (Although the proposal to create a new agency first spoke of a Financial Product Safety Commission or a Consumer Financial Protection Agency, I will use the name of the final entity, the CFPB, throughout.) The Bureau, passed as part of the Dodd-Frank Wall Street Reform and Consumer Protection Act of 2010, enforces a wide range of credit-related statutes and has authority over several previously unregulated types of lenders.

The activist campaign in support of creating the CFPB sported a number of new features for the US consumer movement (Pertschuk 1982). It is true that the campaign took place in a supportive environment—including a public suffering from a prolonged recession, a steady stream of revelations concerning financial wrongdoing by financial institutions, an appealing and media-savvy champion in the person of Elizabeth Warren, and a Democrat-controlled Congress—but consumer organizations made a number of canny moves that helped their cause. I will discuss six such features of the campaign and then point out some absent but potentially important ones. Together, these observations hold important implications for the future of the US consumer movement.

Features of the CFPB Campaign[2]

Going Structural

The first important feature of the campaign to create the CFPB was the nature of the campaign's goal: to create a new, broadly empowered government structure rather than to pass a single, narrow statute. The idea of a new consumer agency dedicated to the interests of consumers of financial products and services was laid out in 2007 by Harvard Professor Elizabeth Warren in an article in *Democracy* (Warren 2007, 2008), but consumer organizations could have easily dismissed her proposal as unrealistic and overly ambitious. Instead, these organizations (and those in other social movements) were smart enough to recognize a good idea (and a good messenger) when they saw it.

The receptivity of consumer organizations to seeking a structural change in consumer protection was no doubt abetted by the general optimism surrounding the election of President Obama and a Democrat-controlled Congress. Consumer advocates looked forward to a more activist government with a more pro-consumer orientation, but the receptivity of consumer activists to the idea of seeking an entirely new consumer protection agency had an additional source: advocates had grown tired of eking out partial reforms of large, decades-old problems.

The Credit Card Accountability, Responsibility and Disclosure Act (Credit CARD Act) passed in early 2009, while warmly welcomed by advocates, exemplified to them the limits of a piecemeal approach in which specific abuses in specific industries were addressed by specific legislation. Abuses of credit consumers had been building for many years. The laundry list of industry practices included: shortening grace periods to maximize late fees, reordering of purchases to maximize over-the-limit fees, charging interest rates far in excess of economy-wide interest rates and invoking universal default (under which one lender raises interest rates when a borrower misses a payment or exceeds a credit limit to a second lender). The Credit CARD Act had forty sections, each taking on a particular abuse by proscribing a creditor practice, requiring a disclosure or mandating a study.

Reflecting on the credit card campaign, Ed Mierzwinski, Consumer Program Director for US PIRG and ACCI's 2010 Colston Warne Lecturer, felt that there had to be a better way of going about reform. Consumer groups were playing "a game of Whack-A-Mole" in which specific abuses were addressed but only after the lending industry had figured out ways of nullifying any new protections (Mierzwinski 2010). Plus, if it took so much lobbying work to pass legislation reining in credit card issuers, an industry that virtually everyone hates, what would be the chances of taming banks, insurers, investment firms or real estate companies one at a time? Advocates like Mierzwinski concluded that they needed a more structural solution in the form of an agency that could respond quickly to both abuses themselves and industry efforts to evade new rules.

Going Coalitional

The goal of a new agency dedicated to protecting financial consumers was highly ambitious. Harvard history professor Lizabeth Cohen did not exactly call the goal unobtainable in her 2009 Colston Warne Lecture to ACCI, but she was circumspect (Cohen 2010). First, Cohen drew numerous parallels between the campaign to create the CFPB and the unsuccessful campaign during the 1970s to create an overarching Consumer Protection Agency that would represent consumers within all federal agencies. (The proposed new agency also went by the names of the Office of Consumer Representation and the Agency for Consumer Advocacy.) Second, she predicted that business opposition would be broad, sophisticated and well financed. Organizations like the Chamber of Commerce and the American Financial Services Association were already leading the charge against the new agency, claiming that any new regulations would end up harming consumers. Business opponents would eventually launch a multimillion dollar advertising effort to discredit the idea of a new agency. Finally, Cohen took as a "bad sign" that Federal Reserve Board Chairman Ben Bernanke was not supportive of the new agency. Surveying the landscape, Cohen observed that "the fight promises to be nasty and the outcome uncertain" (p. 242).

If consumer advocates were going to overcome strong opposition, they would need partners and perhaps a formal coalition. During the campaign to pass the Credit CARD Act, an organization was launched—Americans for Fairness in Lending (AFFIL)—that brought together two dozen consumer, labor, civil rights, fair housing and faith-based organizations to "raise awareness of abusive credit and lending practices and to call for re-regulation of the industry ... using a unified and consistent national message" (Americans for Fairness in Lending 2008). AFFIL never became a formidable, well-financed lobbying force, but it did set the precedent for a multimovement coalition in pursuit of financial reform.

In late 2008, a small group of organizers including Ed Mierzwinski, Travis Plunkett (Legislative Director of the CFA) and Maureen Thompson (a consultant to AARP) took informal soundings among many of the groups involved in AFFIL and uncovered a strong inclination to campaign for broad, comprehensive financial regulatory reform rather than narrow, incremental changes (Plunkett 2010). These leaders established that there was provisional support for a campaign to address fair lending, consumer and investor protection, financial systems reform and related matters.

Although several preliminary meetings confirmed a widespread feeling among progressive-leaning organizations that "we had better all be in this time," champions of the CFPB faced two major risks. First, while working on a broad financial reform bill gave them powerful allies like the AFL-CIO and the Leadership Conference on Civil and Human Rights, a coalition approach also raised the ante substantially. Business groups that might not care very much about stopping a new consumer financial protection agency might oppose a comprehensive financial reform bill because of provisions about derivatives trading, compensation for the executives of financial services firm or limits on the ability of banks to make certain kinds of speculative investments.

The second risk was that in all the horse trading involved in getting a broad bill passed, the CFPB might be excessively watered down or dropped entirely. Although consumer financial protection and a strong, independent regulator ranked as the number one priority for many of the groups involved in the discussions (e.g., the CRL, CU, the CFA, the NCLC, US PIRG, AARP and the National Association of Consumer Advocates), there were a number of other groups with different priorities. For labor organizations such as the AFL-CIO, SEIU and AFSCME, issues of corporate governance, shareholder rights and the problem of "too big to fail" were more important than the consumer agency. Alternatively, strengthening the Community Reinvestment Act and addressing mortgage discrimination took top billing for fair lending and community development organizations.

In short, if supporters of the CFPB were going to work as members of a coalition, they would find themselves in a high-stakes game involving some complex financial issues on which they had little expertise. By the same token, groups for whom consumer financial protection was a secondary priority would also have to work on the consumer protection issues if a coalition approach was to work. Despite these challenges, advocates for financial reform decided in spring 2009 to create a formal coalition and name it Americans for Financial Reform (AFR).

In April 2009, the members of the nascent AFR steering committee made a strategic decision that would influence the rest of the campaign (Plunkett 2010). They adopted a set of guiding principles contained in a special report issued in January 2009, by the Troubled Asset Relief Program Congressional Oversight Panel (COP). The COP, headed by Elizabeth Warren and Damon Silvers, took a broad view of financial reform, spanning the regulation of financial firms and markets, control of systemic risk as well as consumer and investor protections (Congressional Oversight Panel 2009).

The leaders of AFR observed that the COP's eight principles of reform corresponded, at least qualitatively, to the range of interests expressed by the groups attracted to the coalition (Abrecht 2011). By taking ownership of the entire range of financial reform issues, AFR hoped to build a powerful, energized membership organization.

Finding Skilled Leadership

It was going to take a very special person to lead a large and diverse coalition in taking on the entire financial services community. The coalition found its leader in Heather Booth, the most accomplished community organizer you have never heard of. Her life is a short course in the various progressive social movements of the 1960s to the present—civil rights, antiwar, organized labor, feminism and economic justice.

Booth is perhaps best known for helping to found the Midwest Academy in the 1970s. (Booth is still president of its board of directors.) Inspired by the ideas of master community organizer Saul Alinsky, Booth and her husband Paul—a leader of Students for a Democratic Society in the 1960s and later a top labor union—founded the Academy in 1973. The Academy's aim was to train leaders and staff members of community organizations, reinforce interorganizational and intermovement cooperation and, in the long run, build a broad-based movement in support of the all-American goals of freedom, democracy and justice for all. Booth provided the initial funding for the Academy; it came from a successful lawsuit against a former employer who had fired her for complaining about the conditions under which the company's secretaries worked. In the Academy's first ten years, more than 16,000 people attended its training sessions (Reitzes and Reitzes 1987).

In early 2009, Heather Booth was directing a non-governmental organization, Rebuild and Renew America Now, devoted to passage of the first Obama budget. Before that campaign was over, though, Booth was approached by Gary Kalman of US PIRG and Steve Abrecht of the Service Employees International Union. They told her that there had been three meetings of groups interested in a financial reform campaign. There was enormous potential, but the organizing effort was not advancing. "And if it was not advancing, people were going to leave" (Booth 2011).

According to Kalman, Booth wanted to know whether the campaign to enact financial reform would be serious, that is, whether there would be adequate funding for it. He responded, "No. Not only don't we have a little bit of money, we don't have any money. So, if we hired you, we couldn't actually pay you" (Kalman 2011). To Kalman's delight, Booth turned back to him and said, "You know, this kind of economic issue, the restructuring of financial systems, is why I do what I do. I can't *not* work on this issue. I will do it" (Kalman 2011). The opportunity to rein in the banks and other financial institutions that had crashed the economy and destroyed so many people's lives was simply irresistible.

Abrecht and other members of AFR's Steering Committee set to work raising funds. In relatively short order and with the key assistance of some foundations, AFR had a $2 million budget with which to work. With initial funding committed, Booth recruited Lisa Donner as her deputy director. Donner, whom Booth had not met previously, came from a younger generation of organizers but had activist credentials that no doubt appealed to Booth. After graduating from Harvard, Donner cut her political teeth as an organizer for the Service Employees International Union, spending most of her time on its Justice for Janitors campaign in Washington, DC. As the campaign name suggests, it was a city-by-city effort begun in the mid-1980s to improve the working conditions and remuneration for janitors. For the following eleven years (1995–2006), Donner worked for ACORN, including a stint as head of its Financial Justice Center. There, she tackled such issues as payday lending, refund anticipation loans and subprime home loans (Donner 2010). Thus, Donner had command of some of the financial issues that would be crucial during the campaign to establish the CFPB.

Involving Younger Leaders

In Booth and Donner, AFR had its top guns. The two were experienced professionals capable of leading and coordinating a multifaceted campaign. The combination of the older Booth and the younger Donner was emblematic of a larger feature of the campaign. AFR forged the savvy of experienced leaders with the energy and skills of a younger cohort of activists.

Many progressive organizations are headed by activists who earned their first political stripes during the 1960s. Thus, transitioning leadership to a new generation of activists is a challenge for many contemporary social movements, including the consumer movement. For example, CU is led by Jim Guest, who gave the Colston Warne Lecture in 2002. Jim is dynamic and baby faced, but he is 71 years old. Steve Brobeck, the 1988 Warne Lecturer, has led the CFA since 1980. He, too, is going strong at the age of 67, but he will not direct CFA forever. The same is true of Ken McEldowney, who has been the director of San Francisco-based Consumer Action since 1980. Will Ogburn, executive director of the NCLC, is practically a baby among consumer group directors at the age of 64.

In putting together its executive committee, steering committee and staff team, AFR emphasized youth. Key roles were played by activists in their forties, thirties, and even twenties: Eileen Toback, Heather McGhee, Janis Bowdler, David Arkush, George Goehl and Dan Geldon. These "youngsters" had the opportunity to learn from some masters of progressive politics, including Heather Booth, Nancy Zirkin and Ed Mierzwinski—lessons that could well pay off in future campaigns.

Moving Outside Beltway Politics

Although the campaign to enact the Dodd-Frank Act and include a strong CFPB boiled down to getting the necessary number of votes in the House and Senate, AFR viewed mobilizing the grassroots as integral to its legislative goals. It has been several decades since consumer groups have been able to get people into the streets for rallies and picket lines, but these political tactics are still part of the stock and trade of labor and civil rights groups. Thus, the campaign to create the CFPB had a "people power" element that consumer groups alone probably would not have been able to provide.

In October 2009, AFR worked with National People's Action, the SEIU and other groups to organize a "Showdown in Chicago." An estimated five thousand protestors made life uncomfortable for the attendees of the American Bankers Association annual meeting in The Windy City (Moberg 2009). The Chicago protesters had a diverse agenda, but creating a new agency to protect consumers was high on it. During a speech to the protesters, Illinois Senator Dick Durbin asked bankers to stop opposing the CFPB. FDIC Chairman Sheila Bair delivered the same message. At another venue, a call and response involving 700 people was heard. One person yelled: "Tell me what you want, what you really want." Hundreds of voices shouted back, "Our homes back!" Then again: "Tell me what you need, what you really need." The crowd answered back: "CFPA!" (Kaplan 2009).

AFR provided a small portion of its very tight budget to local groups in exchange for their efforts to mobilize grassroots and "grasstops" support for the financial reform campaign. Although grassroots campaigning aims at energizing everyday voters and consumers, grasstops lobbying focuses on local influentials—clergy, union leaders, newspaper editors and television news directors—who are capable of communicating with legislators from their districts. Members of the media were particularly important lobbying targets. Gary Kalman of US PIRG expressed the view that "the minute that the banking lobby sensed that this [set of issues] was to going fall out of the media, that people weren't paying attention, that's when they come to win" (Kalman 2011).

AFR benefitted, however, from some free publicity for its CFPB campaign in the form of media appearances by Elizabeth Warren and two viral videos produced by Academy award–winning director Ron Howard. Warren was a frequent guest on television programs such as *The Daily Show with Jon Stewart, Real Time with Bill Maher* and *The Colbert Report,* always making sure to tout the CFPB. Building on her growing celebrity, Warren posted a video on YouTube in mid-July 2009. Appearing at her professor's desk at Harvard attired in a soft-pink blouse, she began by mentioning that she had testified before Congress on President Obama's plan to create a new agency for consumers. Now, she wanted to share her "thoughts directly with anyone who wanted to hear them" (Warren 2009). Warren explained that the job of the new agency would be to "set up basic rules so that no one gets tricked or trapped again." She concluded by urging viewers to contact their representatives in Washington: "Tell them you support change. Tell them you want a consumer agency, someone in Washington who's on your side."

Two additional videos stemmed partially from a conversation Warren had with director Ron Howard. He told her he "would try to get together with a few people who might be able to get the word out [about the CFPB]" (Stelter 2010). The "few people" turned out to be some of the most famous comedians in the United States, including Jim Carrey, Will Ferrell and Dan Aykroyd.

In the first video, actors impersonating former US presidents visit the bedroom of a putative President Obama and his wife Michelle. In a dream sequence, the former presidents tell President Obama to show some gumption and support the creation of a strong CFPB, regardless of the personal political consequences. The video's release on March 3, 2010 was clearly meant to influence the Senate Banking Committee negotiations: it ends with a voiceover by Ron Howard, urging people to contact their senators.

The second video, released a few days later, features Heidi Montag, a blonde bombshell of an actress known for her numerous plastic surgeries. In self-deprecating fashion, she ties the dangers of plastic surgery to that of another kind of plastic—credit cards. She says:

> With hidden fees and standard interest rate increases, that $11,000 jaw line could end up costing you upwards of $50,000. ... Being in debt for elective surgery is bad enough, but when I think about the thousands of Americans whose only method of paying for food is their credit cards—it's enough to make me cry without moving my new face (Montag 2010).

Moving to solutions, Ms. Montag says, "A consumer agency will stop banks and credit card companies from being such sleazy jerks." The video concludes with Ms. Montag, reclining seductively in a bathtub, suggesting that viewers call Senators Christopher Dodd (D-CT) and Richard Shelby (R-AL).

At that point, cardboard heads of the senators emerge from her bubble bath, and viewers are urged to call a phone number splashed on the screen. As much of a darling of the mass media and general public as Ralph Nader was during the 1960s and 1970s, it was never this cool being a supporter of a new consumer agency.

Keeping the President Firmly on Their Side

A final feature of the CFPB campaign that had generally eluded consumer groups in the past was strong support from the US president, in this case President Obama. Back in the 1970s, President Carter initially agreed on the need for a new federal consumer protection agency, but his support flagged and the agency was never created (Schwartz 1979; Vogel 1989).

President Obama, in contrast, remained steadfast in his support for the new agency. He began by including the new agency in his financial reform package. He made Michael Barr, Assistant Secretary of the Treasury and an experienced political insider, his point-person in the effort to enact financial reform. Barr had long-standing and positive relations with many of the organizations within AFR and was committed to a strong and independent CFPB. The President spoke out repeatedly in favor of the CFPB. The most notable occasion was in October 2009. In reference to ads sponsored by the US Chamber of Commerce suggesting that the new agency would destroy small businesses, the President described the claim as "completely false" (Obama 2009).

For its part, AFR went out of its way not to antagonize the Administration when the inevitable compromises on the CFPB's independence and authority were made. For example, when Senator Dodd, with the President's blessing, proposed locating the CFPB in the Federal Reserve rather than making it a free-standing agency, Congressman Barney Frank derided the proposal as "a joke" (Chan and Wyatt 2010). Some members of AFR howled as well, but most held their fire, choosing to examine quietly whether the agency's independence was really at stake.

All told, the advocates who pulled together via the AFR played a vital role in the public policy process. They helped secure passage of the Dodd-Frank Act and ensured inclusion of a new consumer agency with substantial authority and independence.

THE ROADS NOT TAKEN

From a legislative point of view, the campaign to create the CFPB was a major success. Despite powerful opposition and a deeply divided Congress, the agency emerged with substantial authority and independence, including a funding mechanism that sidesteps most of the congressional appropriations process. Nevertheless, there may be some value in noting campaign features whose absence may reflect vulnerabilities of the US consumer movement. These features may be summarized as alliances not forged, tools not employed and passions not ignited.

Alliances Not Forged

The coalition among consumer, labor, community development and civil rights organizations was a fairly natural one. Not only had these groups worked together recently on the Credit CARD Act, but also they had worked together sporadically since the 1960s. This time the collaboration was different in intensity and quality. The advocates brought in seasoned professionals to coordinate the campaign, paid attention to mobilizing grassroots public support and formulated a broad agenda of financial reform.

AFR had limited success in creating alliances beyond those that had come together in fighting for the Credit CARD Act. Several military service organizations joined with AFR in insisting that auto dealers not be exempt from the CFPB's jurisdiction over lenders. The confluence of interests between consumer groups and military groups was a replay of a successfully waged battle in 2006 to cap interest rates on payday loans to military personnel and their dependents (Department of Defense 2007).

On April 15, 2010, The Military Coalition, a federation formed in 1996 of thirty-four military, veterans and uniformed services organizations representing 5.5 million people, sent a letter to the chair and ranking member of the Senate Banking, Housing and Urban Affairs Committee. The letter opposed an amendment to exempt auto dealers and their lending practices from CFPB jurisdiction (The Military Coalition 2010). In May, the Secretaries of the US Army and Air Force added their prestige to the debate, arguing in letters to Congress that failure to protect men and women in uniform from predatory lenders undermined military preparedness. This was a very unusual step given that the military is generally leery of lobbying Congress on issues without a clear and direct connection to military readiness.

Unfortunately for the CFPB's advocates, the support from the military began and stopped with auto lending. Representatives of the military did not raise their voices with respect to mortgage lenders or providers of student loans. Nor did any military organizations join AFR.

In addition to its narrow alliance with military groups, AFR made some connections to members of the academic community. Many of these linkages dealt with Dodd-Frank issues far removed from the CFPB, such as debt swaps, commodities futures and other derivatives. For example, Michael Greenberger, a law professor at the University of Maryland and a former division director at the Commodities Future Trading Commission, and Jane D'Arista, a research associate at the University of Massachusetts (Amherst), testified before legislators and regulators on the more arcane issues addressed by the Dodd-Frank Act (D'Arista 2009; Greenberger 2009). D'Arista, in turn, was one of several academics associated with a group called SAFER, A Committee of Economists and other Experts for Stable, Accountable, Fair and Efficient Financial Reform, that advised AFR.

With respect to the CFPB, ACCI members Norman Silber and Jeff Sovern were the principal drafters of a letter signed by seventy-two other law professors specializing in consumer and banking matters. In addition to expressing general support for a new consumer financial protection agency, the professors waded into the controversial issue of federal preemption of state regulatory authority, coming out strongly for giving states greater powers as "laboratories" for trying out different approaches to lending problems (Silber and Sovern 2009).

Partnerships between AFR and academics ended pretty much there. Neither mainstream members of basic disciplines such as political science or economics nor members of applied professional associations, such as urban planning, public administration, financial counseling and consumer economics, lifted a finger in support of the CFPB. AFR failed to adequately reach out to these groups, and no help was spontaneously offered to AFR by such groups.

Tools Not Employed

The proof of the pudding with respect to the effectiveness of AFR's political methods is that its campaign produced a strong, new consumer agency. As mentioned above, AFR also had at least a modest grassroots and grasstops presence. Still, at the grassroots level, an important technique—the consumer boycott—was not part of the campaign.

For several centuries now, the use of consumer buying power to reward or punish corporate behavior has been employed in pursuit of emancipation of slaves, improvement of labor conditions, environmental protection and other progressive causes (Glickman 2009). (It has also been used, although less frequently, in support of conservative issues, such as discouraging sponsors of television programs featuring gay characters.) In the domain of financial services, an online petition and fear of a boycott appear to have played a role in Bank of America's decision to roll back a $5 per month charge for the use of debit cards. On the floor of the US Senate, Richard Durbin (D-IL) lent his support to a Bank of America boycott, saying: "Bank of America customers, vote with your feet … Get the heck out of that bank" (Kim 2011). Using Facebook, a Los Angeles art gallery owner set off "Bank Transfer Day," an event to encourage people to move their accounts from big banks to smaller financial institutions, such as credit unions. Between talk of a boycott and calls for account transfers, about 650,000 people opened accounts at credit unions, according to the main credit union trade association (Rapport 2011).

Boycotts are difficult to organize, and they often fizzle, but they can have symbolic and/or tangible benefits (Friedman 1999). When testifying before Congress, leaders of AFR claimed that their coalition represented 250 groups with 50 million individual members. Given that virtually all of these people have at least one relationship with a financial institution (and typically several), the opportunity to use the power of the pocketbook was available but left essentially unused in the campaign to create the CFPB. For example, when Arianna Huffington and Rob Johnson called for a boycott of big banks in December 2009, AFR did not pounce on the idea (Huffington and Johnson 2009). The boycott never became an important tactical element for AFR.

Although boycotts in the United States stretch back at least to the eighteenth century, use of the Internet as a tool of consumer power is recent and evolving rapidly. AFR's use of the Internet was unimaginative, confined largely to easing communication among its leaders and organizing online letter-writing campaigns. AFR did not use the Internet to promote and synchronize consumer boycotts. Nor did it take advantage of the Internet to "crowdsource" feedback on potential messaging strategies, collect compelling stories of consumer mistreatment by lenders, organize virtual sit-ins or even raise funds. In short, the CFPB campaign barely tapped the burgeoning possibilities of using the Internet to inform and organize consumers (Van Laer and Van Aelst 2010).

Passions Not Ignited

The deep and broad (and now long) Great Recession has wreaked havoc on workers, investors, homeowners and consumers. Although the economic meltdown had many causes, opaque and unsuitable mortgages are one of, if not the, most fundamental. One might expect, then, that the public would rally around the general idea of financial reform and the more specific notion of a new agency dedicated to protecting borrowers. Opinion polls showed that members of the public were generally sympathetic to the idea of a new agency, but the idea hardly ignited their passion.

In late 2008, President Obama's chief of staff Rahm Emanuel told a group of corporate executives, "You never want a serious crisis to go to waste" (Seib 2008). Although the crisis no doubt helped secure passage of the Dodd-Frank Act and other pieces of legislation, there was precious little public outrage and few calls for fundamental change. There are many possible reasons. People were hunkering down, protecting what little financial security was left to them after their investment accounts and home values tumbled by trillions of dollars. Also, if the public bought AFR's main argument that government inaction had contributed to the financial crisis, why then should people believe that yet another government agency would be the answer to their problems? If anything, the government seemed more intent on bailing out big financial institutions than helping workers, homeowners and consumers. Yet, a third, more speculative barrier to public anger is connected to the nature of credit transactions. As much as some advocates liked to portray lenders forcing loans on unwary borrowers, consumers were not completely blameless in the mortgage meltdown. Borrowers could have been more wary of the you-can't-pass-this-up nature of many mortgage sales pitches. The general public recognizes this, and so do many people who got in trouble with credit. A new government protector might help unmask schemes that are too good to be true, but most consumers recognize that it is ultimately their responsibility to resist the temptation to get something for nothing.

CONCLUSION

During its origins in the United States at the turn of the twentieth century, the consumer movement tapped an ardent sense of responsibility on the part of members of the upper middle class toward less fortunate members of society (Nathan 1986; Sklar 1998). As affluence spread further, the movement turned to providing benefits for middle-class consumers in the form of legal and informational supports for a comfortable lifestyle (Hilton 2009). Consumers were asked to do little other than to be efficient in the exercise of their purchasing power.

As early as the 1980s, some people wondered whether the consumer movement had outlived its usefulness, a victim of its many successes (Cook 1983; Smith and Bloom 1986). The Great Recession revealed, however, that the need for a robust consumer movement was far from extinguished. Indeed, as CU's President Jim Guest has argued, a lack of effective consumer protection in mortgage markets was a root cause of the financial meltdown (Guest 2011).

In seeking to prevent future financial catastrophes, consumer advocates appealed to a sense of victimization that stretched from subprime borrowers in inner-city Cleveland to middle-class suburbanites in Orange County, CA. The advocates faced off against the most powerful forces in our society—the financial industry and its government allies—and won. The movement was innovative in its organization, base broadening and resource mobilization, but it was still essentially an expression of third-wave consumerism (Herrmann and Mayer 1997). It sought traditional, market-oriented remedies for consumers who had been tricked and trapped. It created a new agency to root out abusive lending practices and equip consumers—via information disclosure—to drive bad actors from the marketplace.

If the movement is to build on its recent achievement of helping to establish the CFPB and open the door to the long-awaited fourth era of the consumer movement, it will have to appeal to something stronger than the desire for safe and affordable products as well as honest selling practices (Rotfeld

2010). Drawing on its recent work with the civil rights and labor movements, the consumer movement will have to articulate a vision of a just society in which consumers play a central role through employing their buying power in pursuit of environmental and workplace responsibility, using new technologies to inform and organize, and improving the situation of less fortunate consumers at home and around the world. In short, advocates must lead consumers in more than a struggle for transparent and competitive markets but also toward realizing a larger vision of consumer interdependence and justice—what Ralph Waldo Emerson called "the infinite enlargement of the heart" (Emerson 1941).

NOTES

1. This does not include the budgets of its local affiliates.
2. Many of the ideas in this section of the address were developed with ACCI member Larry Kirsch as part of a book-length manuscript of the CFPB campaign.

REFERENCES

Abrecht, Steve. 2011. Interview with the Author, May 23.

Americans for Fairness in Lending. About Us. http://americansforfairnessinlending.wordpress.com/about-2/. (Accessed on June 12, 2008)

Bloom, Paul, and Stephen Greyser. 1981. The Maturing of Consumerism. *Harvard Business Review,* 59 (November–December): 130–139.

Blumenthal, Richard. 2012. Consumer Protection Speech to the U.S. Senate. C-SPAN, March 15. http://www.c-spanvideo.org/appearance/601410290.

Booth, Heather. 2011. Interview with the Author, January 11.

Chan, Sewell, and Edward Wyatt. 2010. Gridlock May Be Ending on Consumer Protection. *New York Times.* http://www.nytimes.com/2010/03/03/business/03regulate.html.

Cohen, Lizabeth. 2010. Colston E. Warne Lecture: Is It Time for Another Round of Consumer Protection? *Journal of Consumer Affairs,* 44 (1): 234–246.

Congressional Oversight Panel. 2009. Special Report on Regulatory Reform, January 29. http://cybercemetery. unt.edu/archive/cop/20110402010517/http://cop.senate.gov/documents/cop-012909-report-regulatoryreform.pdf.

Consumer Reports. 1962. An Official Consumer Voice in Washington (September): 463–465.

Consumers International. 2010. *Consumers International: 50 Years of the Global Consumer Movement.* http://www.consumersinternational.org/media/33263/ci50ebook-english.pdf.

Cook, Louise. 1983. Poll Indicates Consumerism May Be a Victim of Success. *Spokane Chronicle,* February 28.

D'Arista, Jane. 2009. Prudential Matters, Resolution Authority and Securitization. Testimony Before the U.S. House Financial Services Committee on Systematic Regulation, Washington, DC, October 29. http://democrats.financialservices.house.gov/media/file/hearings/111/darista.pdf.

Department of Defense. 2007. Limitations on the Terms of Consumer Credit Extended to Service Members and Their Dependents. *Federal Register*, 72 (169): 50580–50594.

Donner, Lisa. 2010. Interview with the Author, December 1.

Downs, Anthony. 1972. Up and Down with Ecology—The "Issue Attention Cycle." *Public Interest*, 28 (Summer): 38–50.

Emerson, Ralph Waldo. 1941. *Essays*. Boston: James Munroe & Co.

Friedman, Monroe P. 1999. *Consumer Boycotts*. New York: Routledge.

Glickman, Lawrence B. 2009. *Buying Power: A History of Consumer Activism in America*. Chicago: University of Chicago Press.

Greenberger, Michael. 2009. Testimony on Behalf of Americans for Financial Reform Before the Commodities Future Trading Commission on Excessive Speculation, Washington, DC, August 5. http://www.cftc.gov/ucm/groups/public/@newsroom/documents/file/hearing080509_greenberger.pdf.

Guest, James A. 2011. Remarks at G20 French Presidency/OECD High-Level Seminar on Consumer Financial Protection, Paris, October 14. http://es.consumersinternational.org/media/844439/jguest-remarks-for-oecd-panel-october-2011.pdf.

Guest, James A. 2012. Fighting for Consumer Rights, Fifty Years After Kennedy's Call. Huffington Post, March 15. http://www.huffingtonpost.com/jim-guest/jfk-consumer-rights_b_1347471.html.

Herrmann, Robert O., and Robert N. Mayer. 1997. U.S. Consumer Movement: History and Dynamics. In *Encyclopedia of the Consumer Movement*, edited by Stephen Brobeck (584–601). Santa Barbara, CA: ABC-CLIO.

Hilton, Matthew. 2009. *Prosperity for All: Consumer Activism in an Era of Globalization*. Ithaca, NY: Cornell University Press.

Huffington, Arianna, and Rob Johnson. 2009. Move Your Money: A New Year's Resolution. *Huffington Post*, December 29. http://www.huffingtonpost.com/arianna-huffington/move-your-money-a-new-yea_b_406022.html.

Kalman, Gary. 2011. Interview with the Author, February 10.

Kaplan, Esther. 2009. Anger, At Last. *The Nation*, October 26. http://www.thenation.com/blog/anger-last.

Kennedy, John F. 1962. Special Message to the Congress on Protecting the Consumer Interest, March 15. http://www.presidency.ucsb.edu/ws/?pid=9108#ixzz1mZQg3iQr.

Kim, Seun Min. 2011. Dick Durbin Urges Customers to Leave Bank of America, *Politico*, October 3. http://www.politico.com/news/stories/1011/65038.html.

Mayer, Robert N. 2005. The Financial Ingenuity of U.S. Consumer Organizations: 4 Case Studies, Review of Consumer Co-operative Studies. *Journal of the Consumer Co-operative Institute of Japan*, 355: 37–42.

McCallum, Helen. 2012. Is It Time Again to Look at Consumer Rights? *Consumers International Blog*, March 14. http://consumersinternational.blogspot.com/2012/03/is-it-time-to-look-again-at-consumer.html?utm_source=feedburner&utm_medium=email&utm_campaign=Feed%3A+ConsumersInternationalBlog+%28Consumers+International+Blog%29.

Mierzwinski, Edmund. 2010. Interview with the Author, December 31.

The Military Coalition. 2010. *Letter to Honorable Christopher J. Dodd and Honorable Richard C. Shelby.* Alexandria, VA: U.S. Senate Banking, Housing & Urban Affairs Committee, April 15. http://www.nclc.org/images/pdf/special_projects/military/letter-auto-exemption.pdf

Moberg, David. 2009. 5,000 Protest Bank Power, Abuses, as 'Showdown' Culminates. *In These Times,* October 27. http://inthesetimes.com/working/entry/5103/5000_protest_bank_power_abuses_as_showdown_culminates/.

Montag, Heidi. 2010. Video: http://www.funnyordie.com/videos/a1da6ff653/heidi-montag-says-no-to-plastic.

Nathan, Maud. 1986. *The Story of an Epoch-Making Movement.* New York: Garland.

Obama, Barack. 2009. Remarks by the President on Financial Protection. White House Office of the Press Secretary, October 9. http://www.whitehouse.gov/the-press-office/remarks-president-consumer-financial-protection.

Obama, Barack. 2012. Consumer Data Privacy in a Networked World: A Framework for Protecting Privacy and Promoting Innovation in the Global Digital Economy. Washington, DC, February. http://www.whitehouse.gov/sites/default/files/privacy-final.pdf.

Olson, Mancur Jr. 1965. *The Logic of Collective Action: Public Goods and the Theory of Groups.* Cambridge, MA: Harvard University Press.

Pertschuk, Michael. 1982. *Revolt Against Regulation.* Berkeley, CA: University of California Press.

Plunkett, Travis. 2010. Interview with Author, December 21.

Rapport, Marc. 2011. Bank Transfer Day: CUNA Says 650,00 Have So Far. *Credit Union Times,* November 3. http://www.cutimes.com/2011/11/03/bank-transfer-day-cuna-says-650000-have-so-far.

Reitzes, Donald C., and Dietrich C. Reitzes. 1987. *The Alinsky Legacy.* Greenwich, CT: JAI Press.

Rotfeld, Herbert J. 2010. A Pessimist's Simplistic Historical Perspective on the Fourth Wave of Consumer Protection. *Journal of Consumer Affairs,* 44 (2): 423–429.

Schwartz, George. 1979. The Successful Fight Against a Federal Consumer Protection Agency. *MSU Business Topics,* 27 (Summer): 45–57.

Seib, Gerald. 2008. In Crisis, Opportunity for Obama. *Wall Street Journal,* November 21. http://online.wsj.com/article/SB122721278056345271.html.

Silber, Norman I., and Jeff Sovern. 2009. A Communication to Congress from Academic Faculty Who Teach Courses Related to Consumer Law and Banking Law at American Law Schools: Statement in Support of Legislation Creating a Consumer Financial Protection Agency, September 29. http://www.stjohns.edu/academics/graduate/law/pr_law_090929.news_item@digest.stjohns.edu%2facademics%2fgraduate%2flaw%2fpr_law_090929.xml.

Sklar, Kathryn Kish. 1998. The Consumers' White Label Campaign of the National Consumers' League. In *Getting and Spending: European and American Consumer Societies in the Twentieth Century,* edited by Susan Strasser, Charles McGovern, and Matthias Judt (17–35). Cambridge, UK: Cambridge University Press.

Smith, Darlene Brannigan, and Paul N. Bloom. 1986. Is Consumerism Dead or Alive? Some Empirical Evidence. In *The Future of Consumerism,* edited by Paul N. Bloom and Ruth Belk Smith (17–22). Lexington, MA: Lexington Books.

Stelter, Brian. 2010. Fake Former Presidents Use Comedy for a Cause. *New York Times,* March 5. http://www.nytimes.com/2010/03/06/arts/television/06funny.html?_r=2&dbk.

Van Laer, Jeroen, and Peter Van Aelst. 2010. Internet and Social Movement Action Repertoires. *Information, Communication & Society,* 13 (December): 1146–1171.

Vogel, David. 1989. *Fluctuating Fortunes.* New York: Basic Books.

Warren, Elizabeth. 2007. Unsafe at Any Rate. *Democracy*, 5 (Summer): 8–19.

Warren, Elizabeth. 2008. Product Safety Regulation as a Model for Financial Services Regulation. *Journal of Consumer Affairs*, 44 (3): 452–460.

Warren, Elizabeth. 2009. Professor Elizabeth Warren Speaks about the Consumer Financial Protection Agency, Video, YouTube.com, July 16, 2009. http://www.youtube.com/watch?v=lYd08e5Cjvs.

INTERNET FRAUD

Michael Bachmann and Brittany Smith

ABSTRACT

This article provides an introduction into the topic of Internet fraud. A precise definition and detailed descriptions of the most prevalent Internet fraud schemes are provided. The entry presents a history of frauds committed on the Internet and introduces the leading scholars on the subject Predominant areas of research are discussed, and future directions of the problem of Internet fraud schemes are outlined. The entry concludes with a critique of current limitations and advancements needed to better address the increasing problem of online frauds.

INTRODUCTION

In legal terms, "fraud" is typically defined as a false representation by means of any act, expression, omission, or concealment made knowingly or recklessly to deceive another to one's advantage. The terms "Internet fraud" or "e-fraud" generally denominate any usage of interconnected computerized or computer-assisted electronic networks or services for any type of fraudulent scheme that intentionally deceives prospective victims through false representation, thereby intending to solicit, obtain, or transmit fraudulent transactions that deprive victims of personal property or any interest, estate, or right. Simply stated, Internet fraud can be understood as any usage of computerized networks, oftentimes in conjunction with social engineering tactics intended to deceive or manipulate a victim in order to give the offender a material advantage at the victim's expense.

Michael Bachmann and Brittany Smith, "Internet Fraud," *Encyclopedia of Cyber Behavior*, ed. Zheng Yan, pp. 931–943. Copyright © 2012 by IGI Global. Reprinted with permission.

Unlike victims of violent crime, fraud victims are not forced to give up their possessions; rather, they are deceived, coerced, or otherwise manipulated into giving them up voluntarily (Gottfredson & Hirschi, 1990).

Internet frauds largely mirror previous fraud schemes perpetrated over the phone or through the mail (Computer Crime Research Center, 2005).

While some researchers (e.g. Wall, 2001) argue that from a strictly legal standpoint, Internet fraud schemes are essentially the same as 'old-fashioned' frauds committed with new toots and nothing more than the "same old wine in new bottles" (Grabosky, 2001, p. 243), there is broad consensus among criminologists who examine the social-structural conditions of electronic environments that society is confronted with a qualitatively new generation of fraudulent schemes. The improved quality of online scams arises primarily from three general features of social interactions taking place within the world of connected computers that render them markedly different from the ones taking place in the 'meatspace' (Pease, 2001, p. 23).

Most notably, the Internet "variously 'transcends', 'explodes', 'compresses', or 'collapses' the constraints of space and time that limit interactions in the 'real world' (Yar, 2006, p. 11). It represents the most important element for the "time-space compression" of globalization in that it allows instantaneous interactions between spatially distant actors (Harvey, 1989). This feature of cyberspace has important implications for fraud schemes because it grants "e-fraudsters" unprecedented access to potential victims from all around the globe.

Secondly, the Internet offers varying degrees of automatization in interaction (Shields, 1996). Among other aspects, automated interactions within computer-mediated communication networks extend both the scope and scale of fraudulent schemes. Many-to-many communications inexorably alter the relationship between fraudsters and their victims and they hinder the efforts of criminal justice systems to investigate, counteract, or resolve the scams (Capeller, 2001). On the one side, Internet users are instantaneously targetable by a substantially large pool of potential fraudsters from all over the world. Concurrently, the offenders are no longer bound by the limits of physical proximity and can launch their schemes through highly automated routines. They possess a multitude of software tools in their cache that permit them to distribute deceptive or misleading information, to create increasingly sophisticated websites that contain fraudulent material or fake logins, and to remain undetectable to law enforcement.

A third criminogenically relevant feature of computer networks is that they allow for easy creation, alteration, and reinvention of the social identity. Internet users can create arbitrary virtual avatars, electronic personas that are often markedly different from their 'real world' identities (Turkle, 1995). The ability to disguise social identity in the electronic realm is of high criminological relevance because it allows potential fraudsters to remain largely anonymous (Snyder, 2001). The increased anonymity in computerized networks reduces the offender's perception of the risks involved in the commission of Internet frauds, which ultimately increases the likelihood that the fraud is committed (Joseph, 2003).

Combined, these three aspects of social interactions in online environments exponentially multiply the possibilities for potential offenders to target vast numbers of potential victims and their property to a previously unknown degree. They render the Internet the ideal "breeding ground for fraud" (Fried, 2001, p. 1). While the crime of fraud is not new and has been around for centuries, the invention and proliferation of the Internet has opened a Pandora's Box for a new breed of criminal to take advantage of unsuspecting or unaware victims.

OVERVIEW

Intellectual History of Internet Fraud

Prior to the commercialization of the Internet in the early 1990s, only a few computer-mediated or computer-oriented fraud cases, usually committed through impersonation or other social engineering methods, had been recorded. A notorious case originated in 1970 when Jerry Neal Schneider began gathering documents from the Pacific

Telephone and Telegraph (PT&T) company. He then proceeded to set up an elaborate reselling scheme for company equipment that cost PT&T more than a million dollars. The scheme was finally discovered in 1973 when one of his ten employees denounced him (Whiteside, 1978).

In addition to the use of social engineering methods, many classic computer-related fraud schemes are perpetrated through illegal or unauthorized data alterations, known as "data diddling." One of the largest data diddling fraud cases involved the Equity Funding Corporation of America. In 1964, the company's president ordered the head of data processing to print the annual report with fictitious profits. In 1972, the scam had grown so vast that the head of data processing calculated that if the current fictional growth rates continued, Equity Funding would have insured the entire population of the world and its assets would surpass the gross national product of the planet. As in Schneider's case, it was again an angry operator who ultimately alerted the authorities to the scam (Trumbore, 2004). Both of these cases represent rare occurrences of early fraud schemes involving computers and electronic data; however, they cannot be considered e-fraud cases in a narrow sense. At the times of their commission, the modern, TCP/IP-based Internet had not yet been established an d its preceding network, the Arpanet, had been designed for the distribution of information, not for monetary transaction.

The prevalence of e-fraud schemes dramatically increased when the Internet began to become commercialized in the early 1990s. The evermore mission-critical nature of computer networks to many industries and the expanding popularity of electronic financial transactions opened up innumerable opportunities to defraud and exploit unsuspecting users. Typical early Internet fraud schemes included auction and retail fraud, securities fraud, and identity theft. The substantial rise in the variety of Internet fraud schemes represents a co-evolutionary relationship between newly introduced, legitimate uses of the Internet and new uses of the same technologies for fraudulent purposes.

While various Internet fraud schemes emerged soon after the Internet was made public in the early 1990s and it began being used for financial transactions, the study of Internet fraud as a new phenomenon did not emerge until several years later. Much of the research conducted in the mid-to late-1990s was produced by law enforcement agencies interested in what appeared to be a growing crime trend. Carter and Katz (1996) were among the first researchers to systematically study early Internet fraud schemes and their benchmark findings revealed how far law enforcement agencies had already fallen behind in policing cybercrimes and Internet fraud. Carter and Katz showed that in the late 1980s, targets of computer crimes were largely limited to government agencies and academic institutions, simply because they were the primary users of networked computers at the time. This changed around 1991 when a United Nations study predicted a massive increase in computer crimes in coming years due to the proliferation of Internet use among private users and corporate networks. The study identified the theft of information as the fastest growing type of Internet crime (Carter and Katz, 1996). Such thefts incorporated various kinds of information, including intellectual property and sensitive user data which were then being sold for substantial profits.

Another pioneering researcher, Groover (1996), revealed that at the time, many law enforcement agencies believed they had little to no computer-related crime within their jurisdictions. This finding was an early indicator of the jurisdictional challenges to come in the investigations of Internet frauds experienced today (Burns, Whitworth & Thompson, 2004). Groover (1996) further suggested that unless more law enforcement agents go through significant training to improve their knowledge, it will be increasingly more difficult for them to identify and trace experienced online criminals.

TYPES OF INTERNET FRAUD

Today, experts contend there are at least 18 distinct types of Internet fraud that meet the legal definitions (Internet Crime Complaint Center, 2011). For consumers, it is particularly important to understand the different forms of e-fraud in order to avoid becoming victimized. The most relevant and common fraud schemes will be outlined below.

Internet Auction Fraud

Throughout the history of Internet fraud, auction fraud has been the most frequently reported among the various fraud schemes (Dolan, 2004; Internet Crime Complaint Center, 2011). Auction fraud refers to fraudulent activities committed on bidding sites such as eBay, eBid, eCrater, or Bonanzle. Auction fraud consistently ranks as the most common online fraud type due to its ability to impact vast, wide-ranging networks of international buyers and sellers engaged in the hundreds of millions of transactions that take place on auction sites each day. Auction fraud schemes are particularly rampant nowadays despite the best efforts of site administrators and governmental organizations to contain such threats. There are simply too many means and opportunities for motivated offenders to easily commit frauds on online auction sites without garnering much attention from law enforcement. EBay, the leading auction site by a large margin, currently offers a daily average of more than 115,000,000 items up for bid. While auction sites offer users some protection from scams, eBay identifies only 0.01 percent of transactions that occur on their site as scams. While this does not appear to be a large percentage of transactions, this amounted to 3,000 fraudulent transactions per day in 2006 (Yar, 2006). According to the Consumer Reports Web Watch (2007) report on fraud committed on eBay auctions, almost half of the respondents who made eBay purchases in the last year said they had experienced at least one type of apparent deceptive scam. Respondents identified scams ranging from a seller's failure to disclose relevant information about the product (15%), the merchandise received differing significantly from the seller's description (13%) to the more egregious cases of counterfeit items or bogus merchandise (5%). Six percent of respondents also indicated they had participated in auctions that had been closed by eBay administrators due to of suspected fraudulent activity.

Chua and Wareham (2004) identify several forms of Internet auction fraud and offer suggestions on how best to combat them. They claim that Internet auction fraud accounted for almost half of all fraudulent activities conducted via the Internet in 2002 and conclude that, despite the significant challenges involved in accurately assessing the prevalence and incident rates of cybercrimes, the best assessments indicate that the high percentage of Internet fraud attributable to auctions applies globally and cross-culturally (Chua and Wareham, 2004). One of the most frequently seen auction fraud schemes is shill bidding or shilling (Nikitkov & Bay, 2008). Shilling denotes auctions where the seller is bidding on his or her own item in an attempt to artificially inflate the price and make the auctioned item more attractive to other bidders. Fraudsters typically employ multiple fake accounts in order to bid on their own items. Victims are usually unaware of the fact that the seller is bidding against his or her own auction.

Another common auction fraud scheme involves the seller's purposive misrepresentation of auction items. It is a scarily common practice for items to be advertised as new when they are actually used, damaged, or dysfunctional. Misrepresentation schemes also incorporate the selling of counterfeit and stolen items. Similarly, some deceptive buyers purchase from in legitimate auctions in order to replace their defective possessions with functional units. Buyers claim to have received a broken item, keep the functioning one, and are reimbursed for their phony investment. Failure to ship and failure to pay are similar frauds where either the seller or buyer does not fulfill his or her end of the transactional agreement. Such scams are usually committed when a buyer claims a loss or damage on an item they actually received in standard working condition.

Chua and Wareham (2004) conclude their investigation into online fraud with the assessment that, since its conception, Internet fraud has become more sophisticated and innovative, and they suggest further research and the application of evidence-based practices by law enforcement and industry leaders to combat its growth. They propose several community based strategies for combating the growing trends. For instance, Chua and Wareham recommend enacting a process of intermediation whereby a highly rated intermediary purchases items from lower rated buyers and uses his or her expertise to decrease the number of fraudulent auctions by verifying seller reliability. As large-scale traders, these intermediaries would be better equipped to absorb the losses from the few fraudulent cases they do incur. Sites such as traderlist.com and consumerist.com are unique in that they work collectively to combat auction fraud, re port offenders, and alert potential victims through consumer education campaigns (Gavish & Tucci, 2008).

While there are many ways consumers may detect and avoid fraudulent auctions. Internet fraud experts typically warn users against engaging in any form of vigilantism. Private Internet users should not attempt retaliation upon the offending party. For instance, if injured parties are purposively sabotaging auctions they suspect are fraudulent by over-bidding or failing to pay, they are in fact committing fraud themselves by violating the terms of service on the sites and in some cases, the law.

Snyder (2000) suggests five steps the Federal Trade Commission (FTC) should take to better protect consumers from auction fraud. Most significantly, Snyder recommends the FTC mandates auction sites to confirm every buyer's and seller's identity through a credit agency, authenticate the quality of the merchandise, provide an escrow service to confirm transactional completion, and expand the penalties for engaging in auction fraud. While these suggested policies would no doubt reduce the number of fraudulent transactions, they would also render online transactions significantly more expensive and cumbersome for both users and operators. Such a highly protected and regimented system would be required to regulate more than 30 million transactions per day. The shear volume of transactions would significantly compromise the ease and efficiency of online transactions thereby rendering Internet auction sites less attractive for consumers.

Credit Card Fraud

Credit card fraud involves the use of fraudulent or stolen credit and debit card information in order to obtain money or property. Credit card information is frequently stolen from insecure websites or by means of identity theft, through skimming (the act of reading out the information contained on the magnetic strip of the card), or by physical theft (Cukier & Levin, 2008). Fraud involving stolen credit and debit cards is most notable in so-called 'card not present' transactions. The label 'card not present' applies to all online transactions and, more generally, to all transactions that do not necessitate the physical presence of the card. The theft of credit card information can be especially harmful to victims by lowering their credit scores, making it more difficult to purchase homes and vehicles.

Advanced Fee Fraud

Fraudsters and conmen have been using fee schemes for far longer than the Internet has been in existence. However, this type of fraud has seen unprecedented increases with the explosion of the Internet and the force multiplication powers the Net provides. Advanced fee fraud involves an imposter claiming to require a fee advance in order to unlock funds stored in an overseas bank account, a percentage of which the offender offers to their targeted victim in exchange for their assistance with the up-front fees. The scammer then disappears with the victim's money, often without a trace (Ampratwum, 2009).

One advanced fee scheme that gained the attention of mainstream media was the Nigerian prince scam that emerged around 1993 (Smith, 2009). In this well-known fraud, scammers sent mass emails to random addresses portraying themselves as wealthy Nigerian aristocrats who needed a free citizen's assistance in gaining access to their bank accounts currently locked to them by their corrupt, third world government. Scammers would sell their sob stories to sympathetic web users via email correspondence, and when they succeeded in gaining the victims' trust, they would empty their bank accounts by using the financial information provided by the victims. According to U.S. Secret Service data, the perpetrators of the landmark Nigerian prince advanced fee scams acquired more than five billion dollars in stolen funds during the years these online scams were fully operational (Smith, Holmes & Kaufmann, 1999). Like other crimes that require victim manipulation through deception or coercion, the type of online offender who engages in Advanced fee fraud utilizes multiple social engineering practices in order to achieve their goals (Edelson, 2003).

Online Securities Fraud

Baker (2002) contends that online securities or investments fraud are not so different from their terrestrial counterparts in that they both rely on cunning, motivated offenders who target potential investors by offering them profit-sharing rights in a start-up business that promises to be successful. Baker cites four main varieties of investment and securities fraud perpetrated over the Internet, each of which is detailed below.

The pump-and-dump scheme involves scammers who distribute emails claiming to provide inside information about small companies that would make excellent investment opportunities for interested individuals. They direct potential investors to secure their interest in this "sure-bet" business as quickly as possible if they wish to maximize their profit-making potential. This email is sent to thousands of people simultaneously and if enough choose to invest in the start-up, its stock prices skyrocket. The scammer then sells his shares at the right time, taking advantage of the temporary boost provided by the surge of investments. Before investors are even aware they have been used, the company's stock plummets, leaving them out of pocket on the money they invested and with zero profit-making potential.

Most well known to the public of all fraud scams and closely related to the pump-and-dump is the classic pyramid scheme. The online version of the pyramid scheme involves scammers emailing potential investors with offers to become independent owner-operators in a sales or service business that relies on recruiting new owner-operators in order to build the base ranks of the corporation's organizational structure. Oftentimes these types of pyramid businesses sell legitimate goods or services, although the bulk of their profits come from the large up-front "membership" dues and revenue fees they charge each new owner-operator they bring into the organization. This results in certain profit for those closest to the peak of the pyramid and frequent losses for the newer investors who represent the majority of owner-operators situated in the base ranks of the pyramid organization. Once the rank-and-file investors realize only those at the top are making a profit, the pyramid scheme usually falls apart as more disillusioned owner-operators leave the business (Baker, 2002).

Baker (2002) continues by describing a type of online fraud known as the "risk-free" plan. This type of fraud involves a scam where prospective investors are lured into handing over start-up funds to be used as capital for a nonexistent company. As with other forms of fraud, the scammer appropriates the victim's resources through misrepresentation and manipulation and disappears with the investor's money before their scheme has been uncovered. Baker cites wireless cable projects, prime bank securities investments, and eel farms as the most common types of fraudulent corporations scammers use to entice individuals to invest in these "risk-free" business plans.

The last type of internet investment fraud Baker (2002) discusses is those schemes involving the transfer of victims' funds to off-shore bank accounts. Offenders involved in this form of online fraud lure investors into wiring money to off-shore companies or accounts in jurisdictions that do not have stringent laws regulating securities exchange. This type of fraud is especially challenging for law enforcement to track which makes them highly attractive to scammers. Yar (2006) estimates that more than seven million Americans were already using the Internet to make online investments in 2001, and this number will only continue to rise as the Internet becomes the world's primary marketplace and forum for social interaction. Although it does not exist in the physical realm, the virtual marketplace is not immune to the pick-pockets and snake oil salesmen lurking around the dark corners of the Internet (Buchanan, J., & Grant, A. J. 2001).

Baker (2003) suggests that Web users are best able to avoid becoming victimized by online scammers and to protect online purchases and investments by verifying the security and authenticity of websites by looking for the Webstrust™ logo. Webstrust™ identifies online businesses that are in compliance with current standards regulating the e-exchange of goods and services.

Phishing

Phishing and the more targeted version of the scam known as spear Phishing represent another online scam used by fraudsters to secure personal financial information from unwitting victims. Phishing scammers create fraudulent websites and emails that appear to be from legitimate banking and credit card companies. Offenders create highly elaborate fake websites that purport to be the official sites of financial institutions and lure users into resubmitting their account information by sending them email notifications claiming there has been fraudulent activity on their accounts. Once clients follow the email link to the fake banking site and input their account information, Phishing scammers have all the information they need to empty victims' bank accounts and steal their identities (Edelson, 2003). Although online security experts continually warn web users that no legitimate financial institution will request secure account information and passwords via email, Phishing continues to be one of the most prevalent forms of online fraud seen today.

FUTURE RESEARCH DIRECTIONS

The increasingly immense quantity of monies exchanged every day via global online transactions has anticipated the respondent development of lucrative platforms ripe for exploitation by ambitious scammers and thieves. These online conmen have every motivation to be creative and innovative in their efforts to remain a step ahead of law enforcement. Despite the continued efforts of law enforcement to pursue multiple countermeasures in their own attempts to outsmart fraudsters on the Internet, experts agree that Internet fraud schemes will present an even greater problem for anti-fraud units in coming years.

Countermeasures currently undertaken to better combat, contain, police, and prevent Internet fraud schemes address various different dimensions related to the scams and the investigations of fraud cases will have to be improved to provide an effective and comprehensive response to this growing problem. Strategies relating to the policing of fraud cases will have to center primarily on increasing the training for law enforcement agents. One of the most pressing current issues is the lack of agents with the technical skills required for cybercrime investigations. Currently, most Internet fraud cases are investigated by small economic crime units in local police departments. Providing additional resources for the recruitment, retention, and continued education of specialized agents in local, state, and federal agencies are critical for the fight against online fraudsters. Furthermore, the cooperation and coordination between agencies within the United States as well as the collaboration with foreign agencies has to be improved to streamline investigations of global crimes such as Internet frauds. The establishment of Europol's cybercrime law enforcement bodies ENISA represents a first important step toward this goal. More concerted international efforts are required to establish transnational collaboration between law enforcement agencies.

In order to be more successful, transnational investigations into Internet fraud cases also require continued effort to harmonize international cybercrime legislations (Ambratwum, 2009). Currently, the Convention on Cybercrime of the Council of Europe, signed by the United States and 29 other states, is the first and only binding multilateral instrument that also serves as a guideline for other countries seeking to develop comprehensive national legislation against cybercrime. Drafted specifically to address jurisdictional problems in the fight against international computer crimes, this treaty requires underwriters to establish laws against cybercrime that ensure that law enforcement agencies have the necessary procedural authorities to investigate and prosecute international e-fraud cases effectively. More concerted efforts to harmonize international legislation and cooperation are the two most pressing issues to ensure a more effective response to the growing problem of Internet fraud. Ideally, such efforts might even lead to the establishment of a centralized international agency similar to Interpol that would be best suited to combat Internet fraud and eliminate interagency jurisdictional disputes.

Outside of law enforcement, an effective battle against Internet fraud requires the continued education of Internet users to avoid them falling prey to the various scamming tactics and to get users who have been victimized to report their victimization. Online-based merchants and industries must further ensure continue lobbying for the promotion of new trusted e-business standards and regulations, while at the same time focusing on advancing technologies for the stealthy deployment of the latest anti-fraud countermeasures. Secure online identification technologies that will improve the authentication of unique web users, in particular, will make it more challenging for scammers to steal the information of unsuspecting Internet users. Unfortunately, there are no simple solutions or policies to contain the problem of Internet fraud. The continued developments of existing fraudulent schemes as well as the emergence of new schemes are directly correlated to the degree with which more financial transactions are being conducted in online environments—and are thus likely to intensify in the near future.

REFERENCES

Ampratwum, E. F. (2009). Advance fee fraud "419" and investor confidence in the economies of sub-Saharan African (SSA). *Journal of Financial Crime, 7*(5(1), 67–79. doi: 10.1108/13590790910924975

Baker, C. R. (2002). Crime, fraud and deceit on the internet: Is there hyperreality in cyberspace? *Critical Perspectives on Accounting, 73*(1), 1–15. doi: 10.1006/cpac.2001.0494

Baker, W. E., & Faulkner, R. R. (2003). Diffusion of fraud: Intermediate economic crime and investor dynamics. *Criminology, 41(4),* 1173–1206. doi: 10.1111/j. 1745-9125.200J!tb01017.x

Buchanan, J., & Grant, A.J. (2001). Investigating and prosecuting Nigerian fraud. *United States Attorneys' Bulletin, November,* 29–47.

Burns, R. G., Whitworth, K. H., & Thompson, C. Y. (2004). Assessing law enforcement preparedness to address Internet fraud. *Journal of Criminal Justice, 32(5),* 477–493. doi: 10.1016/j. jcrimjus.2004.06.008

Capeller, W. (2001). Not such a neat Net: Some comments on virtual criminality. *Social & Legal Studies,* 10, 229–242.

Carter, D., & Katz, A. (1996). Computer crime: An emerging challenge for law enforcement. *FBI Law Enforcement Bulletin,* 65(12), 1–8.

Chua, C. E. H., & Wareham, J. (2004). Fighting Internet auction fraud: An assessment and proposal. *Computer,* J7(10), 31–37. doi:10.1109/ MC.2004.165

Computer Crime Research Center. (2005). *Fraud in the Internet.* Retrieved May 10, 2011, from http://www.crime-research.org /articles/Internet_fraud_0405/

Cukier, W., & Levin, A. (2008). Internet fraud and cybercrime. In Schmalleger, F., & Pittaro, M. (Eds.), *Crimes of the Internet* (pp. 251–279). Upper Saddle River, NJ: Pearson, Prentice Hall.

Dolan, K. M. (2004). Internet auction fraud: The silent victims. *Journal of Economic Crime Management, 2(1),* 1–22.

Drinkhall, J. (1997). Internet fraud. *Journal of Financial Crime, 4(3),* 242-244. doi:10.1108/ eb025785

Edelson, E. (2003). The 419 scam: Information warfare on the spam front and a proposal for local filtering. *Computers & Security,* 22(5), 392-401. doi: 10.1016/SO167-4048(03)00505-4

Fried, R. (2001). *Cyber scam artists: A new kind of con.* Retrieved May 2,2011, from http://crime-scene-investigator.net/CyberScam.pdf

Gavish, B., & Tucci, C. (2008). Reducing Internet auction fraud. *Communications of the ACM, 51(5),* 89–97. doi: 10.1145/1342327.1342343

Gottfredson, M., & Hirschi, T. (1990). *A general theory of crime.* Palo Alto, CA: Stanford University Press.

Grabosky, P. N. (2001). Virtual criminality: Old wine in new bottles? *Social & Legal Studies, 10(2),* 243–249.

Grazioli, S., & Jarvenpaa, S. L. (2000). Perils of Internet fraud: An empirical investigation of deception and trust with experienced Internet consumers. *IEEE Transactions on Systems, Man, and Cybernetics. Part A, Systems and Humans,* 30(4), 395–410. doi: 10.1109/3468.852434

Grazioli, S., & Jarvenpaa, S. L. (2003). Consumer and business deception on the Internet: Content analysis of documentary evidence. *International Journal of Electronic Commerce,* 7(4), 93–118.

Groover, R. S. (1996). Overcoming obstacles: Preparing for computer-related crime. *FBI Law Enforcement Bulletin, 65(12),* 8–10.

Harvey, D. (1989). *The condition of postmodernity.* Oxford, UK: Blackwell.

Internet Crime Complaint Center. (2010). *2009 Internet crime report.* Retrieved May 10, 2011, from http://www.ic3.gov /media/annualreport/2009_ic3 report.pdf

Internet Crime Complaint Center. (2011). *2010 Internet crime report.* Retrieved May 11, 2011, from http://www.ic3.gov/media/annualreport/2010_IC3Report.pdf

Joseph, J. (2003). Cyberstalking: An international perspective. In Jewkes, Y. *(Ed.), Dot.cons: Crime, deviance and identity on the Internet.* Cullompton, UK: Willan.

Nikitkov, A., & Bay, D. (2008). Online auction fraud: Ethical perspective. *Journal of Business Ethics, 79(3),* 235–244. doi:10.1007/sl0551-007-9374-8

Pease, K. (2001). Crime futures and foresight: Challenging criminal behaviour in the information age. In Wall, D. S. (Ed.), *Crime and the Internet.* London, UK: Routledge.

Rusch, J. J. (1999). *The usocial engineering" of Internet fraud.* Paper Presented at the Internet Society Annual Conference, San Jose, CA.

Shields, R. (1996). *Cultures of the Internet: Virtual spaces, real histories, living bodies.* London, UK: Sage.

Smith, A. (2009). Nigerian scam e-mails and the charms of capital. *Cultural Studies, 23(1),* 27–47. doi: 10.1080/095 023 80802016162

Smith, R., Holmes, M., & Kaufmann, P. (1999). *Trends and issues in crime and criminal justice No. 121: Nigerian advanced fee fraud. Australian Institute of Criminology Trends and Issues in Crime and Criminal Justice.* Canberra: AIT.

Snyder, F. (2001). Sites of criminality and sites of governance. *Social & Legal Studies, 10,* 251–256.

Snyder, J. M. (2000). Online auction fraud: Are the auction houses doing all they should or could stop online fraud? *Federal Communications Law Journal, 52(2),* 453–472.

Trumbore, B. (2004). *Ray Dirks and the equity funding scandal.* Retrieved May 10, 2011, from http://www.buyandhold.com/bh/en/education/ history/2004/ray_dirks.htmI

Turkle, S. (1995). *Life on the screen: Identity in the age of the Internet.* New York, NY: Simon and Schuster.

Wall, D. (2001). Cybercrimes and the Internet In Wall, D. (Ed.), *Crime and the Internet.* London, UK: Routledge.

Whiteside, T. (1978). *Computer capers: Tales of electronic thievery, embezzlement, and fraud.* New York, NY: New American Library.

Yar, M. (2006). *Cybercrime and society.* London, UK: Sage.

ADDITIONAL READING

Burns, R. G., Whitworth, K. H., & Thompson, C. Y. (2004), Assessing law enforcement preparedness to address Internet fraud. *Journal of Criminal Justice, 32(5),* 477–493. doi: 10.1016/j. jcrimjus.2004.06.008

Cukier, W., & Levin, A. (2008). Internet fraud and Cybercrime. In Schmalleger, F., & Pittaro, M. (Eds.), *Crimes of the Internet* (pp. 251–279). Upper Saddle River, NJ: Pearson, Prentice Hall.

Internet Crime Complaint Center. (2011). *2010 Internet Crime Report.* Retrieved May 11,2011, from http://www.ic3.gov/media/annualreport/2010_IC3 Report.pdf

The Silver Lake Editors. (2006). *Scams and swindles: Phishing, spoofing, ID theft, Nigerian advance schemes investment frauds: How to recognize and avoid rip-offs in the Internet Age.* Aberdeen, WA: Silver Lake Publishing.

Thomas, J. T. (2000). *Dotcons: Con games, fraud & deceit on the Internet.* San Jose, CA: Writers Club Press.

Wall, D. (2001). Cybercrimes and the Internet. In Wall, D. (Ed.), *Crime and the Internet.* London, UK: Routledge/

Wells, J. T. (2010). *Internet fraud casebook: The World Wide Web of deceit.* Hoboken, NJ: Wiley.

Yar, M. (2006). *Cybercrime and society.* London, UK: Sage.

CONSUMER TOPIC 3.1

Tips and Resources to Resolve Consumer Complaints

Source: California Department of Consumer Affairs (2012). Consumer Self-Help—Tips & Resources to Resolve Consumer Complaints. Retrieved from: http://www.dca.ca.gov/publications/consumer-selfhelp.shtml

The best way to protect yourself from fraud, scams, or problems is to be aware of potential pitfalls ahead of time. If that isn't enough, you should also know what you can do to resolve complaints. Here are some tips for both:

Before You Buy

- Make sure any professional you hire has the required license:
  - For professionals licensed by the Department of Consumer Affairs (health care providers, accountants, security guards, cosmetologist, auto repair shops, contractors and more), visit the license lookup web page or call 800.952.5210.
  - For other types of California professional licenses, visit www.consumers.ca.gov/. Click the "license verification" tab.
- Get a written copy of guarantees and warranties.
- Ask about the refund, return and exchange policy.
- Don't sign any contract or legal document until you read and understand it. Insist that any extras you are promised are put in writing.

After You Buy

- Save the paperwork: contracts, sales receipts, cancelled checks, owner's manuals, warranty documents, etc.

- Be sure to follow the service and use instructions in the owner's manual. The way you use or take care of a product could affect your warranty.

Solving a Problem

- Check with your credit card company. You may have the right to withhold payment if the product or service is unsatisfactory.
- Complain as soon as possible. A letter to the manager of the business that sold the product or performed the service is usually effective. Keep copies of all correspondence.

Filing a Complaint

If a letter to the manager does not resolve the problem, you may want to file a complaint with the following:

- Department of Consumer Affairs. File a complaint online at www.dca.ca.gov/ or call 800.952.5210 to have a complaint form mailed to you.
- California Attorney General's Office. File a complaint online at http://oag.ca.gov/.
- The Better Business Bureau. Go to www.bbb.org/, or consult your phone directory for a local office.
- The District Attorney's Office in your county. Consult your phone directory under "county offices."

Other Options

A neutral third party may be able to help resolve a dispute between a consumer and a business. For more information about complaint resolution services, visit www.dca.ca.gov/ or call 800.952.5210.

Small Claims Court

If other attempts to resolve your dispute have failed, you may be able to file a claim in Small Claims Court. Consult DCA's publication The Small Claims Court: A Guide to Its Practical Use.

The online California Courts Self-Help Center, sponsored by the Judicial Council, also has information on Small Claims Courts.

CONSUMER TOPIC 3.2

Consumer Complaint Data Book

Source: Federal Trade Commission (2012). Consumer Sentinel Network Data Book. Retrieved from: www.ftc.gov/.../sentinel-cy2011.pdf

C onsumer Sentinel Network (CSN) is the unique investigative cyber tool that provides members of the Consumer Sentinel Network with access to millions of consumer complaints. The network is working based on the premise that sharing information can make law enforcement even more effective. The data is free and available to any federal, state or local law enforcement agency.

HIGHLIGHT OF CONSUMER SENTINEL NETWORK DATA BOOK 2011

Identity theft was the number one complaint category in the CSN for calendar year 2011 with 15% of the overall 1.8 million complaints, followed by Debt Collection (10%); Prizes, Sweepstakes and Lotteries (6%); Shop-at-Home and Catalog Sales (5%); Banks and Lenders (5%); Internet Services (5%); Auto Related Complaints (4%); Impostor Scams (4%); Telephone and Mobile Services (4%); and Advance-Fee Loans and Credit Protection/Repair (3%). The complete ranking of all thirty complaint categories is listed on page six of this report.

Fraud

A total of 990,242 CSN 2011 complaints were fraud-related. Consumers reported paying over $1.5 billion in those fraud complaints; the median amount paid was $537. Sixty-eight percent of the consumers who reported a fraud-related complaint also reported an amount paid.

Source: Consumer Sentinel Network Data Book for January-December 2011. Copyright © 2012 by California Department of Consumer Affairs. Reprinted with permission.

Sixty percent of all fraud-related complaints reported the method of initial contact. Of those complaints, 43% said email, while another 13% said an Internet website. Only 7% of those consumers reported mail as the initial point of contact.

Identity Theft

Government documents/benefits fraud (27%) was the most common form of reported identity theft, followed by credit card fraud (14%), phone or utilities fraud (13%), and bank fraud (9%). Other significant categories of identity theft reported by victims were employment fraud (8%) and loan fraud (3%).

Complaints about government documents/benefits fraud increased 11 percentage points since calendar year 2009; identity theft-related credit card fraud complaints, on the other hand, declined 3 percentage points since calendar year 2009.

Florida is the state with the highest per capita rate of reported identity theft complaints, followed by Georgia and California.

CASE STUDY

Maya is not happy; actually she is angry that a credit card statement ruined her Sunday morning. Reviewing those financial statements is not Maya's habit; however, she has decided to spend a whole day to sort them out after a holiday shopping season. After three bank statements and a dozen bills, Maya finds two charges on her bank credit card account that she and John could not have made. The charges were for a rental car and a hotel room for 2 days in St. Louis, MO. Those charges totaled $419 out of the couple's $738 balance for the month.

What actions would you suggest Maya take to solve the problem?

Once the problem is resolved, what action would you recommend Maya do to ensure that her credit record is not negatively affected by this error?

CONSUMER RESOURCES

California Department of Consumer Affairs: http://www.dca.ca.gov/cic
Consumer Action: http://www.consumer-action.org
Council of Better Business Bureaus: http://www.bbbonline.org
National Consumer Law Center: http://www.nclc.org
National Fraud Information Center: http://www.fraud.org

CHAPTER 4

BUDGETING AND CREDIT: MANAGING YOUR MONEY

CHAPTER 4 INTRODUCTION

In 2012, American consumers owed $11.3 trillion, which was equivalent to 72% of the U.S. GDP of $15.7 trillion. Among the debts there were about $8 trillion in mortgage debt, $850 billion in credit card debt, and $990 billion in student loans. Many households saw their wealth shrinking, with income continue falling since 2007 and high unemployment rate, and found it harder to meet the debt obligations. Consumers need to take actions to deal with the challenges from this 'New Normal' of the economic environment. Read the chapter and see what we can do to manage our money.

FINANCIAL EDUCATION IN 2010 AND BEYOND

Helping Consumers Adapt to a "New Normal"

Barbara O'Neill, Rutgers Cooperative Extension

This paper describes how recent changes in the economy have affected consumer finances and financial education. Specifically, it describes 10 areas of personal finance that have been impacted by the "Great Recession" and implications for education and practice. While none of these topics are new, they deserve a fresh look as a result of recent economic events. Since the financial crisis erupted, consumers have been adapting to a "new normal" in their financial lives. The aftermath of severe financial crises typically results in three negative occurrences that impact consumer finances: deep and prolonged asset market collapses (e.g., housing prices and equity indexes), significant declines in output and employment, and a dramatic increase in government debt as tax revenues decline (Reinhart & Rogoff, 2009).

Baby boomers, those born from 1946 to 1964, and older members of Generation X behind them, are especially adjusting to a "new financial normal." These are Americans who fully experienced not only one major asset bubble, but two, during long stretches of their working lives. First there was the extraordinary run of high double-digit annual returns in the U.S. stock market during the late 1990s. This was followed by the housing bubble during much of the decade of the 2000s. As noted by Regnier (2009, p. 112), "A generation of Americans grew into middle age thinking that they had more wealth than they really did and that their future was a lot more secure than it really was."

Barbara O'Neill, "Financial Education in 2010 and Beyond: Helping Consumers Adapt to a 'New Normal,'" *The Journal of Consumer Education*, vol. 27, pp. 1-15. Copyright © 2010 by Illinois Consumer Education Association. Reprinted with permission.

LITERATURE REVIEW

Given the relatively short time frame since the financial crisis began, literature regarding post-crisis financial behavior is limited. In one study, conducted after the financial crisis began by the FINRA Investor Education Foundation (2009), nearly half of 1,488 respondents reported difficulty paying monthly expenses and bills and a majority did not have funds set aside for emergencies or savings for predictable life events (e.g., retirement). Only 49% of respondents reported that they had set aside funds sufficient to cover expenses for three months. Across all age groups up to age 60, one-third of respondents reported that they were not saving. In addition, nearly one-quarter (23%) engaged in high-cost "alternative" forms of borrowing (e.g., payday loans, pawn shops, and rent-to-own stores).

The 2009 MetLife Study of the American Dream (2009) was also conducted during the financial crisis and included 2,243 online survey responses. One of its key findings was a marked shift in consumer focus from material accumulation to near-term survival. Respondents reported paring spending and focusing more on personal relationships. Nearly half of the respondents, and 66% of those born before 1946, said they already had all of the possessions they needed. Half of the sample said they could only meet their financial obligations for one month if they were to lose their job.

The Nielsen Company (2009) conducted research to assess changes in consumer behavior following the economic downturn. They found evidence that consumers sought safer places to keep their money (i.e., cash equivalent assets), even if it meant a trade-off of lower interest rates. Deposits in all types of investments, except 529 college savings plans, fell between late 2007 and early 2009. Consumers also reduced their spending during this period, leading to a phenomenon known as the "paradox of thrift." This means that, when individuals collectively spend less and save a larger portion of their income, the economy slows down from a reduction in demand, resulting in a loss of jobs.

O'Neill and Xiao (2010) studied consumers' performance of 20 recommended financial practices before and during the financial crisis. An online self-assessment tool was used to collect data between January 2007 and June 2010. The sample of 6,700 respondents was divided into pre- and post-December 2008 cohorts for purposes of comparison. There was evidence of a modest positive difference in the performance of five financial practices following the December 2008 escalation of the financial crisis.

Two recent studies of financial behaviors of college students included a comparison of pre- and post-financial crisis data. Shim and Serido (2010) found that 95% of a sample of 748 students changed their money management practices in response to the recession. On the positive side, the practice of budgeting rose slightly (3%). However, other statistics were somewhat alarming, including a 60% increase in average credit card debt from $95 to $152 and an 85% increase in average educational loan debt from $1,041 to $1,932. There were also large increases in "risky" behaviors, including dropping classes, taking leaves of absence, postponing health care, and using one credit card to pay off another. Richter and Prawitz (2010) found that, even following instruction about credit in a personal finance class, students still reported a desire to acquire more credit cards after the financial crisis had started. Perhaps, this is because credit provides a viable short-term solution for meeting a semester's expenses during tough economic times.

KEY FINANCIAL EDUCATION TOPICS

The term "new normal" has increasingly been used to describe what is predicted to be an extended period of slow U.S. economic growth, low single-digit annual stock returns, high unemployment, increased frequency of consumer savings and debt repayment, and ultimately, when the financial crisis abates, higher inflation (Hughes & Seneca, 2009; Reinhart & Rogoff, 2009; Wolverson, 2009). In this environment, consumer educators have a rare opportunity to teach financial concepts at a time when public and media interest is high. The following is a description of 10 areas of personal finance that consumers may need to address as they navigate their way through the "new normal."

Area #1: Planning and Goal-Setting

Past research (Consumer Federation of America, 2008; The Hartford Financial Services Group, 2009; Lusardi & Mitchell, 2007; Updegrave, 2009) has found a positive relationship between financial planning and goal-setting, including higher savings levels, higher wealth accumulation, and greater feelings of control and happiness, compared to those who do not make specific plans. However, other studies have found that relatively few people develop specific written financial goals with a time deadline and a dollar cost as experts recommend (Hogarth, Hilgert, & Schuchardt, 2002; O'Neill & Xiao, 2006, 2010). Financial practitioners may be able to use anxiety resulting from the economic crisis, as a "hook," to encourage consumers to set goals and develop specific plans as a way to maintain some semblance of control over their finances during difficult times. In other words, educators can use consumers' pre-crisis financial status as a reference point for future planning and positive action (e.g., saving). A simple "paper and pencil" *Financial Goal-Setting Worksheet* is available for downloading at http://njaes.rutgers.edu/money/pdfs/goalsettingworksheet.pdf. Online financial calculators such as http://www.dinkytown.net/ and http://www.calculatorweb.com can also be used to calculate savings required to fund future financial goals and to determine whether future plans are realistic.

Area #2: Income/Employment

An estimated 20% to 23% of U.S. workers are operating as consultants, freelancers, free agents, contractors, or micropreneurs, with the percentage projected to rise in coming years to about 40% of the U.S. job market (Greenwald, 2010; Revell, Bigda, & Rosato, 2009). Some people choose to be self-employed while others do so following the loss of a job. The rise of a "freelance nation," where secure jobs with benefits and career paths are being replaced by "project-to-project" assignments for contingent workers, has prompted a variety of financial education needs. Those who are in this situation need to know how to develop a business plan and think like an entrepreneur. They also need to understand such concepts as small business tax preparation (e.g., Schedules C and SE and estimated tax payments), self-funded health insurance, and retirement savings plans in lieu of employer benefits. Contingent workers also need to understand the process of developing what Garman & Forgue (2008, pp. 81–84) refer to as a "cash-flow calendar." This is where surplus or deficit situations are identified in advance to smooth out uneven cash flow (e.g., during and in between job assignments). Even workers currently earning a steady paycheck are not immune to "new normal" employment trends.

Consumer educators should encourage all clients to develop their human capital, "save for a rainy day," and develop back-up employment plans, especially as jobs in the private and public sectors become increasingly unpredictable and entrepreneurial.

Area #3: Budgeting

As noted above, income volatility is increasingly part of the "new normal." Even public school and government workers with the most secure paychecks have had their incomes reduced by mandatory furloughs and/or contact rollbacks. Previous studies (Hogarth, Hilgert, & Schuchardt, 2002; O'Neill & Xiao, 2006, 2010) have found that written household budgets are prepared infrequently. Perhaps "new normal" uncertainty will increase the use of budgets (a.k.a. spending plans) as consumers seek ways to economize, reduce debt, and save. Kies (2008, p. 42) noted that, "one of the few things clients and planners can truly influence is the decision-making process involving cash flow." To download a worksheet that can be completed with a pencil and hand-held calculator, visit http://njaes.rutgers.edu/money/pdfs/fs421worksheet.pdf. To download a spreadsheet that uses preprogrammed Excel® software to make income and expense calculations with a computer, visit http://njaes.rutgers.edu/money/templates/Spending-Plan-Template.xls. More tech-savvy consumers may prefer online budgeting tools that integrate budget calculations with other financial data (e.g., loans and investments) and automatically update them. Budgeting Web sites with encrypted user names and passwords are frequently recommended by financial media outlets and include Mint.com (http://www.mint.com), Wesabe.com (http://www.wesabe.com), and Geezeo.com (http://www.geezeo.com), among others.

Area #4: Spending

In the "new normal," frugal living is an important life skill. People used to living beyond their means during an earlier era of easy credit and inflated housing prices may need information to reduce living costs and avoid "frugality fatigue." For consumer educators, this means "back-to-basics" instruction, including needs versus wants, expense prioritization, low-cost substitutions (e.g., clothing from a consignment shop), and living within one's means. Two general approaches to expense reduction include helping consumers reign in small daily expenses, which Bach (2004) refers to as "The Latte Factor™," and helping them trim large monthly expenses such as mortgage payments (e.g., by refinancing) and outstanding debt balances (e.g., by transferring them to lower-rate credit cards or loans or using debt acceleration Web sites such as http://www.powerpay.org).

Area #5: Credit Use

Consumers may find it harder to obtain credit in the "new normal," as creditors have tightened their lending standards. In addition, provisions implemented under the *2009 Credit Card Accountability, Responsibility and Disclosure (CARD) Act* have resulted in many creditors adjusting their interest rate and fee structures to compensate for lost revenue from now-prohibited practices (e.g., universal default and two-cycle billing). A key credit education concept is that revolving consumer debt can be risky behavior for households with reduced or fluctuating income. Compared to households with high debt balances, those with little or no consumer debt have increased flexibility to adjust their lifestyles downward, when necessary, which reduces financial stress. Other relevant credit topics to teach include the following: factors to consider when selecting a new credit card; strategies to increase credit scores; specific provisions of the CARD Act; the high cost of making minimum payments (a "teachable moment" topic now that creditors are required to provide this information on monthly billing statements); and benefits of charging no more than can be repaid immediately.

Area #6: Taxes

Given the exploding federal budget deficit and post-financial crisis stimulus spending, income taxes will most likely increase in the future (McQueen, 2009). Even if no new tax increases are passed, federal marginal income tax rates are scheduled to rise in 2011, because tax reductions in the *2001 Economic Growth and Tax Relief Reconciliation Act* will expire at the end of 2010 (Evans, 2003). Federal estate tax exemptions will also revert back to 2001 levels. On a micro level, consumers will need help readjusting to higher tax rates. In particular, they may need assistance in recalculating their W-4 form withholding allowances so that they correspond to "new normal" income volatility. Some consumers may also need educational assistance with tax issues related to employment transitions such as: making estimated tax payments if they plan to report self-employment income; understanding unemployment insurance benefits; and making tax-related decisions about whether, and when, to convert traditional IRA balances to Roth IRAs. Two other tax-related investment decisions that consumers need to reconsider are related to weighing the pros and cons of making unmatched contributions to tax-deferred saving plans and deciding when to sell appreciated capital assets (given an expected rise in future federal income tax rates).

Area #7: Homeownership

In the late 2000s, the U.S. housing bubble burst. By third quarter 2009, almost one in four U.S. homeowners with mortgages (23%) were "underwater" (Simon & Hagerty, 2009). This means that they owed more on their loans than their property was worth. Meanwhile, those with positive home equity were impacted by declining home values, as foreclosures and short sales depressed housing prices (McQueen, 2009). "New normal" topics related to homeownership include the following: front- and back-end debt ratios; homeownership for shelter versus "flipping" of real estate for a quick profit; buyer qualifications for a mortgage and/or homebuyer incentives; sellers accepting the reality of lower prices; buying versus renting or buying a second home while prices are relatively low; and strategies (e.g., principal prepayment) to pay off a home mortgage prior to retirement to free up cash flow for other expenses (e.g., health care and travel).

Area #8: Saving

As the financial crisis escalated, the U.S. savings rate rose to 4.3% at the end of 2009. Although still low compared to 10%+ savings rates and 20%+ savings rates in the early 1970s and early 1940s, respectively, this was still an increase from previous savings rates in the 1% to 3% range (Employee Benefit Research Institute, 2010). Unfortunately, as people started to save more, interest rates on cash equivalent assets (e.g., certificates of deposit and money market mutual funds) plummeted. In early 2010, some short-term certificates of deposit (CDs) were paying less than 1% as the Federal Reserve cut interest rates to stimulate business, thereby hurting savers (Sloan, 2009). For example, a $100,000 CD that earned 5% ($5,000 annually) in the mid 2000s might be earning 0.75% ($750 annually) in 2010, a decrease of $4,250 in annual income or $354 per month. When savings accounts earn so little, they lose ground to taxes and inflation.

Consumer educators can provide information to consumers about how to shop around for higher-yielding savings vehicles, including cash alternatives such as online bank accounts, credit union CDs and savings accounts, and Series EE and I U.S. savings bonds. There is also a need to continue to motivate people to save for emergencies and future goals and to help them identify ways to "find" money to save from household cash flow (e.g., expense reduction and automation). Innovative savings education programs include *America Saves* (http://www.americasaves.org) and *Save to Win* (http://www.savetowin.org). *Save to Win*, a new program operated by credit unions, is a cross between a CD and a lottery (for more details, see Zweig (2009)).

Area #9: Investing

The financial crisis taught investors valuable lessons such as the need to acknowledge their "true" (bear market) risk tolerance level and adjust expectations about investment rates of return downward. Investors experienced firsthand the extreme volatility of the stock market during times of uncertainty and the limits of diversification as a short-term defensive strategy against market losses (Stovall, 2010). Even target-date mutual funds, which contain several asset classes and adjust their weightings to match the time remaining before a future date, suffered deep losses (McQueen, 2009). Consumer educators need to teach investors about investment characteristics and past historical performance. By doing so, they can help reduce the incidence of fear-driven "panic" selling. Investment education is especially important for young adults so they are not terrified of stocks like many who came of age during the Great Depression were. Otherwise, these young people could lose decades of wealth-building. Other investment lessons that can be learned from the financial crisis include how to: avoid complex and highly leveraged investments; select broadly diversified investments; seek low-cost and tax-efficient investments; rebalance portfolio asset class weightings periodically; and avoid market timing (Reichenstein & Swedroe, 2009). A useful educational resource for investment education is the eXtension *Investing for Your Future* course at http://www.extension.org/pages/Investing_for_Your_Future.

Area #10: Retirement Planning

The "Great Recession" created a new retirement reality, especially for millions of baby boomers who are starting to retire. Many people suffered large losses in retirement savings plan accounts such as IRAs and 401(k)s. In addition, employer supports, such as traditional defined benefit pensions and retiree health insurance, have been eroding over time. Consumer educators can capitalize on consumers' heightened desire to "see where they stand" and "make up what they lost" as entry points for instruction. With respect to the former, a good place to start is a retirement savings needs analysis. According to the Employee Benefit Research Institute's *2010 Retirement Confidence Survey* or *RCS* (Helman, Greenwald, Copeland, & VanDerhei, 2010), less than half of U.S. workers (46%) have tried to calculate how much they need to save to live comfortably in retirement. A simple tool to calculate retirement savings is the American Savings Education Council's *Ballpark Estimate* at http://www.choosetosave.org/ballpark/.

With regard to the latter, studies to determine the best retirement recovery strategies have found that measures need not be drastic. Working a few years longer than planned (T. Rowe Price, 2008) and suspending annual inflation adjustments on asset withdrawals (Fahlund, 2009) are among the most effective methods. Financial advantages of extending one's working years include the following: fewer years of retirement left to finance; more years in which to accumulate savings for retirement; more years to earn Social Security and/or defined benefit pension benefits; and continued eligibility for health insurance benefits (National Endowment for Financial Education, 2010).

Of course, a question remains whether older workers will be able to find work. Helman, Greenwald, Copeland, and VanDerhei (2010) found a large disconnect between expectations and reality. In the *2010 RCS*, 41% of retirees reported that they left the workforce earlier than planned for reasons such as health problems, downsizing, and family caregiving. The current economy exacerbates this problem, making investments in human capital and networking with colleagues essential to increasing an older worker's chances of remaining employed.

SUMMARY AND IMPLICATIONS

This article reviewed 10 areas of personal finance and suggested specific ways that consumer educators can use the current economic climate as a springboard for financial education efforts. The financial crisis and its aftermath have provided an opportunity to revisit basic financial topics that are not new, but may be of greater interest to consumers given recent economic events. This does not mean that financial education in the "new normal" will be easy. Financial educators will continue to face challenges in getting their messages across and will need to use a variety of outreach methods that are tailored to individuals or groups. As always, motivating people to take positive action to improve their finances is a challenge and educational programs must address learners' real and/or perceived fears and obstacles. Teaching personal finance content alone, without addressing the context of target audiences, is simply not enough to be effective.

Another key component of effective financial education programs is addressing emotional and relationship issues that underlie financial decisions. An example is someone who is hesitant to save money because, in the past, it always ended up becoming the "family emergency fund." Financial planning often involves complex decisions that affect a number of people. When household resources are constrained as they are in a tough economy (e.g., reduced income), financial decisions can sometimes pit "doing what is recommended" (e.g., repaying consumer debt) against "doing what is necessary" (e.g., helping a loved one deal with an emergency).

By recognizing learners' needs, hopes, and fears, and incorporating them into motivational financial education programs, consumer educators can impart valuable knowledge and skills necessary for people to manage financial resources effectively during tough times. Where possible, incorporating recommended financial practices directly into financial education programs (e.g., "hands-on" completion of credit report request forms and 401(k) plan enrollment documents) may help facilitate positive action, as can "point of purchase" tools, such as financial calculators, that are available to use when financial decisions need to be made. The years ahead are a "teachable moment." Let's make the most of them.

REFERENCES

Bach, D. (2004). *The automatic millionaire: A powerful one-step plan to live and finish rich.* New York, NY: Broadway Books.

Consumer Federation of America. (2008, November). *Understanding the emergency savings needs of low- and moderate-income households: A survey-based analysis of impacts, causes, and remedies.* Washington, DC: Author. Retrieved October 15, 2010, from http://www.consumerfed.org/elements/www.consumerfed.org/file/Emergency_Savings_Survey_Analysis_Nov_2008.pdf

Employee Benefit Research Institute. (2010). *EBRI databook on employee benefits. Chapter 9: Personal savings.* Washington, DC: Author. Retrieved October 15, 2010, from http://www.ebri.org/pdf/publications/books/databook/DB.Chapter%2009.pdf

Evans, M. W. (2003, April 21). The budget process and the "sunset" provision of the 2001 tax law. *Tax Notes, 99*(3), 405–414.

Fahlund, C. (2009, February). Retirement income: Repairing the damage to assure the flow. *AAII Journal, 31*(2), 5–9.

FINRA Investor Education Foundation. (2009). *Financial capability in the United States: National survey—Executive summary.* Washington, DC: Author. Retrieved October 15, 2010, from http://www.finrafoundation.org/web/groups/foundation/@foundation/documents/foundation/p120535.pdf

Garman, E. T., & Forgue, R. E. (2008). *Personal finance.* Boston, MA: Houghton Mifflin Company.

Greenwald, R. (2010, February 8). How to succeed in the age of going solo. *The Wall Street Journal,* p. R1, R3.

The Hartford Financial Services Group. (2009). *The Hartford investments and retirement survey.* Hartford, CT: Author. Retrieved October 15, 2010, from http://www.hartfordinvestor.com/general_pdf/Hartford_Retirement_Survey_09.pdf

Helman, R., Greenwald, M., Copeland, C., & VanDerhei, J. (2010). The 2010 retirement confidence survey: Confidence stabilizing, but preparations continue to erode. *EBRI Issue Brief No. 340.* Washington, DC: Employee Benefit Research Institute. Retrieved October 15, 2010, from http://www.ebri.org/pdf/briefspdf/EBRI_IB_03-2010_No340_RCS.pdf

Hogarth, J. M., Hilgert, M. A., & Schuchardt, J. (2002). Money managers—The good, the bad, and the lost. In J. M. Lown (Ed.), *Proceedings of the Association for Financial Counseling and Planning Education* (pp. 12–23). Scottsdale, AZ: Association for Financial Counseling and Planning Education.

Hughes, J. W., & Seneca, J. J. (2009). 2009: The shape of "new normal." *Sitar-Rutgers Regional Report, 12*(1), 1–8. Retrieved October 15, 2010, from http://www.policy.rutgers.edu/reports/sitar/sitarfeb09.pdf

Kies, E. H. (2008). Back to basics: Helping clients manage cash flow. *Journal of Financial Planning, 21*(12), 40–42.

Lusardi, A., & Mitchell, O. S. (2007). Baby boomer retirement security: The roles of planning, financial literacy, and housing wealth. *Journal of Monetary Economics, 54*(1), 205–224.

McQueen, M. P. (2009, September 12–13). New rules for personal finance. *The Wall Street Journal,* p. B1.

Metropolitan Life Insurance Company. (2009). *The 2009 MetLife study of the American dream.* New York, NY: Author. Retrieved October 15, 2010, from http://www.metlife.com/assets/cao/gbms/studies/09010229_09AmDreamStudy_WEB.pdf

National Endowment for Financial Education. (2010). *Advantages of working longer before retirement.* Retrieved October 15, 2010, from http://www.myretirementpaycheck.org/Work/AdvantagesofWorkingLonger/tabid/58/Default.aspx

The Nielsen Company. (2009). *Financial behavior trends: Economic downturn triggers consumer change in financial behavior.* New York, NY: Author. Retrieved October 15, 2010, from http://blog.nielsen.com/nielsenwire/wp-content/uploads/2009/05/market-audit-white-paper.pdf

O'Neill, B., & Xiao, J. J. (2006). Financial fitness quiz findings: Strengths, weaknesses, and disconnects. *Journal of Extension, 44*(1). Retrieved October 15, 2010, from http://www.joe.org/joe/2006february/rb5.php

O'Neill, B., & Xiao, J. J. (2010). *Financial behavior before and during the "great recession": Evidence from an online survey.* Manuscript submitted for publication.

Regnier, P. (2009, April). Where the next 'normal' will take us. *Money, 38*(4), 112.

Reichenstein, W., & Swedroe, L. (2009, July). Bear market grads: What you should learn from the financial crisis. *AAII Journal, 31*(6), 5–9.

Reinhart, C. M., & Rogoff, K. S. (2009). The aftermath of financial crises. *American Economic Review, 99*(2), 466–472.

Revell, J., Bigda, C., & Rosato, D. (2009, July). Five big changes and what they mean for you. *Money, 38*(7), 56–61.

Richter, J. & Prawitz, A. D. (2010). Attitudes of college students toward credit cards: A comparison of credit card user types. In A. Carswell & C. Robb (Eds.), *Proceedings of the Eastern Family Economics and Resource Management Association.* Retrieved October 15, 2010, from http://mrupured.myweb.uga.edu/pdfs/Credit_Card_Study_Poster_Abstract_EFERMA_2010_submission_FI.pdf

Shim, S., & Serido, J. (2010). *Arizona pathways to life success for university students. Wave 1.5 economic impact study: Financial well-being, coping behaviors and trust among young adults.* Tucson, AZ: University of Arizona. Retrieved October 15, 2010, from http://aplus.arizona.edu/wave1_5_report.pdf

Simon, R., & Hagerty, J. R. (2009, November 24). 1 in 4 borrowers under water. *The Wall Street Journal,* p. A1, A4.

Sloan, A. (2009, November 9). Thanks for nothing, Uncle Sam. *Fortune, 160*(9), 22.

Stovall, S. (2010, March). Diversification: A failure of fact or expectation? *AAII Journal, 32*(3), 25–29.

T. Rowe Price. (2008, Summer). Working longer and other ways to optimize retirement income. *T. Rowe Price Report, 100, 14–18.* Retrieved October 15, 2010, from http://www.troweprice.com/gcFiles/pdf/2A41.pdf?src=Media_Near_or..&t=lgcy

Updegrave, W. (2008, October). Save for tomorrow, Be happy today. *Money, 37*(10). 41.

Wolverson, R. (2009, October). Term of the month: The new normal. *Smart Money, 18*(10), 22.

Zweig, J. (2009, July 18–19). Using the lottery effect to make people save. *The Wall Street Journal,* p. A1.

Barbara O'Neill is Extension Specialist in Financial Resource Management, Rutgers Cooperative Extension, Cook College Office Building Room 107, 55 Dudley Road, New Brunswick, NJ 08901; (732) 932-9155 (x250); E-mail: oneill@aesop.rutgers.edu

BUDGETING

Julia A. Heath

Budgeting your money is something you need to do. It is really the only way to get a handle on your financial life and to ensure that you can reach your goals. But it is not very exciting, is it? In fact, it is a lot like flossing—you know you should, but ...

While this chapter probably will not make you excited about budgeting, it will at least help you understand how important it is and how to do it. Think of it this way: You have an idea about where you want to go in terms of your financial goals. You have a general idea of what steps you need to take to achieve them. So, you have a rough map of your journey to get you from here to there. What you do not yet know is do you have enough gas in the car to get there? Having goals is essential—you cannot achieve what you do not have—but you also need the ability to move toward those goals. If you do not have enough gas, you will not get there.

This chapter is about making sure you have as much gas in the car as possible. By doing some planning and making smart decisions you can maximize your ability to achieve your goals. So do not think of budgeting as drudge work. Think of it as the key to getting where you want to go.

INCOME

A *budget* basically consists of two parts: money coming in and money going out. The first step in establishing a budget is to recognize how much money you have coming in and seeing if you can increase that amount. While getting a raise or inheriting a small fortune are certainly ways to increase the money flowing in, we are not going to base our budget on future events that may or may not occur. We will deal with the here and now and talk about how to increase income.

The first thing to recognize is that you do not really have just one income—you have two. Your *gross income* is the income you earn before taxes are taken out. If you earn $10 an hour and work a 35-hour week, your gross income is $350 for the week. However, if you have ever had a job, you know that your paycheck is not made out in the amount of $350. Many things are deducted from your gross pay to get to your check amount—your *net income*. Some of the deductions are required by law, others are optional and vary by situation and choices. Here are some of the most common.

Income Taxes

A big portion of your deductions are federal (and in some cases state and local) taxes. When you earn an income, you must pay the government money in the form of taxes. Rather than face a large tax bill on April 15 of every year, employers are required to take out a portion of your bill each pay period. Because state and local taxes vary, we will focus on federal income taxes here.

Although your employer is required to withhold federal taxes from your paycheck, you have some control over how much is withheld. When you start working, you will fill out a *withholding allowance form* (W-4). The number of allowances you claim on this form determines how much federal income tax your employer will take out of your paycheck. These allowances, or *exemptions*, are designed to reflect the cost of living (food, clothing, housing). For example, if you are married with three children, the amount of tax you owe will be adjusted downward to reflect the cost of running a household with three children in it. The more allowances you claim, the less tax will be deducted. If you can be claimed as a dependent on someone else's tax return (for example, your parents), you cannot claim any withholding allowance and would enter zero. In other words, they are incurring the cost of "maintaining" you, so they get the exemption. If you are not claimed as a dependent on someone else's tax return and you are single, you would normally claim one allowance, but you can claim more. The IRS.gov Web site has online withholding calculators to help you decide how many allowances to claim.

Many people try to claim as few allowances as possible so they will get a large tax return when they file their tax returns. While getting a big check from the IRS is nice, think about why you are getting that check. You are getting the check because too much was taken out of your paychecks throughout the year. In effect, you have given the government your money—an interest-free loan. They give the excess back, but wouldn't you rather have had use of that money throughout the year? If you increased the number of your allowances, your tax refund check would be smaller, but your net pay each pay period would be higher.

In fact, you want your tax refund check (or payment) to be as close to zero as possible. You should change your withholding allowances as your circumstances change. Since tax laws also change, you should check to make sure that your current withholdings are still optimal for your situation.

To summarize, while you cannot wave a magic wand and suddenly have more income coming in, you can control, to some extent, the amount of federal income taxes taken out of your paycheck. The result is the same—your net pay is higher. What is you want is the highest net pay as possible, meaning the smallest amount of taxes taken out of your paycheck as possible. In turn, low taxes mean that you take as many exemptions as possible on your W-4 form without owing a large tax bill at the end of the year.

FICA

By law, everyone must pay into both *Social Security* system and *Medicare*. These taxes comprise the *FICA (Federal Insurance Contributions Act)* tax. Taxes collected through FICA fund Social Security retirement payments, survivors and disability benefits, and hospital insurance.

The total FICA tax is 15.3 percent of your pay, which is split evenly between you and your employer. A portion of that (12.4 percent) goes to Social Security *(Old-Age, Survivors, and Disability Insurance, or OASDI)*. The other 2.9 percent goes to Medicare. That means that your portion of the FICA tax is 6.2 percent plus 1.45 percent for Medicare, for a total of 7.65 percent. If you are self-employed, you must pay the entire 15.3 percent yourself. In addition to OASDI and Medicare having different tax rates, there is another important difference between the two. The Medicare tax is applied to all income levels, regardless of what your earnings are. On the other hand, OASDI is only applied to earnings up to a certain level. After you reach that level of income, you are not taxed on the income over that level. For example, the Social Security income level for 2010 is $106,800 (the Social Security Administration typically increases the cap each year). Let us assume that you earn $130,000. Your Medicare taxes withheld would be $1,885 ($130,000 × 1.45 percent). Your Social Security (OASDI) taxes would be $6,621.60 ($106,800 × 6.2 percent). You are only taxed on the first $106,800 of your income for Social Security purposes. Therefore, your total FICA tax on an income of $130,000 would be $8,506.60 ($1,885 + $6,621.60). Therefore, those with the highest incomes pay a lower overall percentage of their incomes than those whose incomes do not reach the cap.

Pretax Deductions

The discussions above about income and FICA tax deductions are actually a little out of order. Taxes are not taken out of gross pay; they are taken out of gross pay less any *pretax deductions*. A qualified pretax deduction is taken out of your gross pay before taxes (federal, state, local, and FICA) are applied. Because these deductions shelter your income from taxes, they lower your tax liability.

One of the most common forms of pretax deduction are the premiums paid for medical, dental, and/or vision insurance offered through an employer. *Flexible spending accounts* (FSAs) also qualify for pretax deductions. An FSA is an account that you contribute to with pretax dollars and that you use to pay for eligible expenses. You can set up an FSA for medical expenses, dependent care expenses, and/or the costs associated with getting to and from work (parking, mass transit, or vanpool). You contribute money to one or more of these accounts, then when you incur qualified expenses (for example, your share of the payment when you go to the doctor), you can get reimbursed out of your FSA. Therefore, the money you pay into an FSA is not counted as income for tax purposes.

Let us assume you make $50,000 a year, and you contribute a total of $5,000 to these flexible spending accounts. Let us further assume that your combined tax rate (FICA plus federal, state, and local) is 25 percent. By using FSAs, your taxable income has been reduced from $50,000 to $45,000, and you have saved $1,250 ($5,000 × 25 percent)! What a great deal, right? Well ... maybe.

Remember what FICA taxes are for—6.2 percent of them go toward your Social Security benefits. Therefore, anything that reduces your FICA contributions also lowers the amount that you have paid into the Social Security system, potentially reducing the level of benefits you receive from the system when you reach retirement age. The lower your income over your working life, the more of an effect this issue may have. Remember that Social Security taxes are only taken out of income up to a cap—once your income is over that cap, you no longer pay Social Security taxes. For those with high incomes over their working lives, their FICA wages can be reduced and still be above the cap. For example, if you earn $150,000 a year and participate in an FSA that reduces your taxable income to $140,000 a year, your contributions to FICA do not change since the cap is $106,800. For most people, the benefits of saving on taxes today will outweigh the cost of a reduction in Social Security benefits later. To make sure, you can see what the effect of FSA contributions will have on your Social Security benefits by using the calculator at the Social Security Web site (ssa.gov).

Another type of qualified pretax deductions is a contribution to a *401(k)*, or *403(b)* plan. These plans are retirement accounts that employees can contribute to out of pretax dollars. A 401(k) is typically available to employees of for-profit corporations, while 403(b) accounts are usually offered to employees of nonprofit institutions (hospitals, schools, etc.). Actually, contributions to these plans are only *tax deferred*. You can contribute to them with pretax dollars, but when you make withdrawals, you must pay tax on them. In addition, contributions are sheltered from federal, state, and local taxes, but not from FICA taxes. For 2010, employees can contribute up to $16,500 per year. For example, let us assume that you earn $50,000 per year and contribute $6,000 per year to a 401(k) retirement plan. You would pay income taxes on $44,000, and you would pay FICA taxes on $50,000.

Other Deductions from Your Paycheck

While federal taxes and pretax deductions are the largest (and most common) deductions from your paycheck, there are circumstances under which other things might be subtracted as well. These could include such things as state income taxes, union dues, or any payments to a life insurance or a disability policy. All told, deductions typically lower your gross pay by about 25 percent–35 percent, depending upon your filing status (for example, married or single), your pretax, and other deductions.

To summarize this section on income, let us talk about an example. Assume you have been offered a job for $35,000 a year. That sounds really good to you, and you are already thinking about all the stuff you can buy with all of that money. Let us see how that breaks down.

GROSS PAY V. NET PAY (SINGLE TAXPAYER, NO DEDUCTIONS)	
Monthly Gross Pay ($35,000/12)	$2,916.67
Health Insurance	$267.00
Flexible Spending Account (Medical)	$50.00
Federal Withholding	$251.10
Social Security	$161.18
Medicare	$37.70
401(k)	$300
Net Pay.	$1,849.69

Suddenly, your gross monthly income of $2,917 has been replaced by a net income of only $1,850. Here is how that happened. First, your pretax deductions of health insurance premiums and contributions to your flexible spending account are subtracted, leaving you with $2,599.67 ($2,916.67 – $267 – $50). Your Social Security and Medicare taxes are computed on this amount. The Social Security tax (6.2 percent × $2,599.67) is $161.18; your Medicare tax is $37.70 (1.45 percent × $2,599.67). Because you are making contributions to a tax-deferred 401(k) account, that amount is subject to FICA taxes, but not federal income taxes. Therefore, the amount that is withheld for federal tax purposes is based on $2,299.67 ($2,599.67 – $300). The federal tax on that amount is $251.10 (for single, no dependents). Your net pay, therefore, is about 63 percent of your gross salary.

Note that if you had not made a $300 payment to a 401(k) account, your net pay would be higher—but not $300 higher. Why not? If you were not contributing to a 401(k) account, your net pay would be $2,104.69, a difference of $255. The reason is because the 401(k) contribution reduces your tax liability by reducing your taxable income. If you had not made the $300 contribution, your federal taxes withheld would have been $296.10—$45 more than with the contribution. Likewise, if you had not made a contribution to a flexible spending account, your net pay would be $1,888.37, an increase of not $50, but only $38.68. Look at it this way: If you put $50 in the FSA, you will be able to use that money to pay $50 worth of medical expenses. If you do not put it into an FSA, you will get $38.68 more in net income, which you can use to pay medical (or any other expenses). If you put $300 into a 401(k), you have put that money toward retirement where it will accrue interest. If you do not, you will increase your take-home pay by $255. So, which is better: $50 or $38.68? $300 or $255? That is the beauty of tax exempt and tax-deferred contributions.

It is helpful to know what effect various deductions and contribution amounts will have on your net pay. There are many online calculators (for example, at paycheck.com) to help you decide what kinds of contributions (and in what amounts) will work for you.

EXPENSES

Preparing a budget requires that you be mindful of money that is coming in and money that is going out. The previous section discussed how you can, to some extent, control the money coming in (short of a magic wand) by manipulating exemptions and other deductions. This section will discuss getting control of the money going out.

The first step in controlling the money going out is to be aware of what it is. For a month, keep track of everything you spend. Everything. This includes the vending machine snacks, the coffees, the music downloads—everything. Carry a little notebook around with you and jot down the amount, the date, and what you bought. Also write down why you bought what you did. When you bought that new pair of jeans, were you with a group of friends who were buying things? Were you bored? Did you really need them? Did you later regret buying them? Basically, what you are doing is keeping a spending diary. Also write down how much cash you have spent that you cannot remember spending—cash that you have no record of spending, that is just gone. You will probably be surprised at how much you just lose track of. Maybe that amount will decrease as you become more thoughtful about your spending.

Next, get a handle on where your money goes by creating categories of spending. The first two categories are broad: fixed and variable expenses. *Fixed expenses* are those that you cannot change in the short run. Examples of fixed expenses would be rent (or mortgage) payments, student loans, car payments, insurance premiums—anything that is a consistent amount, month after month. The other broad category is *variable expenses*. This category includes things like food, clothing, entertainment, health, and beauty items. You have much more control over how much you spend on these purchases. A daily sample diary could look like this:

FIXED EXPENSES			VARIABLE EXPENSES			
TYPE	AMOUNT	DATE	TYPE	AMOUNT	DATE	NOTES
Rent	$350	4/1	Gas	$30	4/6	
Car Pmt	$257	4/3	Jeans	$57	4/6	With friends at mall
Car Insurance	$76	4/4	Starbucks	$3.50	4/7	Didn't finish all of it
			Subway	$6	4/8	Could have packed lunch
			Movies	$13	4/9	Movie was great
			Lotion, etc.	$21	4/10	Name brands
			????	About $10	4/12	
			Etc.			

Once you have kept track of everything you have spent your money on, make subcategories of your variable expenses—group all the clothes purchases together, all the entertainment, etc., then enter totals for each subcategory. You can continue to do this with your notebook and a pencil or enter your information into a spreadsheet. Your diary with monthly totals could look like this:

FIXED EXPENSES		VARIABLE EXPENSES	
TYPE	AMOUNT	TYPE	TOTAL AMOUNT
Rent	$350	Gas	$98
Car Pmt	$257	Clothes	$129
Car Insurance	$76	Entertainment	$78
		Groceries	$189
		Restaurants	$103
		Unknown????	$52
		Etc.	

It is at this point that you can start understanding where your money is going. Most of the time, people are very surprised at how much they are spending in certain categories. For example, when you are spending money over the course of the month, it is easy to not realize that you are spending over $100 on restaurant meals. Or that you simply lost track of $52. And that is the whole point of keeping the spending diary and adding up your totals for the month. Once you know where your money *actually* goes, you can then decide if that is where you *want* it to go.

Now it is time for the really tough part—how does your actual spending plan jive with what your spending plan should look like? Or, if you are just starting out and do not really have an existing budget yet—what should your budget look like? How much rent can you afford to pay? How much can you spend on a car loan? There is a lot of advice out there about how much you should be spending in each category, but you want something that is easy to understand, easy to implement, good for any income level as your circumstances change, and that will build financial security along the way. Elizabeth Warren and Amelia Warren Tyagi have developed a good, easy-to-follow plan that meets all these criteria, called the 50/30/20 budget plan.

Here is how the 50/30/20 plan works. Take your gross income and subtract any taxes (such as federal, state, local, FICA). This is your *after-tax-income*. Notice that this is not the same as your net income. Your net income was arrived at by also subtracting out 401(k) contributions, health insurance premiums, disability insurance premiums—all the deductions we talked about previously. Your after-tax income only has wage-based taxes taken out.

Now that you have a figure for your after-tax income, you want your must-have expenses to be no more than 50 percent of that number. What is a must-have expense? A must-have expense looks very much like a fixed expense. It includes things like housing, utilities, minimum loan payments, child care, or anything you are contractually obligated to pay (at least for right now). If you can put it off (that new shirt, for example), then it is not a must-have. Remember that since things like health insurance premiums are not included in your after-tax income, they should be included here.

The money you spend on the other things—that new shirt, going to the movies—those kinds of expenses are wants and should be no more than 30 percent of your after-tax income. In other words, all of the things that you could really do without would fall into this category.

The final 20 percent is savings and debt repayment. Any payment you make to a credit card balance that is more than the minimum payment required belongs in this category. Notice that contractual payments (car loan, mortgage, etc.) fall into the 50 percent category. It is the *extra* payments you make on loans that go into this 20 percent category. Any other funds you are allocating to a 401(k) or toward a specific goal should go in this category. Here is a list of what should be in each category:

THE 50/30/20 BUDGET		
50 PERCENT OF YOUR BUDGET	**30 PERCENT OF YOUR BUDGET**	**20 PERCENT OF YOUR BUDGET**
• Rent/mortgage • Property taxes • Insurance (home, health, life, auto) • Out-of-pocket medical • Car payments • Gas, transit, parking • Child care/support • Tuition/school expense • Utilities/phone • Groceries • Credit card minimums • Loan minimums (student, etc.) • Other legal obligations (alimony, judgments) • Union dues, other work expenses	• Clothes • Vacation • Dining out • Entertainment • Recreation/gym • Internet/TV/optional phone services • Misc. cash spending • Household items • Charity/gifts • Personal care • Lessons/tutoring • Subscriptions/fees	• 401(k) • IRA • Emergency fund • College savings • Other savings • Extra payments on loans (mortgage, home equity, car, student, credit cards)

If you pay your credit card balances off in full every month, you do not have any credit card debt, but you are spending money in the 50 percent and/or 30 percent categories. So, if you pay in full, allocate individual charges to the proper category. For example, if you went on a shopping spree and bought $150 worth of new clothes but paid the bill off in full at the end of the month, you would put $150 in the 30 percent category.

It is very possible that your must haves comprise much more of your budget than 50 percent. Here is where you start asking yourself the tough questions. Is your apartment/house too much for you to comfortably handle? Is your car payment too much? Can you reduce your insurance premiums by increasing your deductibles? How about the 30 percent category? You could eliminate cable, call-waiting on your phone, Internet access. You could take your lunch to work. You could stop buying lattes and bottled water. Once you have kept track of your spending, put it into categories, and entered your amounts into the 50/30/20 framework, you may be shocked at how far away from this ideal you are. But at least you now have the information you need to make changes. You will not be able to achieve this ideal budget overnight, but you will have a much better idea of where you need to readjust your spending.

Let us take another look at the last category, the saving and debt reduction. Remember the financial goals you developed in chapter 2? Pull those out and look at the steps you need to take to reach your short- , medium- , and long-term goals. The secret to achieving those goals is here, in this last column. How can you start addressing those goals with this budget? Let us assume that you have a goal of buying a new car. You need $2,000 for a down payment. When this goal is broken down into steps, you need to save $167 a month for a year. Take a look at your spending categories. Where is that $167 going to come from? Can you cut down on restaurant meals? Entertainment? There are no right or wrong answers here—the point is to give you as much information as possible so you can achieve your goals.

Suppose you do not have an apartment yet (or any of the other categories). You are just starting out and want to know how much you can afford to spend on a place to live, etc. Let us go back to our earlier example. You make $35,000 a year, with a net monthly income of $1,849.69, but remember, we need to look at after-tax income only. Your monthly gross income is $2,916.67, federal withholding is $251.10, Social Security is $161.18, and Medicare is $37.70. So, your after-tax income is $2,466.69. To conform to the 50/30/20 budget, your rent (or mortgage), your car payment, all your insurance premiums, utilities, groceries—all of your must-haves should add up to no more than $1,233.35 a month. You are already spending $267 a month on health insurance and $50 per month in an FSA, so that leaves $916.35 for all the rest of it. For your wants, you have 30 percent of your after-tax income, or $740. Your savings and debt reduction each month should be $493.34. If you are putting $300 into a 401(k), you have another $193.34 to save for something else (look back at your goals), and/or make extra payments on some outstanding loans.

Challenging, isn't it? Again, do not be discouraged if you are not at 50/30/20—this is a goal. More important than the actual percentages is that you are being thoughtful about how you spend your money.

SUMMARY

Developing and sticking to a budget can seem overwhelming, boring, unrealistic, and downright impossible. In fact, it does not have to be any of these things. Think of developing a budget as a way to give yourself power over your own future, a way to achieve your goals. You can get a handle on your finances no matter where you are starting from. Financial matters, in particular, seem to have a way of spinning out of control when we are not paying attention. On the other hand, with a little oversight and managing, they can lead us to where we want to go.

KNOW YOUR SCORE

California Department of Consumer Affairs (2007). Know your score. Retrieved from: http://www. dca.ca.gov/publications/knowyourscore.shtml

Think Your Grade Point Average Is Your Only Score That Matters?

Think again! There's another score that's important as you go through life. It's called a credit score. And whether you know it or not, someone is already keeping track.

WHAT IS A CREDIT SCORE?

In simplest terms, a credit score is a single number that helps lenders and others decide how likely you are to repay your debts. It is based on an analysis of the information in your credit report, which lists your debt and repayment history.

Did You Know?

Credit scores are based solely on credit history and don't include in the calculation factors like race, religion, national origin, gender, age, education level or marital status.

Do you have any credit cards? A car loan? A student loan or bank loan in your name? A department store charge account? If you answered "yes," you likely have a credit report. If you have a credit report, then you likely have a credit score that goes with it.

Your credit score changes over time. Every time you apply for, use, make or miss a payment on a loan or credit card, you build another entry on your credit report—and raise or lower your credit score. More recent activity carries more weight.

WHAT GOES INTO A CREDIT SCORE?

Your credit score is based on several types of information contained in your credit report.

- Your payment track record.
- How long you've used credit.
- How often you've applied for new credit and whether you've taken on new debt.
- The types of credit you currently use, such as credit cards, retail accounts, installment loans, finance company accounts and mortgages.

HOW TO GET YOUR CREDIT SCORE AND MORE

Your Credit Score: For a fee, you can order your FICO® credit score and learn more about your credit scoring by going to: www.myfico.com.

Did You Know?

Higher credit scores can mean lower interest rates-and big cost savings-for buying big-ticket items such as cars. Here's an example. For a five-year, $20,000 car loan, a good credit score may get you a lower annual interest rate-say 8 percent. But if your credit score is low, your loan may cost you more-say a 14 percent interest rate. What's the difference? With the higher interest rate, you'll wind up paying about $3,600 ($60/month) in additional interest costs.

Your Credit Report: To obtain a copy of your credit report or to report errors, you can contact the three major credit repositories:

1. **(800) 685-1111 www.equifax.com/home/en_us**
2. **(888) 397-3742 www.experian.com**
3. **(800) 888-4213 www.transunion.com**

In some situations, such as when you've been denied credit, you can get your report for free. Otherwise, there may be a fee.

For more information about how you can successfully manage credit, go to www.freddiemac.com/creditsmart. CreditSmart^SM is a new Freddie Mac educational program to help consumers use credit wisely.

For more information about credit, debt and savings, go to www.consumerfed.org, the web site for the Consumer Federation of America.

WHY DOES MY CREDIT SCORE MATTER RIGHT NOW?

Because your credit score can be a factor in some of the most important financial events of your life.

Buying a car or a home: Lenders may look at it before deciding whether you are a good risk for a car loan or home mortgage-or how much interest to charge you if you get the loan.

Did You Know?

One recent study from Nellie Mae found that undergraduate students carry an average of almost $2,800 in credit card debt. If you owed that much on a card with an 18 percent interest rate, and paid $50 each month, you'd wind up paying a total of $6,154. Moreover, it would take you more than 10 years to pay off that debt.

Getting affordable credit when you need it: Credit card issuers use credit scores to help decide whether to approve your application for a new card and if you should get a low interest rate on that card.

Keeping credit affordable: Credit card issuers continue to look at your credit scores after they issue a credit card to you-they may raise your interest rate if your credit score gets significantly worse. Or, they may raise your credit limit if your credit score improves.

Renting an apartment: Landlords may check it before deciding whether to rent to you.

Phone and electric line set-up: Utility companies may check it before deciding whether you have to pay a deposit.

WHAT IS CONSIDERED A "GOOD" CREDIT SCORE?

The higher the number, the better your credit score. FICO® credit scores-developed by Fair, Isaac and Company, Inc., and today's most commonly used scoring system-can range from 300 to 850. Most people score in the 600s and 700s.

Other scoring systems may use different numerical scales, but most use similar methods and factors to determine scores.

HOW CAN I BUILD A STRONG CREDIT RECORD AND A GOOD CREDIT SCORE?

Establish a credit record. Open a credit account-such as a credit card-in your name, and use it wisely.

What An Example?

Meet Tina. Take a look at the ups and downs of Tina's credit score. Tina is a fictitious person, but what happens to her credit score is a realistic example. Tina has just arrived at college ready to take on a new life full of opportunities. She's got her money saved up for the semester, and thus far has never had a loan or a line of credit of her own. She signs up for a new credit card at the bookstore her first week at school, where they are giving away free T-shirts for every completed application.

Here is how her credit management decisions affect her credit score in our hypothetical story.

Pay your bills consistently and on time. BEFORE the due date, pay as much as you can, but never less than the minimum amount due. Always follow the terms you agreed to when you opened the account.

Remember that a little late is bad—and a lot late is worse. If you miss the due date on a payment, send it as soon as possible-the late fees, interest penalties and harm to your credit score increase as the payment becomes more overdue.

"Maxing out" credit lines is never a good Idea. Use your credit sparingly and keep well within the credit limit on the account.

Pay off card balances instead of moving debt to other cards. Opening new accounts you don't really need can lead to more debt, and too many open accounts may lower your credit score.

Finally, check your credit report regularly to make sure it is error-free. You can do that by contacting any of the three major reporting agencies. (Phone numbers are on the back panel of this brochure.)

BEHAVIOR OR ACTION	CHANGE IN SCORE	CURRENT FICO SCORE	THE CREDIT SCORE CURVE
Freshman Year Her new credit card arrives in the mail with a $1000 credit limit. She breaks it in by buying her books and supplies over the semester. She pays at least the minimum due as soon as the bill arrives every month.	—	780	A+
Tina starts Spring Break in a great mood. She throws a party for all her friends and maxes out her card.	−180	600	C−
She pays the minimum balance every month on time until the year ends.	+30	630	C−
Tina applies for and gets a second credit card.	−10	620	C−
SUMMER She works hard and pays off her balance on her first card.	+180	800	A+
Sophomore Year In September, Tina's car needs major repairs so she can get to her job. The bill maxes out both cards.	−180	620	C−
In October, Tina forgets to tell one credit card company that she has moved, so her payment on her account, including late fees, is $100 and 30 days past due.	−130	490	F
In December, Tina's old, uninsured car is totaled when a tree falls on it. To buy a car, Tina needs a loan. She applies with two lenders who look at her credit score and credit record. One lender simply says "no" and the other offers her a high interest loan at 29% APR. She takes the bus until she can save enough money to buy another car.	0	490	F
She makes up the late payment and pays just the minimum amount due on time on both cards for the rest of the year.	+110	600	C−
Junior Year Tina works very hard to pay down her debts by paying $50 more than the minimum payment on each credit card every month and by using her cards sparingly for the rest of the school year.	+70	670	B−
Senior Year Tina does some self-reflection and decides to take better control of her credit. She tapes her credit cards into her wallet to limit the urge to use them spontaneously. Tina pays off almost all of her debt by graduation, and, since she has also paid her bills on time for a solid two years, her credit is once again excellent.	+100	770	A+

Credit scoring information used here is provided courtesy of Fair, Isaac and Company, Inc. The FICO® scores cited in Tina's story are simplified for purposes of illustration and are hypothetical. Your actual scores may differ.

CONSUMER TOPIC 4.1

Budgeting Mistakes to Avoid

Michael Kling

Making a budget is a great idea for the majority of us. But many people draw up budgets that have fairly obvious oversights that render their work useless. To create a realistic budget, avoid these common pitfalls.

1. NOT PLANNING FOR YEARLY EXPENSES

You plan for typical ongoing bills expenses: groceries, utilities and gasoline. But oops, you forget about yearly expenses, like car insurance and property taxes. For planning purposes, simply divide yearly lump sums by 12 and allocate that amount for annual expenses every month.

Yes, it's easy to forget about bills that don't show up at your door every month, but you're probably better off paying the total bill at once, since most companies levy an extra charge for monthly payments. Remember to also plan for other non-monthly expenses, like school supplies, pet care and gifts.

2. NOT EXPECTING THE UNEXPECTED

Many people don't set aside money for medical expenses, car repairs and home maintenance. But are these so-called irregular costs really unexpected? Almost all cars and homes eventually need repairs. The amount of repairs depends on age, quality of construction and maintenance.

Michael Kling, "11 Most Common Budgeting Mistakes," http://www.investopedia.com/financial-edge/0909/11-most-common-budgeting-mistakes.aspx#axzz2BZHHQCOT. Copyright © 2009 by ValueClick, Inc. Reprinted with permission.

Sure, unexpected breakdowns happen. But you can predict some costs, at least roughly. When shingles on your 25-year-old roof with a 25-year-warranty are curling up, it's time to start setting aside money. Save money by shopping around and getting quotes, instead of hiring the first contractor who returns a call.

3. NOT TRACKING PAST EXPENSES

A good way to get a handle on irregular expenses is look at past expenses. How often you went to the doctor or mechanic last year can indicate how much you'll go next year. Plus, some costs are seasonal. Gas and oil bills are higher in the winter, and electric bills are frequently higher in the summer when air conditioners run.

4. DISREGARDING SAVINGS

Many people contribute to savings only what they happen to have left after they've bought everything they want. A better way is to reverse that thinking. Decide what you will contribute to savings and stick to that amount, then buy what you really need.

5. NOT HAVING AN EMERGENCY FUND

Paying attention to savings will help build an emergency fund. Financial planners recommend building up two or three months' worth of emergency savings, in case of job loss or severe illness.

6. NOT INCLUDING SMALL BUT ONGOING ITEMS

Small items, like eating out for lunch, add up quickly. A $3 cappuccino every workday comes to $75 a month—would buying a coffee machine be a better option? Look at these types of items, if your budget isn't paying off the way you'd hoped.

7. PUTTING TOO MUCH WORK IN

Some people write down every amount they spend everyday and track every penny. You should be able to maintain a budget with a reasonable amount of record-keeping.

8. NOT BEING FLEXIBLE

You don't have to be too restrictive—trade amounts in different categories. For instance, spend less on eating out in one month and buy some new shoes the next.

9. NOT WRITING IT DOWN

Numbers in your head can be amorphous and inaccurate. Writing down the budget can add discipline and authority. Try a spreadsheet or online software.

10. NOT CHANGING IT

Some people drop their budget instead of changing it. You should be able to change it as new income and expenses arise, or you find that your previous planning wasn't accurate.

11. NOT BEING REALISTIC

Some people set down unrealistically low spending limits, and then become discouraged when they run out of money and can't meet their goals. The point of a budget is not to stop you from spending money at all or from treating yourself once in a while. Instead, it is meant establish your priorities and you give you sense of control, and free you from guilt about spending. Budgeting is meant to empower, not cripple. Work within your means to create a budget that best fits your lifestyle. After all, it's your money, and you should have control over it.

CONSUMER TOPIC 4.2

Credit Card Mistakes to Avoid

Kay Bell

Whether you're in a financial crunch or just lack a second Ferrari, credit card offers landing in your mailbox might look like an answer to a prayer.

Don't succumb to temptation, says Cate Williams, vice president of financial literacy for Money Management International in Chicago.

"The first thing consumers need to do is walk from their mailbox to their shredder," says Williams. "A new credit card might give you that sparkling feeling for about 24 hours, but as a way to clean up your finances, borrowing money to pay back other money is not a solution."

Experts' advice can steer you away from the top 10 credit card mistakes.

1. GETTING TOO MANY

Bypass the shredder and you could make one of the most common credit card blunders by collecting too many credit cards.

"Ask yourself," says Williams, " 'Do I need another credit card?' Probably 95 percent of us don't need another one to keep in the sock drawer or in the little metal box in the kitchen."

Howard S. Dvorkin, founder and president of Consolidated Credit Counseling Services, a non-profit debt management company in Fort Lauderdale, Fla., agrees. "The worst mistake is that people don't know when to stop. Too many credit cards is not a good thing."

Even if the cards have zero balances, multiple open accounts could cause a lender to question what could happen if the account holder gives in to temptation and maxes out on all that plastic.

Kay Bell, "10 Worst Credit Card Mistakes," http://www.creditcards.com/credit-card-news/help/worst-credit-card-mistakes-6000.php#ixzz2BZFa4LIq. Copyright © by CreditCards.com. Reprinted with permission.

2. MISUNDERSTANDING INTRODUCTORY RATES

But, you argue, that new card will help you manage your money better because you can transfer other balances to a no-interest account. Welcome to credit card mistake No. 2: being misled by introductory rates.

"People don't look at what the rate's going to be once the teaser is over," says Daniel Wishnatsky, certified financial planner and owner of Special Kids Financial in Phoenix. "The assumption is that it's going to be a reasonable rate. But with these particular loans, it's not unusual for it to go up to 18 to 20 percent. They're surprised six months later when it expires. But if they'd done their homework, they wouldn't be."

3. NOT READING THE FINE PRINT

That homework is reading the offer's fine print. Not doing so is credit card blunder No. 3.

That tiny text insert is where you'll discover when the zero-percent or very low interest rate expires. It's also how you can find out about any balance transfer fees, as well as any offer limitations. In most cases, the introductory rate applies only to balance transfer amounts or new purchases for a certain period of time, says June A. Schroeder, a CFP with Liberty Financial Group Inc. in Elm Grove, Wis., a private financial planning and advisory firm.

4. CHOOSING A CARD FOR THE WRONG REASONS

You might be tempted to ignore the fine print because the card has other attractions, such as a rebate or rewards program. Don't, or you'll make credit card mistake No. 4: choosing a card for the wrong reasons.

"Credit card granters are not a consumer's friend. It is a business," says Dvorkin. "They don't know what's right for you. Their job is to extract as much money from you as they can. Your job is to not let that happen. People need to go through and find a card that's right for them. There's every sort of card out there—points, cash back, donations to your college."

5. NOT RATE SHOPPING

Look for the best possible interest rate. Not shopping around is credit card mistake No. 5.

It's especially important to note the rate on unsolicited offers. If you're struggling financially, you're not likely to get the most favorable rates or terms. You'll be paying higher interest rates. So comparison shop for a credit card.

6. MAKING MINIMUM PAYMENTS

OK. You do need another card. You read the fine print, you completely understand the terms and you got a competitive rate. But even after choosing the perfect credit card, people still make mistakes, such as No. 6 on our list, making minimum-only payments.

"Credit cards are not a form of supplemental income," says Dvorkin. "They're for convenience, and should be paid off at the end of every month. Paying the minimum is not going to get you anywhere. It's going to get you in trouble, that's where it's going to get you."

And it's going to get you into trouble for a long, long time. "People don't realize how difficult it is to pay off loans at a high rate," says Wishnatsky. "You're going to be paying it for your next three lifetimes."

CreditCards.com's calculator can show how long it will take to pay off a bill if you send only the minimum each month.

7. PAYING YOUR BILL LATE

Making late payments, blunder No. 7, is better than not paying at all, but not by much. Not only will you face a late-payment charge, which could be higher than your minimum payment, your tardiness will show up on your credit report, damage your FICO score and make it harder to get better terms for future loans and accounts.

Check your account statement for the due date and make sure you send your check in plenty of time. But the date alone isn't enough, says Liberty Financial's Schroeder. Some companies have cutoff times. If your check arrives on the 22nd as required, but in the afternoon mail, your payment is counted as late because your account terms called for payment by 9 a.m. that day.

If you've set up an automatic payment via your bank, make sure the time and date are taken into account, says Schroeder. And find out your bank's payment policy when the due date falls on a weekend or holiday.

8. IGNORING YOUR MONTHLY STATEMENT

You can avoid late payments by checking your credit card statement. Not doing so is mistake No. 8. Checking your statement will help you pay your bill promptly, as well as allow you to make sure that the charges on it are correct. "In these days of ID theft, you need to check your bills religiously," says Schroeder. And you need to do so as soon as the statement arrives. If you wait too long to dispute a charge, says Schroeder, "you're essentially accepting it."

9. EXCEEDING YOUR CREDIT LIMIT

Checking your statements also can keep you from exceeding your credit limit, mistake No. 9. "If you're near the top of your credit limit, try really hard to pay in cash for subsequent purchases or get an increased credit line," says Schroeder. "If you don't, you'll get over-the-limit charges, which are costly and look bad on your credit report."

10. BUYING THINGS YOU DON'T NEED

Careful statement examination also could prevent the 10th credit card blunder, using plastic to purchase things you don't need." Go over your credit card bills every month and you'll be amazed at the number of items that, upon reflection, you could have done without," says Wishnatsky. "It's surprising how many purchases we make that we think are needs, but are impulse buys."

The Phoenix financial planner tells his clients who are considering a significant purchase to wait 48 hours, if at all possible. "If you still want it, wait another 48 hours," Wishnatsky says. "Then if you have to get it, then get it."

Also use your statements to help you create a budget. Wishnatsky realizes many people cringe at the "B" word, but he says control of your spending and your credit card usage doesn't have to be a way to deprive yourself. Instead, it can be a way to make things happen in financially positive ways.

"Once you get control, even to a degree, it frees you from this constant money worry," says Wishnatsky. "You might find there are things that you can actually end up having if you just have a plan, if you get your financial desires in tune with your financial resources."

CASE STUDY

"Honey, I am out of cash and I need $50.00." Maya tells John as he's walking down the hall.

"Honey, what happened to the $100 I gave you yesterday for stuff?" John asks.

"I spent it"

"On what?"

"Stuff."

"What stuff? You told me you were going to Target for toilet paper." John says.

"I did get toilet paper."

"Honey, you didn't get $100 worth of toilet paper, you only got 4 rolls and those are not that expensive at Target." John says.

"I bought the cutest pair of boots at DSW." Says Maya with a smile.

"Honey you have about 50 pairs of boots in your closet barely worn." John says.

"Yeah, but I didn't have these in dark green suede, and they were on clearance for only $85!" Mays says.

"Ok, I have to run and we'll talk more about this later, when I get home from work." John gives her a kiss and heads out the door for work.

He goes to work, and all day he thinks about their money and financial issues. He doesn't want to fight with Maya and doesn't want to be in debt either. Plus, he has been thinking of getting a new car for a long time, and their retirement account barely has any money in it. Also, he and Maya have be talking about having a baby and want to be financially ready. He decides to write out a budget on an excel worksheet, so he can see it in black and white, where everything is coming and going.

What do you recommend to John for his talk with Maya?

What preparing their budget, what should they pay attention?

What strategies and processes would you recommend to them for their budget development?

CONSUMER RESOURCES:

Auto loans, credit cards, and other loans: http://www.bankrate.com

College financial aid information: http://www.finaid.org

Credit report: http://www.annualcreditreport.com

Equifax (800-685-1111): http://www.equifax.com

Experian (888-397-3742): http://www.experian.com

TransUnion (800-916-8800): http://www.transUnion.com

Federal Reserve consumer information: http://www.federalreserve.gov/consumerinfo/default.htm

National Foundation for Credit Counseling: http://www.nfcc.org

CHAPTER 5

CONSUMER MAJOR PURCHASES

CHAPTER 5 INTRODUCTION

Consumer purchases in the U.S. account for about 70% of the economy. The average U.S. resident, in a year, consumes 280 pounds of meat, uses 640 pounds of paper, and uses energy equivalent to 8 metric tons of oil. We are living in a consumer society. Indeed, the 4.5% of the world population in this country contribute one third of the consumer spending in the global market. In the U.S., there is almost one passenger car for every one people. Europeans have about one passenger car for every three people. Developing countries have, on average, about one passenger car for every 50 people. Housing is no doubt one of the largest spending categories for American households. Homeownership is a symbol of realizing the American Dream; and then people realize there is a huge financial burden, $8 trillion mortgage loan, on their shoulders. Let us be careful and responsible when we spend our limited budgets. Read this chapter and understand our major purchases.

WHAT VEHICLE FEATURES ARE CONSIDERED IMPORTANT WHEN BUYING AN AUTOMOBILE?

An Examination of Driver Preferences by Age and Gender

Brenda H. Vrkljan and Dana Anaby

ABSTRACT

Introduction: Certain vehicle features can help drivers avoid collisions and/or protect occupants in the event of a crash, and therefore, might play an important role when deciding which vehicle to purchase. The objective of this study was to examine the importance attributed to key vehicle features (including safety) that drivers consider when buying a car and its association with age and gender. *Methods:* A sample of 2,002 Canadian drivers aged 18 years and older completed a survey that asked them to rank the importance of eight vehicle features if they were to purchase a vehicle (storage, mileage, safety, price, comfort, performance, design, and reliability). ANOVA tests were performed to: (a) determine if there were differences in the level of importance between features and; (b) examine the effect of age and gender on the importance attributed to these features. *Results:* Of the features examined, safety and reliability were the most highly rated in terms of importance, whereas design and performance had the lowest rating. Differences in safety and performance across age groups were dependent on gender. This effect was most evident in the youngest and oldest age groups. *Conclusions:* Safety and reliability were considered the most important features. Age and gender play a significant role in explaining the

Brenda H. Vrkljan and Dana Anaby, "What Vehicle Features Are Considered Important When Buying an Automobile? An Examination of Driver Preferences by Age and Gender," *Journal of Safety Research*, vol. 42, issue 1, pp. 61–65. Copyright © 2011 by Elsevier Press. Reprinted with permission.

importance of certain features. *Impact on Industry:* Targeted efforts for translating safety-related information to the youngest and oldest consumers should be emphasized due to their high collision, injury, and fatality rates.

1. INTRODUCTION

Advancements in automotive design, including crash avoidance technologies (e.g., anti-lock brakes, traction control, stability control, night vision) and structural enhancements (e.g., steel safety cages, energy absorbing crumple zones, airbags, seatbelts, energy absorbing steering columns, padded instrument panels, and side door guide beams) have played a role in reducing the number of fatalities and injuries among vehicle occupants. Translating safety-related information to prospective consumers who ultimately purchase these vehicles has become the focus of governments and other motoring organizations. For this purpose, New Car Assessment Programs (NCAP) have been established in many industrialized nations, including Europe (Euro NCAP), the United States (National Highway Traffic Safety Administration [NHTSA]), Canada (Transport Canada), and Australia-Asia partnership (ANCAP). These programs evaluate the crashworthiness of new private vehicles. 'Star ratings' are then awarded based on a vehicle's respective performance during crash simulations involving frontal, side, and rear impacts, as well as roll-over and pedestrian collisions. The top overall rating is five stars.

While consumers have reported using collision rating systems and other safety-related information to inform their private vehicle purchase, other features, including cost, design, and reliability, have consistently outranked safety during the buying process (DesRosiers Automotive Reports, 2002; Market, Opinion Research International [MORI], 2005). Much research on new vehicle purchasing decisions has focused on the influence of safety during the buying process. Results from a series of European-based surveys suggest that safety-related information from reputable sources remain paramount when purchasing a private vehicle but that the importance attributed to safety in comparison to other features can differ depending on the characteristics of the driver.

A consumer survey conducted on behalf of Euro NCAP (MORI, 2005) indicated underlying age and gender differences with how safety was perceived during the vehicle purchase process. Older consumers (i.e., aged 75 and older) were slightly less concerned about safety (82%) than other age groups (92%). Female and male respondents were equally concerned about safety, but females were often not responsible for final purchase decisions (34% vs. 68%). In a study of the purchasing preferences of Swedish consumers aged 18 to 65, Johansson-Stenman and Martinsson (2006) found that 85% of consumers rated safety as "very important" (using a 4-point continuum), but that other features, including reliability (79%) and fuel consumption (60%), were rated just as highly. However, their survey was not designed to specifically explore vehicle purchase decisions, rather to understand consumer behavior more generally, with automobiles serving as the product of choice. Johansson-Stenman and Martinsson concluded that consumers seek to purchase products that enhance their self-image, meaning their purchases reflect a desire to maintain or improve this image.

Studies that specifically address vehicle purchase decisions have usually involved prospective buyers and, as such, Koppel, Charlton, Fildes, and Fitzharris (2008) identified that participant responses might be influenced by hypothetical bias. To account for this potential for bias, Koppel et al. surveyed consumers in Spain and Sweden *after* their vehicle purchase. Consistent with previous research, participants in both countries ranked safety-related factors as most important. Using regression analysis, attributes of drivers who were most likely to prioritize safety-related features included: those aged 55 years and older; female; highly educated (i.e., post-secondary); drove a moderate number of kilometers per annum; and were purchasing their first vehicle. Koppel et al. (2008) reported that vehicle purchase decisions often involve "difficult tradeoffs, such as those between price, intended use, reliability, and safety" (p. 995). By asking participants to rank their priorities from a combined list of safety features (advanced braking systems [ABS], front passenger air bag) and non-safety related features (e.g., navigation system, air conditioning), results indicated that safety took the top spot when it comes to making the final determination of which vehicle to purchase.

With the exception of Koppel et al. (2008), most surveys on vehicle purchase decisions do not identify the process by which participants are recruited for the study. Many of these studies have been based on preferences reported by European consumers. To our knowledge, there is limited information in the peer-reviewed literature addressing the needs of North American consumers.

Age and gender have been identified as significant factors in previous studies. However, there is conflicting evidence. For example, the survey conducted by MORI (2005) suggested that female and male respondents were equally concerned about safety, whereas Koppel et al. (2008) identified that females were more likely to prioritize safety during the vehicle purchase process.

Consideration of how drivers of different genders across the lifespan perceive the importance of safety and other features when buying a car is worth further investigation given their differential needs and associated crash risk. For instance, drivers aged 70 years and older have the highest risk of collision, injury, and fatality, comparable only to drivers aged 16 to 24 years when distance driven is considered (see Brorsson, 1989; Cotrell & Wild, 1999; Gresset & Meyer, 1994; Stutts & Wilkins, 2004). In this context, it is also important to consider the profile (i.e., age, gender) of drivers who identify features that might be considered the converse of safety (such as vehicular performance or design) as important when purchasing an automobile.

To address the gap in the literature, there is a need to further examine the interaction by driver age and gender related to particular vehicle features. Such findings can inform methods used to target safety-related information to particular segments of the consumer market. Using a random sample of over 2,000 drivers in Canada, the purpose of this study was to describe the importance attributed to certain features (e.g., storage, mileage, safety, price, comfort, performance, design, and reliability) if the drivers were to purchase a vehicle (see Table 1). Further, the aims of this study were to examine: (a) the differences in the level of importance attributed to vehicle features, and (b) the effect of age and gender on the perceived importance of these features.

2. METHOD

2.1. Participants

A secondary analysis of a stratified random national survey of Canadian drivers was conducted by telephone between March 16th and April 5th, 2005. A total of 2,002 Canadians aged 18 and older

Table 1: A list of the eight features drivers rated in terms of importance when purchasing a vehicle on the telephone survey.

"On a scale of 1–7 where 1 indicates not important at all and 7 indicates extremely important with 4 being somewhat important, please indicate the importance of ["1–8"] in deciding what kind of car to buy."
1. "Seating capacity and storage space" [STORAGE]* 2. "Getting good mileage" [MILEAGE] 3. "Safety features" [SAFETY] 4. "Purchase price" [PRICE] 5. "Comfort" [COMFORT] 6. "Performance, speed and power" [PERFORMANCE] 7. "Design and style" [DESIGN] 8. "Reputation, reliability & warranty" [RELIABILITY]

*Bracketed word indicates the short form of the identified feature used in analyzing the results.

who had driven a motor vehicle in the past month were interviewed. The sample was determined through a random selection of households across Canada, using Random Digit Dialing (RDD). The sample provides a margin of error of +/− 2.2 percentage points, 19 times out of 20. The sample was divided into six age groups: 18–24 (48% women), 25–34 (54% women), 35–44 (52% women), 45–54 (54% women), 55–64 (55% women), 65 years and older (55% women).

2.2. Survey Instrument

The survey was conducted through a joint partnership between Transport Canada and National Resources Canada aimed at gathering information from a representative group of Canadians about their driving experiences. The plan was to use this information to inform public education and awareness campaigns. The survey was weighted by age, gender, and geographical region. The survey instrument was developed in consultation with funding partners (i.e., Transport Canada, National Resources Canada). As part of the survey, each respondent was asked to rank the importance of eight vehicle features (see Table 1) they consider when purchasing a car using a 7-point scale where 1 indicates *not important at all* and 7 indicates *extremely important.* Unfortunately, it is not known what percentage of the sample (whether those surveyed) had ever actually ever purchased a vehicle.

A mean was calculated for each vehicle feature where higher scores indicate greater importance attributed to the respective feature. The vehicle characteristics surveyed are similar to those used in previous studies that analyzed vehicle purchasing behavior among prospective consumers (e.g., DesRosiers Automotive Reports, 2002; MORI, 2005; Johansson-Stenman & Martinsson, 2006).

2.3. Statistical Analyses

Box plots were used to examine the distribution of the ratings for the eight features, including mean, median, range, and interquartile. To determine whether there was a difference in the level of importance attributed to these features, a repeated measures Analysis of Variance (ANOVA) was performed using a polynomial approach. Post-hoc analysis using the Tukey method was conducted to identify the source of the difference between these features. For those features identified as most important and least important based on post-hoc results, Two-Way ANOVAs were conducted using the following design: 2 (gender) X 6 (age groups). Finally, Effect Size (ES) was calculated using the partial eta square (η^2_p) values based on the following formula: $\eta^2_p = SS_b/(SS_b + SS_w)$. These values were interpreted according to Cohen's classification (Cohen, 1977) where $\eta^2_p = .01$ considered as a small effect, $\eta^2_p = .06$ as medium, and $\eta^2_p = .14$ as a large effect size. Level of significance was set at 0.05 for all statistical tests. SPSS version 17.0 was used for this analysis.

3. FINDINGS

The sample was almost equally split between male (47%) and female drivers (53%) aged 18 years and older, with 35% having a university education or higher and 35% having high school or less. The majority (53%) drove at least seven times per week. Of all survey respondents, 53% drove over 10,000 kilometers per year, with one in two indicating their car was no more than five years old.

As detailed in Fig. 1, drivers rated certain features as more important than others when considering the purchase of a vehicle. The maximum value for importance (i.e., 7) was selected by more than 50% of the sample for three of the eight features surveyed, specifically: safety; reliability; and mileage. Repeated measures using a polynomial approach indicated that there is a significant difference amongst all features $F(7,13790) = 534.249$, $p < 0.001$. Post-hoc analyses revealed that safety had the highest importance rating as compared to all other features with the exception of reliability $(p = .014)$. The importance attributed to the feature of reliability (mean = 6.28, $SD = 1.10$) was similar to that given to safety (mean = 6.19 $SD = 1.21$, $p = .061$). Overall, these two features (i.e., safety, reliability) were found to be significantly more important than all other features. The least important features were performance (mean = 4.81, SD = 1.60) and design (mean = 4.71 SD = 1.60). The following analyses further explored the association between gender and age for those vehicle features rated as most important (i.e., safety, reliability) and least important (i.e., performance, design) if the driver were to purchase a car.

A two-way ANOVA indicated a significant interaction effect between age group and gender on the rating of safety and performance (see Table 2). Gender differences in the importance attributed to safety and performance were dependent on the age of the driver. Across all age groups, women rated safety as significantly more important than men. Women tended to rate safety similarly across the lifespan, whereas men showed a different pattern (see Fig. 2). With age, the importance attributed to safety when considering a vehicle purchase increased steadily for male drivers, although there was a slight decrease noted for male drivers aged 55–64. However, this rating then increased again among men in the oldest age group (i.e., aged 65 and older). When examining the feature of performance, the results indicated that (see Fig. 2) men and women aged 35–54 rated the importance of this feature similarly whereas the youngest and oldest groups exhibited differences based on gender. Interestingly, men in the youngest age group and women in the oldest age group rated performance as more important as compared to other age groups with respect to this feature.

Table 2: Two way-ANOVA of features identified as most important (Safety, Reliability) and least important (Performance, Design) when buying a vehicle.

	GENDER		AGE GROUPS		GENDER* AGE GROUPS	
	F	ES	F	ES	F	ES
Safety	151.6**	0.07	8.6**	0.02	2.89*	0.007
Reliability	17.5**	0.09	5.51**	0.01	1.9	0.005
Performance	0.01	0.00	2.1	0.005	2.99*	0.008
Design	5.4*	0.003	0.87	0.002	1.44	0.004

$*p < 0.005$ $**p < 0.01$.

When examining reliability, a main effect was found between male and female drivers and across age groups with no interaction effects. Post-hoc analysis revealed that the youngest group of drivers rated reliability significantly lower than the two oldest groups (i.e., aged 55–64, 65 years and older). Women rated reliability as significantly more important than their male counterparts, except between the ages of 45–54 when their ratings were similar.

For the feature of design, a main effect was found only between genders with no interaction effect. Overall, male drivers tended to rate the importance of design significantly higher than women. Although the change in importance across the driver lifespan was not significant, there is a trend indicating that, with age, men rate vehicle design as less important (see Fig. 2). Effect size values were low across all the significant main effects and interactions that were found.

4. DISCUSSION

This study examined differences in the level of importance attributed to certain vehicle features, including safety, and the effect of age and gender on the reported importance when considering a vehicle purchase. Safety and a vehicle's reliability were rated highest of all features surveyed. While this finding was consistent with those from other surveys that involved actual consumers (e.g., MORI, 2005; Koppel et al., 2008), the results of the present study further suggest that the level of importance attributed to certain vehicle features were dependent on age and gender. The younger the driver the less important safety was when considering a vehicle purchase, although this feature was still highly valued across all age groups. Young male drivers rated safety lowest, while the level of importance attributed to safety among female drivers was highest of all age groups and remained relatively constant across the life span. Among male drivers, safety gradually increased in importance with age. This increase might reflect lifestyle changes, which can have a corresponding effect on features deemed important. For example, transporting passengers, including children and/or an aging family member, might increase the importance of safety-related features on vehicle purchase decisions. However, there is limited evidence on the influence of passengers and/or other extraneous factors on vehicle purchase decisions. For example, future studies could account for passenger characteristics when examining this decision-making process.

The features of performance and design were rated as least important. In this context, a vehicle's performance (i.e., speed) is considered the converse of safety. Hence, age and gender of those who considered this feature important were also examined. Male drivers in the youngest group and women in the oldest group rated performance highest of all respondents. This result raises concerns given that drivers in both these age groups have the highest collision, injury, and fatality rates when distance driven is considered (Williams & Shabanova, 2003). For instance, young male drivers (aged 18 to 24) are more likely to be found responsible for crash-related fatalities, as are female drivers aged 50 and older when compared to their male counterparts (Williams & Shabanova).

Johansson-Stenman and Martinsson (2006) identified that consumer preferences for certain features can be influenced by a desire to maintain or even improve self-image. Hence, younger drivers may be trying to establish their image by purchasing a higher performance automobile. Male drivers in the youngest age group perceived safety-related features as least important amongst all those surveyed, yet the role of these features in helping drivers avoid collisions and/or protect occupants in the event of a crash cannot be overstated. While public education campaigns must emphasize the importance of safety-related features for all prospective vehicle buyers, results from this study indicate that particular focus should be on the youngest and oldest consumers who have the highest crash risk per kilometer driven. Safety-related features may not only protect vehicle occupants from fatality or serious injury, but such enhancements to vehicle design may circumvent a crash from happening in the first place.

This study should be considered in light of a few limitations. As a cross-sectional design, we cannot claim causality with respect to our findings, rather association only between age and the importance of vehicle features. Future studies might use a longitudinal approach in order to capture changes in perceived importance over time. Another limitation is that the survey used only one item to measure the importance of each feature. For example, safety is considered a multifaceted variable when it comes to vehicle safety (Koppel et al., 2008). It seems plausible that there may have been more variance in responses generated if each feature was captured by more than one item and, consequently, greater variability might yield different results. Finally, additional factors might have influenced the rating of particular vehicle features, including the behavioral characteristics of the driver, such as their attitude and risk, as well as the driving environment, such as traffic policy and regulations. Such considerations should be incorporated in future surveys that investigate the vehicle purchasing behavior amongst consumers.

Koppel et al. (2008) raised concerns that consumers could be influenced by hypothetical bias and, as such, surveyed drivers after their vehicle purchase. However, their results were similar to those found in the present study as well as other surveys, which found that safety was rated highly when it came to vehicle purchase decisions (MORI, 2005; Johansson-Stenman & Martinsson, 2006).

5. CONCLUSIONS

The results of the present study suggest that certain vehicle features are considered more important than others when considering the purchase of an automobile and that the level of importance attributed to these features can differ depending on the driver's age and gender. With regard to safety, the analysis indicated that those at the highest risk of collision (i.e., younger males) rated this feature as least important compared to all other age and gender groupings. Interestingly, older females rated a vehicle's performance highest of all respondents when questioned about the importance of this feature on their purchase decision. This feature is considered the converse of safety. Nevertheless, findings suggest that safety, along with reliability, are considered most important if purchasing a vehicle amongst drivers as a whole.

Findings from this study provide a snapshot of the importance attributed to certain vehicle features, including safety, among drivers by age and gender. The next step will be to develop a conceptual model that explores the dimensionality of decision-making when purchasing an automobile that more accurately reflects the combination of personal and environmental factors that can influence this decision. Such information can then be used to develop more targeted strategies that can be used by New Car Assessment Programs (NCAP) and other motoring organizations for translating safety-related information to consumer groups most vulnerable to crash, injury, or fatality.

5.1. Impact on Industry

The demographics of the driving population are changing. The baby boom generation has been responsible for every notable trend in automotive sales in North America since the 1960s, including minivan sales in the 1980s and sport utility vehicles (SUV) in the 1990s (Foot, 2009, March 12). Individuals aged 50 and over account for more than 40% of all new cars purchased (Kelly, 2005). Currently, this age group is the fastest growing and most affluent segment of the consumer market in Canada, the United States, and other industrialized nations. Older adults will become the largest segment of potential buyers of automobiles in the marketplace. If automotive manufacturers are to remain competitive, particularly given the recent economic downturn in this sector, understanding the needs of older consumers and incorporating them into the design of the automobile is important. While older drivers represent the fastest growing segment of the consumer market, they also have the highest collision risk, comparable only to the youngest group of drivers when distance driven is considered. The development, design, and marketing of crash avoidance and safety-related vehicular technology to consumers are critical to ensure the vehicle purchased is the best fit with their safety and driving needs.

ACKNOWLEDGEMENT

The authors would like to thank Transport Canada for access to data from the original survey and to Auto21—A Network of Centres of Excellence (NCE) (www.auto21.ca) for funding this research project.

REFERENCES

Brorsson, B. (1989). The risk of accidents among older drivers. *Scandinavian Journal of Social Medicine*, 17(3), 253–256.

Cohen, J. (1977). *Statistical power analysis for the behavioural sciences* (2nd ed.). Hillsdale, NJ: Lawrence Earlbaum.

Cotrell, V., & Wild, K. (1999). Longitudinal study of self-imposed driving restrictions and deficit awareness in patients with Alzheimer disease. *Alzheimer Disease and Associated Disorders, 13*(3), 151–156.

DesRosiers Automotive Reports (2002). *The Need for Dialogue: A Perspective on Vehicle Safety, 16(9), ISSN 0841-9957.* Richmond Hill, Ontario: Author.

Foot, D. K. (2009, March 12). *Who's going to buy this car? [Editorial]. The Globe and Mail* (pp. A19).

Gresset, J., & Meyer, F. (1994). Risk of automobile accidents among elderly drivers with impairments or chronic diseases. *Canadian Journal of Public Health*, 85(4), 282–285.

Johansson-Stenman, O., & Martinsson, P. (2006). Honestly, why are you driving a BMW? *Journal Economics Behavior Organ, 60*, 129–146.

Kelly, M. (2005). How the aging network can work with business: An overnight success after 30 years. *Generations, 28*(4), 64–70.

Koppel, S., Charlton, J., Fildes, B., & Fitzharris, M. (2008). How important is vehicle safety in the new vehicle purchase process? *Accident Analysis and Prevention, 40*(3), 994–1004.

Market, Opinion Research International [MORI]. (2005). *Euro NCAP Consumer Car Buying Survey. Accessed January 15, 2010.* http://www.euroncap.com/content/media/press_releases/november_2.

Stutts, J. C., & Wilkins, J. W. (2004). On-road driving evaluations: a potential tool for helping older adults drive safely longer. *Journal of Safety Research, 34*(4), 431–439.

Williams, A. F., & Shabanova, V. I. (2003). Responsibility of drivers by age and gender for motor-vehicle crash deaths. *Journal of Safety Research, 34*, 527–531.

Brenda H. Vrkljan, O.T. Reg., (Ont.), Ph.D. is an assistant professor in the Occupational Therapy program at McMaster University where her research focuses on driving and community mobility across the lifespan, with a specific focus on older drivers. She is a lead investigator on projects associated with the Canadian Driving Research Initiative for Vehicular Safety in the Elderly (Candrive) research team (www.candrive.ca) funded by the Canadian Institutes for Health Research (CIHR) and co-investigator of the 'Safe Transportation for Seniors' project funded by Auto21 (www.auto21.ca).

Dana Anaby, BOT, Ph.D., is a post-doctoral fellow at the School of Rehabilitation Science at McMaster University.

THE FAST LANE TO THE ADOPTION OF ELECTRIC CARS

Russell Hensley, Stefan M. Knupfer, and Axel Krieger

Large cities may be the ideal test track for the mass market. Catalyzing early adoption could take less than most auto executives and policy makers think.

As more and more electrified vehicles hit the floors of car dealerships, conventional wisdom has it that the market won't get moving without richer incentives and dense battery-charging networks.

Yet our research on demand for electric cars in very large urban areas[1] shows that plug-in hybrid electric vehicles and battery-only electric vehicles could account for 16 percent of overall new-car sales in New York, 9 percent in Paris, and 5 percent in Shanghai by 2015. That's true even with today's financial incentives and limited public charging facilities.[2]

It's not surprising that the market may take root in big cities: nowhere is the need for cleaner air and reduced carbon dioxide emissions more pressing, and nowhere else can you expect to find as many green-minded early adopters who will welcome a clean vehicle that takes them the short distances they need to go on one charge. These characteristics make large urban areas the ideal labs for the next phase of electric-vehicle development. Our research offers insights that can guide auto companies, battery makers, infrastructure providers, and city governments alike as they consider moving forward with this technology and the networks that support it.

Large markets are waiting to be served. We found big clusters of potential early adopters—30 percent of all car buyers in Shanghai and 20 percent in New York—who were distinguished by their green thinking and would consider buying an electric car.

For early adopters, the charging problem isn't as big as it seems. Unlike other groups of car buyers in New York and Shanghai, early adopters were willing to adjust their driving and parking habits to own an electric car. In fact, they indicated that a dense public charging infrastructure would

173

only modestly increase their interest in buying such cars and that they were willing to cope with more limited charging options. This attitude reduces the need for public investments in the start-up stage, though a broad plug-in infrastructure will no doubt be critical as electrified vehicles migrate to mass adoption in large cities and elsewhere.

This is also good news for automakers, which have the opportunity to overcome another major obstacle: battery limits. Since many drivers in large cities travel only short distances—to and from work, for instance—the near-term cost and duration of electric-car batteries is less of a problem there than it is elsewhere. Rather than offering only all-purpose electric vehicles, automakers can segment buyers according to their driving missions and develop attractively priced models with no more battery energy storage than many of their city drivers need.

Technology preferences vary between cities. Shanghai buyers overwhelmingly preferred plug-in hybrid electric vehicles, which can drive some 60 kilometers (about 40 miles) on one charge and then switch to a gasoline-powered engine. The reason is the large share of first-time car buyers in Shanghai who demand family-size cars with full functionality. In New York, though, small electric city cars—a type of battery-only vehicle that can go 60 to 90 kilometers on a full charge—turned out to be very popular (exhibit).

Design matters, but in different ways. Most buyers in New York and Shanghai look for status: being the first with the latest technology and standing out from the crowd. But residents of Shanghai would like a novel and distinctive design, while New Yorkers prefer a more conventional design, albeit with the attributes that identify a vehicle as an electric car.

Nonfinancial incentives can be surprisingly effective. The smartest way to get the market going isn't necessarily by increasing financial incentives. We found that monetary incentives, such as the US federal tax credit of up to $7,500 on the purchase of an electric car, will help stimulate initial demand. Yet raising them considerably will not lead to a quantum leap in adoption. In fact, among the 30 financial and nonfinancial measures we tested with New York consumers, some low-cost options—such as electric-vehicle-preferred lanes or conveniently located charging spots—were surprisingly effective.

Consumer education is one such measure that will be critical for catalyzing both early and mass adoption. Forty percent of New York and Shanghai respondents said they didn't know much about electric vehicles and many were anxious about driving-range limitations. Few knew that battery-powered cars are relatively quiet and can potentially accelerate faster than conventional ones. And more important, many weren't aware that electric cars help drivers save money on both fuel and maintenance in the long run.

So what comes next? Highly motivated private users in large cities such as New York and Shanghai—along with other potential early adopters, such as drivers of inner-city delivery vans with fixed routes—will be key to the electric-vehicle market's longer-term development. By tailoring early products to the needs of these segments, automakers can build a strong base of core buyers whose use will spread word of mouth and drive market momentum. This approach, if supported with targeted actions by national and city governments, power providers, and battery makers, could accelerate the mass production and broad adoption of electric vehicles.

NOTES

1. The study of potential private users of electric cars, conducted in late 2009, was a joint effort by McKinsey, the city authorities of New York and Shanghai, and the French government. Efforts in New York and Shanghai focused on consumer research, including qualitative research that involved individual and group interviews, as well as an extensive quantitative survey of more than 1,000 potential buyers in New York and more than 600 in Shanghai. The Paris research team developed a comprehensive market model to project demand for the greater metropolitan region.

2. The projections take into account expert forecasts of key drivers, such as the price of oil and the cost of electric-car batteries, a limited number of electric-vehicle brands and models available for sale during the time period, a set of incentives (for example, in New York a federal tax credit of up to $7,500 on purchases of electric cars), and a lack of existing public infrastructure for charging car batteries.

LESSONS FROM THE HOUSING CRISIS

By Alex Schwartz

Public discourse on the causes and consequences of the housing crisis, and the appropriate policy responses, has been ideological and partisan. The collapse of the housing bubble in 2007 and the subsequent financial crisis and deep recession could and should have prompted the nation to reconsider many core assumptions about the role of the market in the housing finance system and about the value of homeownership, among many other questions, however, this was not to be. In this essay I draw some lessons from the crisis, both for public policy and for education. To frame the discussion, I first sketch out the state of the nation's housing and mortgage markets as of the spring of 2011, and review the actions that the federal government has taken to date to address the crisis and revive the housing market.

I f there ever was a "teachable moment" in housing policy, it would have been the collapse of the housing bubble in 2007 and the subsequent and intertwined mortgage crisis. The steep downturn in housing prices, greatly diminished construction activity, extraordinarily low residential sales volumes, and surging rates of mortgage default and foreclosure could, and should, have prompted the nation to reconsider several core assumptions and values in U.S. housing policy. Most broadly, these assumptions concern the role of the private market in the housing finance system and the desirability of homeownership.

Unfortunately, 4 years after the crisis threatened to plunge the nation into a financial crisis as bad as the Great Depression, it would appear that the only lessons to be drawn have to do with the intransigence of market orthodoxy, and the political resilience of financial institutions. Public discourse over the origins of the housing and mortgage crises and the appropriate policy responses has been unremittingly partisan and ideological. One needs look no further than the Congressionally

Alex Schwartz, "Lessons from the Housing Crisis," *Family & Consumer Sciences Research Journal*, vol. 40, issue 1, pp. 3–14. Copyright © 2011 by John Wiley & Sons, Inc. Reprinted with permission.

mandated investigation of the crisis for an example of this political and ideological rigidity. Despite overwhelming evidence that the crisis derived primarily from wanton market failures, as well as a failure of regulation, the Republican commissioners refused to sign off on the Commission's report and instead issued minority reports that argued that the crisis was either unavoidable or caused by government intervention in the mortgage and financial markets (Financial Crisis Inquiry Commission, 2011).

In this essay, I will draw some lessons from the crisis, both for public policy and for education. To frame this discussion, I will first sketch out the state of the nation's housing and mortgage markets as of the spring of 2011 and review the actions that the federal government has taken to date to address the crisis and revive the housing market.

The failure of many of the nation's most august financial institutions in 2008, including, among others, AIG, Bear Stearns, Fannie Mae, Freddie Mac, Lehman Brothers, Merrill Lynch, and Washington Mutual, demonstrated that what had been seen as a "subprime" mortgage crisis, serious but contained within a single segment of a much larger and more robust financial system, had spread throughout the system and threatened to undermine it completely. Irresponsible mortgage underwriting had infected the entire financial system. Commercial and investment banks, hedge funds, and other institutions had borrowed to the hilt to invest in securities backed by mortgages that were originated with little if any attention to the borrowers' ability to afford them. Billions if not trillions of dollars in additional securities (synthetic collateralized debt obligations) were backed by credit default swaps that were linked to mortgage-backed securities. The securities were complex and opaque, and of very high risk notwithstanding the AAA-ratings accorded to them by the bond rating agencies whose income derived from the investment firms that were issuing the mortgage-backed securities (Financial Crisis Inquiry Commission, 2011; Immergluck, 2009; Zandi, 2009).

When house prices started to fall, and mortgage defaults and foreclosure began to rise as homeowners were unable to refinance or sell their homes, the value of mortgage-backed securities plummeted, wiping out the capital of virtually all major investment firms, putting their very existence at risk. A complete meltdown of the financial system was averted only by Congress's $700 billion bailout program for banks and other financial institutions and related efforts by the Federal Reserve system to provide liquidity (Congressional Oversight Panel, 2011). These actions prevented the United States from collapsing into a Great Depression, but did not forestall the Great Recession, the most severe economic downturn since the 1930s.

THE CURRENT STATE OF THE HOUSING MARKET

Although the housing crisis peaked in 2008, and the recession officially ended in 2009, conditions in the housing market remain dire. Construction activity and housing prices are still very depressed. Mortgage default and foreclose remain at elevated levels. One-fourth of all homeowners with mortgages are "under water," owing more on their mortgages than their homes are worth (Core Logic, 2011). While some measures of housing affordability show improvement, especially in light of very low interest rates, the number of households with excessive housing cost burdens is at record levels (Table 1).

Table 1: Selected housing market indicators: 2000–2010

	2000	2006	2007	2008	2009	2010	Percent Change		
							2000–2006	2006–2010	2009–2010
Housing Starts (000s)	1,231	1,465	1,046	622	445	471	19.0	–67.8	5.8
Existing Home Sales (000s)	877	1,051	776	485	375	323	19.8	–69.3	–13.9
Case Shiller National Price Index (4th Quarter)	108.07	186.58	170.90	139.54	136.15	130.57	72.6	–30.0	–4.1
% All Mortgages Past Due (4th Quarter)	4.54	4.95	5.82	7.88	9.47	8.22	9.0	66.1	–13.2
% Conventional Subprime Mortgages Past Due (4th Quarter)	NA	13.33	17.31	21.88	25.26	23.01	NA	89.9	–5.1
% Foreclosures Started, All Mortgages	0.29	0.54	0.88	1.08	1.20	1.27	86.2	135.2	4.1
% Foreclosures Started, Conventional Subprime Mortgages (4th Quarter)	NA	2.00	3.71	3.96	3.66	3.36	NA	68.0	–8.2

	1999	2001	2003	2005	2007	2009	Percent Change	
							1999–2009	2007–2009
Households with Severe Cost Burdens (000s)								
Total	12,141	13,330	13,188	16,433	17,140	19458	60.3	13.5
Renter	6,301	6,412	6,477	7,891	7,793	9,000	42.8	15.5
Owner	5,841	6,918	6,711	8,542	9,347	10,458	79.0	11.9

1. Sources: Housing Starts: U.S. Census Bureau, 2011; Home Sales, Mortgages overdue and foreclosures started, U.S. Department of Housing and Urban Development, 2011a and previous issues; Case-Shiller price index, S&P/Case-Shiller Home Price Indices, 2011; Severe housing problems, U.S. Department of Housing and Urban Development, 2011b.

2. Note: Households with severe cost burdens spend at least half of their income on housing-related costs.

Conditions in the residential construction and real estate industry have seldom been so dim. Until the onset of the current crisis, annual housing starts regularly exceeded one million units, averaging more than 1.5 million from 1973 to 2007. But housing starts in 2010 totaled just 587.000, which is 6% above the 554,000 posted in 2009, but more than 67% less than the 1.8 million starts recorded in 2006. Similarly, only 323,000 residential sales transactions were recorded in 2010, down 14% from the year before, and 69% from the 1.05 million sales recorded in 2006.

Home prices remain depressed, and as of early 2011 had been declining for several months in a row, wiping out what little improvement had been made previously. Nationally, the Case-Schiller composite index shows that house prices fell by 30% from the 4th quarter of 2006 to the 4th quarter of 2011. While the largest declines took place in 2008, prices fell further in 2009 and 2010. These are national figures. In the metropolitan areas with the most buoyant housing markets during the years of the bubble (e.g., Phoenix, Las Vegas, Miami), prices today are more than 50% below their peak levels (S&P/Case-Shiller Home Price Indices, 2011).

Mortgage default and foreclosure remain very high. As of the 4th quarter of 2010, 8% of all home mortgages were past due, including 23% of all subprime loans. Foreclosures were started on 1.3% of all mortgages, including 3.4% of all subprime mortgages. While the rate of delinquencies decreased from 2009 to 2010 for subprime and prime mortgages, and the rate of subprime foreclosures also decreased, prime mortgage foreclosures continued to increase.

Another, less widely noted, casualty of the crisis was the financing of subsidized housing for low-income renters. The crisis greatly diminished the market for Low-Income Housing Tax Credits (LITHC) and for tax-exempt bonds issued by state housing finance agencies. The LIHTC had been widely perceived to be one of the most effective subsidy programs in the nation's history for low-income renters. From the program's inception in 1987 through 2006, it has helped finance more than 1.6 million housing units, making it the nation's largest supply side housing subsidy program (Schwartz, 2010). Prior to the crisis, housing developers received close to $1 to cover development costs for each tax-credit dollar, compared to < 50 cents per tax-credit dollar in the early years of the program. However, the financial crisis sharply diminished demand for housing tax credits. The dominant investors in the tax credit program had been major banks and Fannie Mae and Freddie Mac. The latter two institutions, which had acquired about 40% of all LIHTCs in recent years, were effectively nationalized by the federal government and were in no position to purchase additional tax credits. Several major banks and investment firms that had been significant players in the tax-credit market had also gone out of business or had been taken over by other institutions (e.g., Washington Mutual, Lehman Brothers).

The remaining institutions in the market became wary of investing in tax credits, because it was unclear whether their annual income over the next 10 years would be sufficient to warrant the need for tax credits (the LIHTC provides tax credits that can be applied against 10 years of income; if an investor incurs a loss during this period, the tax credits are useless; Belsky & Nipson, 2010; Schwartz, 2010, 2011). As a result, the amount of equity developers received from the syndication of tax-credits declined from about $1 per tax-credit dollar to around 65 cents per tax-credit dollar by August 2009 (Ernst & Young, 2009). This decrease in the "price" of tax credits required developers to secure additional sources of subsidy; otherwise, the projects could not proceed.

The market for the LIHTC improved somewhat in 2010, at least for properties located in major metropolitan areas on the east and west coasts (Belsky & Nipson, 2010). However, the program generates less subsidy for developers than before, and the market remains depressed in many parts of the country, particularly in rural and older industrial areas, and for properties that also involve tax-exempt financing.

The crisis also eviscerated the market for tax-exempt bonds. State housing finance agencies issue such bonds to, among other things, help finance low-income rental housing—and use these bonds in conjunction with LIHTCs (they also issue tax-exempt bonds to finance low-interest mortgages for first-time home buyers). The market collapsed for tax-exempt housing bonds in 2008 and has been very slow to recover. Investors became extremely wary of acquiring bonds associated with any type of housing; moreover, the extraordinarily low interest rates set by the Federal Reserve in the wake of the crisis further diminished demand for tax-exempt bonds (Schwartz, 2010).

Finally, although home ownership is more affordable than it has been in years to households that meet today's stiffer mortgage underwriting criteria, thanks to low interest rates and depressed prices, increasing numbers of homeowners and renters struggle to meet their housing costs. From 2007 to 2009, the number of households who spend 50% or more of their income on housing costs increased by more than 3 million, or 14%. From 2001 to 2009, the incidence of severe cost burden increased by more than 60%, with the increase especially pronounced among home owners.

GOVERNMENT POLICY IN THE WAKE OF THE CRISIS

Although the federal government allocated hundreds of billions of dollars to address the crisis, the results have been disappointing. The bank bailout program, Troubled Asset Relief Program (TARP), staved off the complete collapse of the financial system by injecting billions of dollars into the banking sector, and the Federal Reserve system kept interest rates very low and found ways of lending money at favorable terms to investment banks and other institutions that had previously been ineligible for such support. However, the government's efforts to prevent mortgage foreclosures faltered, and the government has done little to revive the moribund housing sector. The government has provided some funding to help states and localities address the many negative consequences of mortgage foreclosure. From a preventative perspective, Dodd-Frank Wall Street Reform and Consumer Protection Act of 2010 bans many of the mortgage lending and securitization practices that precipitated the crisis (http://banking.senate.gov/public/_files/070110_Dodd_Frank_Wall_Street_Reform_com prehensive_summary_Final.pdf).

Foreclosure Prevention and Housing Market Stabilization

The immediate objective of the Bush and Obama administrations in responding to the ever-escalating crisis, especially after the Bush administration and the Federal Reserve decided to allow Lehman Brothers to go bankrupt, was to prevent major banks and investment firms from failing. Washington decided, at least in the short term, that it was more important to shore up the balance sheets of financial firms than to prevent mortgage foreclosures. Thus, the administration channeled $208.6 billion to 18 banks and financial institutions in the late 2008 but devoted far less to foreclosure prevention and did so in a way that was overly complex, cumbersome, and flawed.

The Obama administration launched its mortgage foreclosure prevention program in early 2009. The program aimed to help eligible homeowners restructure their mortgages so that their debt-service expenses on their first mortgage would not exceed 31% of their gross income. Initially, the administration said that the program would prevent 3–4 million foreclosures. By December 2010, the program had provided permanent mortgage modifications to less than 520,000 homeowners (Congressional Oversight Panel, 2010).

The program fell short of its goals for several reasons. First, it was voluntary, relying on the participation of mortgage "servicers." These loan servicers were typically units of large banks and had several conflicts of interest that may have kept them from cooperating fully with the program. Second, the program was originally devised to assist homeowners with high-cost subprime mortgages, and not the much larger number of households who fell prey to foreclosure because of job loss in the Great Recession. Moreover, the program's eligibility criteria were too narrow. Only households who paid more than 31% of their income on their first mortgage were eligible. Yet, many homeowners paid less than this amount on their first mortgage, but also had second mortgages to pay, which combined with their first mortgage brought their total debt-service payments well above 31%, and this does not deal with other debts that many homeowners carried.

Third, many critics argue that the program should have done more to reduce the outstanding debt carried by distressed homeowners. While the program allowed servicers to reduce loan balances as a way of decreasing debt-service costs, servicers overwhelmingly chose to reduce interest rates instead, or in some cases extend the term of the loan. As a result, the program did very little to address the problem of negative equity—which in extreme cases probably promotes mortgage default and foreclosure (Congressional Oversight Panel, 2010, 2011).

Yet another reason for the disappointing performance of the Obama administration's foreclosure prevention program is that the Senate refused to support a key component. When originally announced, the program was to modify bankruptcy law and allow bankruptcy judges to restructure mortgages for principal residences. While mortgages on second homes and investment properties can be restructured in bankruptcy court, mortgages on one's primary residence cannot. If this portion of the program had passed, it would likely have put pressure on mortgage servicers to modify mortgages more expeditiously; if they did not, bankruptcy judges might modify the loans on less favorable terms. The House passed legislation that would have amended the bankruptcy law with regard to principal residences. The Senate, with banks lobbying vigorously against the proposal, defeated the measure, and it was never reintroduced (Immergluck, 2009).

The administration found some initial success in bolstering the housing market in the wake of the crisis, but to no lasting effect. In 2008, Congress approved a tax credit for home purchases. Originally limited to first-time home-buyers, it was later expanded to include all home purchases up to a certain price. The credit helped generate home sales and helped push prices upwards. After the credit expired in 2010, however, sales volumes and prices fell and have yet to rise (Timiraos, 2011). Mortgage foreclosure and housing abandonment have kept the housing market in the doldrums.

Amelioration

Launched in 2008, the Neighborhood Stabilization Program has provided about $7 billion to states and localities to help them address the blight and housing abandonment associated with mortgage foreclosure. Funding may be used for the acquisition and rehabilitation or redevelopment of vacant properties, demolition of vacant properties, and the establishment of land banks for foreclosed properties. The program has been well received, but the amount of funding is very small in relation to the need (Federal Reserve Banks of Boston and Cleveland, 2010).

In 2008, as part of the administration's economic stimulus legislation, the administration created two programs to supplement the LIHTC. One program provided funding to LIHTC projects that had been stalled because the amount of equity they received from the sale of tax credits was less than the amount budgeted. The other program enabled state housing finance agencies to exchange a portion of their tax-credit allocation with cash grants, thereby obviating the need for finding investors for tax credits in weak markets. The administration proposed additional legislation to further strengthen the tax credit program, but these bills did not win Congressional approval (Schwartz, 2010, 2011).

Crisis Prevention

On July 21, 2010, Congress passed the Dodd-Frank Wall Street Reform and Consumer Protection Act. This far-reaching legislation attempts to prevent the recurrence of financial crisis in the future. Among many other things, it established the Consumer Financial Protection Bureau. Housed within the Federal Reserve System, the bureau sets rules for consumer protections governing all financial institutions offering consumer financial services or products. It also examines and enforces regulations for banks and credit unions with assets of over $10 billion and all mortgage-related businesses, payday lenders, student lenders as well as other large nonbank financial companies such as debt collectors and consumer reporting agencies.

In addition to creating the Consumer Financial Protection Bureau, Dodd-Frank also includes measures designed to reform mortgage lending and prevent a reoccurrence of the inappropriate and often abusive lending practices that thrived during the housing boom. Among other things, the law requires that lenders ensure that borrowers can repay their loans, it prohibits the use of financial incentives that encourage lenders to steer borrowers into more costly loans, it prohibits the imposition of prepayment penalties that can trap borrowers in unaffordable loans, it imposes financial penalties for irresponsible lending, it expands the protections available under federal rules on high-cost loans, and it increases the availability of counseling for prospective home buyers. To discourage the sale of unsustainable mortgages to the secondary market, the law also requires lenders to retain a stake in the mortgages they sell, so that they retain some risk in the event of default (for a complete summary of the law, including measures aimed at reforming other aspects of the financial system, see Brief Summary of the Dodd-Frank Wall Street Reform and Consumer Protection Act 2010. (http://banking.senate.gov/public/_files/070110_Dodd_Frank_Wall_Street_Reform_comprehensive_summary_Final.pdf).

It is far too soon to assess the legislation. Its success will depend on the political support it receives in Congress and from future administrations. Republicans in Congress were opposed to the law and have been attempting to weaken it since its passage. They have sought to withhold funding necessary to write essential regulations; they have sought to change the oversight of the Consumer Protection Bureau from a single individual to a bipartisan committee, and they have threatened to filibuster against the appointment of Elizabeth Warren (the Harvard Law School Professor who originally conceived the financial consumer protection agency) as the head of the bureau. Moreover, many of the law's provisions against inappropriate subprime lending have yet to be tested in practice since the subprime market imploded in 2007 and has yet to revive.

TAKING STOCK

To date, the response to the crisis has been highly partisan, and the debate over the crisis's causes and solutions appear to be ideological and doctrinaire. Most startling perhaps has been the refusal of the political mainstream to question the role that the private market should play in housing finance. Rather than examine how mortgage lenders and investment firms instigated the crisis, under the lax supervision of federal regulators, many prominent economists and financial authorities assert that the crisis resulted from excessive government involvement in the mortgage market. Many of the diagnoses of the crisis proffered by opponents of government regulation are dead wrong:

- *The mortgage crisis was caused by public policies that encouraged low-income people to buy homes they could not afford.* The majority of subprime and other risky mortgages did not go to first-time homebuyers, but to existing homeowners, for mortgage refinancing. In addition, many high-risk home-purchase mortgages were taken out by investors, not owner occupants (Immergluck, 2009). Finally, the national homeownership rate reached its peak in 2004, before mortgage lending standards deteriorated the most.
- *Fannie Mae and Freddie Mac were major causes of the crisis.* Although Fannie and Freddie were far from blameless, having acquired large amounts of (AAA-rated) subprime-backed securities and risky alt-A mortgages, their misguided actions did not precipitate the crisis. The vast majority of high-risk mortgages originated during the housing boom did not conform with Fannie and Freddie's underwriting standards and were not guaranteed by them, but were issued and securitized by other financial firms. Fannie and Freddie's' ill-fated investments resulted primarily from pressure to increase their market share not, from their need to meet Congressionally mandated affordability targets. Mortgages guaranteed by Fannie and Freddie have performed far better than subprime loans. The delinquency rate as of the second quarter of 2010 on loans that conformed with Fannie and Freddie's underwriting standards was 6.8%, compared with 28% among subprime loans (Min, 2011; see also Thomas & Van Order, 2011).
- *The Community Reinvestment Act (CRA) pressed lenders to make inappropriate mortgages.* Most of the lenders in the subprime and alt-A markets were not subject to the CRA, because they were nondepository institutions. The CRA was passed in 1977—30 years before the crisis.

Although the crisis exemplifies many aspects of market failure, much of the debate surrounding the causes of the crisis and legislative proposals to reform the housing finance system assumes that the private market should be central to the housing finance system. The debate over the future of the secondary mortgage market illustrates how little the competence of the market is questioned. Virtually every proposal for restructuring the secondary mortgage market envisions that Fannie and Freddie be "wound down" so that they are eventually dissolved or act as much smaller institutions. In their place would be private institutions that would be responsible for the securitization of home mortgages and receive little if any federal support.

In February 2010, the Obama administration issued a report to Congress that called for the eventual closure of Fannie and Freddie and the establishment of a private housing finance system, outlining three options with varying degrees of government-provided support. Except for the continuation of FHA mortgage insurance for low-income home buyers, the housing finance would be very much dominated by private, for-profit institutions.

According to the report,

> the government's primary role should be limited to robust oversight and consumer protection, targeted assistance for low- and moderate-income homeowners and renters, and carefully designed support for market stability and crisis response ... private markets—subject to strong oversight and standards for consumer and investor protection—will be the primary source of mortgage credit and bear the burden for losses (U.S. Department of Housing and Urban Development and U.S. Treasury, 2011).

Nowhere does the report refer to the many problems the private market has shown over the past 100 years in providing a stable basis for housing finance. Time and again the government has had to intervene when the private market ran aground.

- It was of course the failure of the housing finance system during the Great Depression that prompted the federal government to establish mortgage insurance, Fannie Mae, the 30-year fixed-rate mortgage, and other innovations.
- The federal government's decision to deregulate the savings & loan industry in the 1970s and 1980s so that S&Ls could better adjust to new market dynamics led to the collapse and closure of thousands of lenders. The subsequent federal program to address the S&L crisis cost US taxpayers more than $157 billion and led to a new set of regulations (Schwartz, 2010).
- The mortgage crisis of the 2000s also illustrates the failure of the private market to provide affordable and sustainable mortgages. The crisis stemmed overwhelmingly from the mortgage underwriting and securitization practices of private actors in the mortgage market—mortgage banks and brokers, investment banks, and the bond rating agencies. Most of the lending that fueled the crisis was not subject to federal regulation, and most did not involve Fannie Mae and Freddie Mac (Immergluck, 2009).
- In addition to the propensity of the private market to erupt in periodic crises, it has also often failed to provide equitable access to mortgage credit to minorities. There is a long history of racial discrimination in the mortgage and housing markets (Jackson, 1985; Yinger, 1995). The federal government, especially the FHA, promoted and abetted many of these practices well into the 1970s. However, the profusion of subprime lending was not subject to federal regulation and in many cases was racially discriminatory. Mortgage lenders and brokers frequently targeted minority households for loans they could ill afford and failed to inform them of other less risky mortgage products that they could qualify for (Engel & McCoy, 2008; Immergluck, 2009).

The rigidity of thought on housing matters is not confined to adherents of free-market orthodoxy. Just as many policy analysts and political leaders have refused to question the adequacy of the market in the provision and financing of housing, advocates on the left have also shown little inclination to reconsider their core beliefs. This failure is most apparent in the debate surrounding the Obama administration's proposal to restructure the public housing program so that local housing authorities could borrow from banks to fund much-needed renovations and other capital improvements. The administration introduced Preservation, Enhancement, and Transformation of Rental Assistance (PETRA) in 2009. The legislation would have allowed housing authorities to convert public housing to project-based Section 8, so that the housing would be eligible for rent subsidies based on Fair Market Rents. Authorities could then borrow against this stream of revenue and use the proceeds to pay for essential capital improvements.

At present, public housing is funded through a combination of rental payments, operating subsidies, and capital improvement grants. These sources of revenue fall far short of need. As of 2008, public housing suffered from a backlog of more than $22 billion in essential capital improvements (Schwartz, 2010). Capital improvement grants have never been adequate to renovate more than a small portion of the stock. Partly as a result of chronic underfunding and the aging of the public housing stock, housing authorities have demolished more than 200,000 units of public housing, replacing only a portion of these units. Some authorities, most notably San Diego, have deaccessioned their entire inventory of public housing.

Under PETRA, the enhanced revenue stream made possible by converting public housing to project-based Section 8 would enable authorities to rehabilitate the remaining stock of public housing within a much shorter time frame than would have been possible otherwise. Yet, opponents lambasted the proposal as a feckless form of privatization, in which a public housing facility, a public asset, would be mortgaged and put at risk. In the event of default, banks could foreclose and drive the residents away. Instead, the government should provide the necessary funding directly and not risk the future of public housing.

The critics do not acknowledge that (i) public housing has never been funded adequately, and the prospects for increased governmental subsidy for public housing are highly unlikely; (ii) that without immediate investment, public housing will continue to deteriorate, and more and more will be removed from the program, either through demolition or deaccession (e.g., Lakoff, 2010). They do raise legitimate and important points about the need to ensure tenant protection in the event of default, but rather than engage in a productive discussion on how to best preserve public housing in a hostile political environment, some critics of PETRA have focused on defeating the legislation regardless of the broader threats to public housing.

CONCLUSION

If the housing and mortgage crises were treated as a "teachable moment," they could have occasioned frank and wide ranging discussion on many important issues, including the following:

- To what extent and in what circumstances should homeownership be encouraged for low-income households? What is the minimum amount of equity that households should contribute as a down payment?
- To what extent is innovation necessary in the mortgage market? What were the positive, as opposed to illusory, contributions of financial engineering?

- What are the disadvantages and advantages of having the government play a direct role in setting mortgage underwriting standards and guaranteeing securities based on mortgages that conform to these standards?
- How should fair housing and fair lending laws be updated to address new forms of racial discrimination? How should the CRA be modified to reflect structural changes in the financial sector?
- To what extent should subsidies for low-income renters be dependent on tax incentives rather than on direct expenditures?
- How can the large and growing problem of housing affordability be addressed?

I conclude with two comments on the role of education in preventing housing and mortgage crises from erupting again. First, it is essential to instill historical memory of the crisis and its causes. Courses on housing policy, housing finance, and finance more generally should look at the crisis as a cautionary tale of how the mortgage market can run amuck in the absence of effective regulation. If anything, the crisis teaches us that the mortgage and financial industries cannot be counted upon to regulate themselves, and that one should be very skeptical when successors to Alan Greenspan assert otherwise.

Second, and in a related vein, educators need to offer critical perspectives on the role of markets in the provision of housing. This means not only that educators should teach students about standard economic concepts of market failure. In addition, principles of behavioral economics should be taught so that students may understand the importance of how information (e.g., mortgage terms) is presented influences the choices and decisions consumers make in the housing and mortgage markets. The number and complexity of choices home-buyers need to make to obtain financing can determine the likelihood that they will obtain affordable and sustainable mortgages, and home buyers should have a "default option" that would best serve their needs (Thaler and Sunstein 2008). Finally, students should be exposed to the ways in which housing and mortgage markets operate in other developed countries to underscore the variety of ways by which markets may be structured, regulated, and augmented.

REFERENCES

Belsky, E., & Nipson, M. (2010). *Long-term low income housing tax credit policy questions.* Cambridge, MA: Joint Center for Housing Studies of Harvard University. http://www.jchs.harvard.edu/publications/governmentprograms/long-term_low_income_housing_tax_credit_policy_questions.pdf.

Congressional Oversight Panel. (2010). December Oversight Report: A Review of Treasury's Foreclosure Prevention Programs.

Congressional Oversight Panel. (2011). March oversight report: The final report of the congressional oversight panel.

CoreLogic. (2011). New CoreLogic® Data Shows 23 Percent of Borrowers Underwater With $750 Billion of Negative Equity. Press Release (March 8th).

Engel, K. C., & McCoy, P. (2008). From credit denial to predatory lending: The challenge of sustaining minority homeownership. In J. H. Carr & N. K. Cutty (Eds.), *Segregation: The rising costs for America* (pp. 81–124). New York, NY: Routledge.

Ernst & Young. (2009). *Low-income housing tax-credit survey.* New York, NY: Prepared for Enterprise Community Partners, Inc. and Local Initiatives Support Corporation. http://www.enterprise community.org/public_policy/documents/lihtc_legislative_study.pdf.

Federal Reserve Banks of Boston and Cleveland. (2010). REO & vacant properties: Strategies for neighborhood stabilization. Retrieved May 2, 2011, from http://www.clevelandfed.org/Community_ Development/publications/REO/REO_WEB.pdf.

Financial Crisis Inquiry Commission. (2011). *The financial crisis inquiry report, final report of the National Commission on the Causes of the Financial and Economic Crisis in the United States.* New York, NY: Public Affairs.

Immergluck, D. (2009). *Foreclosed: High-risk lending, deregulation, and the undermining of America's mortgage market.* Ithaca, NY: Cornell University Press.

Jackson, K. (1985). *Crabgrass frontier.* New York, NY: Oxford University Press.

Lakoff, G. (2010). HUD is trying to privatize and mortgage off all of America's Public Housing. Huffington Post (May 21). Retrieved May 8, 2011, from http://www.huffingtonpost.com/george-lakoff/hud-is-trying-to-privatiz_b_585069.html.

Min, D. (2011). *Faulty conclusions based on shoddy foundations. FCIC Commissioner Peter Wallison and other commentators rely on flawed data from Edward Pinto to misplace the causes of the 2008 financial crisis.* Washington, DC: Center for American Progress.

S&P/Case-Shiller Home Price Indices. (2011). Home price index levels and U.S. National Index Levels. Retrieved May 5, 2011, from http://www.standardandpoors.com/indices/sp-case-shiller-home-price-indices/en/us/?indexId=spusa-cashpidff-p-us.

Schwartz, A. (2010). *Housing policy in the United States* (2nd ed.). New York, NY: Routledge.

Schwartz, A. (2011). The credit crunch and subsidized low income housing: The UK and US experience compared. *Journal of Housing and the Built Environment, 23*(3).

Thaler, R. H., & Sunstein, C. (2008). *Nudge: Improving decisions about health, wealth, and happiness.* New Haven, CT: Yale University Press.

Thomas, J., & Van Order, R. (2011). A closer look at Fannie Mae and Freddie Mac: What we know, what we think we know and what we don't know. Draft Paper, George Washington University, Department of Finance (March).

Timiraos, N. (2011). Home-buyer tax credits: Worth the cost? Wall Street Journal (June 1). Retrieved June 12, 2011, from http://blogs.wsj.com/developments/2011/06/01/home-buyer-tax-credits-worth-the-cost/

U.S. Census Bureau. (2011). New residential construction. Retrieved May 12, 2011, from http://www.census.gov/const/www/newresconstindex.html.

U.S. Department of Housing and Urban Development. (2011a). Worst case housing needs 2009.

U.S. Department of Housing and Urban Development. (2011b). U.S. housing market conditions 1st quarter 2011 (May). Retrieved May 5, 2011, from http://www.huduser.org/portal/periodicals/ushmc/spring11/USHMC_1q11.pdf.

U.S. Department of Housing and Urban Development and U.S. Treasury. (2011). Reforming America's housing finance market. A report to Congress. (Feb.).

Yinger, J. (1995). *Closed doors, opportunities lost: The continuing costs of housing discrimination.* New York, NY: Russell Sage Foundation.

Zandi, Mark. (2009). *Financial shock: Global panic and government bailouts—how we got here and what must be done to fix it* (Updated ed.). New York, NY: FT Press.

CONSUMER TOPIC 5.1

Lemon Law Q & A

Source: California Department of Consumer Affairs (2012). Lemon Law Q & A. Retrieved from: http://www.dca.ca.gov/publications/consumer.shtml

Q1. Does California's Lemon Law apply to my vehicle?

A. The Lemon Law covers the following new and used vehicles that come with the manufacturer's new vehicle warranty:

- Cars, pickup trucks, vans, and SUVs.
- The chassis, chassis cab, and drive train of a motor home.
- Dealer-owned vehicles and demonstrators.
- Many vehicles purchased or leased primarily for business use.
- Vehicles purchased or leased for personal, family, or household purposes.

Q2. What if the manufacturer or dealer can't fix my vehicle?

A. If the manufacturer or dealer can't repair a serious warranty defect in your vehicle after a "reasonable" number of attempts, the manufacturer must either:

- Replace the vehicle; or
- Refund its purchase price (whichever you prefer)

Q3. What is a "reasonable" number of repair attempts?

A. There is no set number. However, California's Lemon Law Presumption contains these guidelines for determining when a "reasonable" number of repair attempts have been made:

- The manufacturer or dealer hasn't fixed the same problem after four or more at attempts; or
- Your vehicle's problems could cause death or serious bodily injury if it is driven, and the manufacturer or dealer has made at least two unsuccessful repair attempts; or
- The vehicle has been in the shop for more than 30 days (not necessarily in a row) for repair of any problems covered by its warranty. This is called the Lemon Law Presumption.

"California's Lemon Law Q & A," http://www.dca.ca.gov/acp/pdf_files/lemonlaw_qa.pdf. Copyright © by California Department of Consumer Affairs. Reprinted with permission.

Q4. **Do I need to go to court for the Lemon Law to help me?**

A. No. In many cases the manufacturer of your vehicle may offer a state-certified arbitration program that may assist you in resolving your dispute. If so:

- You must request arbitration in order to claim the benefits of the Lemon Law Presumption; and
- You may accept or reject the arbitrator's decision.

Q5. **I bought my vehicle used with no warranty. Does California's Lemon Law still apply to my vehicle?**

A. No. The Lemon Law applies only to disputes involving the manufacturer's new vehicle warranty.

CONSUMER TOPIC 5.2

To Loan or to Lease

There are many important differences to consider when you are deciding whether to get a loan to purchase a car or lease a car from a dealership. Use the chart below to help you make the best choice for your budget and needs:

Car loans versus car leases

FACTORS	CAR LOANS	CAR LEASES
Ownership potential	Car belongs to you and the bank that gave you the loan until you have paid off the loan. Then, the car becomes yours.	You are essentially renting the car from the dealership. The lease is like a rental agreement. You make monthly payments to the dealership for a set number of years. But the car does not belong to you. When the lease ends, you have to return the car to the dealership.
Wear and tear	No additional costs for wear and tear in your loan agreement.	Most leases charge you extra money for any damage found at the end of the lease that goes beyond "normal wear and tear."

(continued)

"Buying a Car: To Loan or to Lease?" http://69.0.254.19/wwMS/english/InfoBooth/011.htm, Federal Deposit Insurance Corporation. Copyright in the Public Domain.

Car loans versus car leases (*continued*)

FACTORS	CAR LOANS	CAR LEASES
Monthly payments	Payments are higher; however, at the end of the loan, you own the car.	Payments are lower because you are not purchasing the car; the dealership still owns it. Once your lease ends, you turn the car back in and the dealership can sell it or lease it to another customer. You may decide to purchase the car at the end of the lease; however, the total cost ends up being more than it would have been if you had bought the car instead of leasing it.
Mileage limitations	No mileage restrictions.	Leases restrict the number of miles you can drive the car each year. If you exceed the mileage allowed, you have to pay the dealer for each mile over the limit, according to your lease. For example, a dealer may charge you 15 cents for every mile that you drive over 24,000 miles in 2 years. If you drive the car an additional 3,000 miles, you would owe the dealer $450 for those miles.
Auto insurance	May cost more during the loan than it will after the loan is repaid because the lender may require more coverage, but usually still less expensive than auto insurance for leased cars.	Usually costs more if you lease a car than it does if you buy. Most car leases require you to carry higher levels of coverage than purchase agreements do. Some insurance carriers may also consider leasing to be higher risk than purchasing.
Cost	Probably will cost more in the short term than a car lease; your total loan and monthly payments are likely to be higher. However, once the loan is repaid, the car is yours.	Probably will cost less in the short term than a car purchase; your total loan and monthly payments are likely to be lower. However, if you exceed the mileage on a leased car and/or decide to buy it outright once your lease has expired, it will end up costing you more.

Make sure you find out what the requirements are and get a cost estimate from your insurance company before you decide whether to lease or buy. Remember, you will have to have insurance coverage for your new car before you can legally drive it away from the dealership.

CONSUMER TOPIC 5.3

Are You Ready to Buy a Home?

The following questions will help you to determine if you are ready to buy a home:

QUESTION	YES	NO
Do you have a steady source of income? This usually means having a job or other source of income.		
Have you been employed on a regular basis for 2–3 years?		
Is your income reliable?		
Do you have a credit history? Have you ever borrowed money for any purpose?		
Do you have a good record of paying bills?		
Are you able to pay your bills and other debts?		
Do you have the ability to make a mortgage payment every month, plus handle additional costs for taxes, insurance, maintenance, and repairs?		
Do you have money saved for a down payment and closing costs?		

The down payment is the portion of the home's purchase price the buyer pays in cash. The more you have for a down payment, the less you will need to borrow. Some states offer first-time homebuyer assistance programs. Lenders prefer that you have 20 percent of the purchase price for a down payment. For example, 20 percent of a $100,000 mortgage is $20,000. However, there are many special programs that you can participate in that require a smaller or no down payment.

"Buying a Home: Are You Ready to Buy a Home?" http://69.0.254.19/wwMS/english/InfoBooth/013.htm, Federal Deposit Insurance Corporation. Copyright in the Public Domain.

Mortgage insurance protects the lender if you default on the loan. It is an additional cost of the mortgage. Closing costs are the charges related to transferring the ownership of the property. The lender must tell you what these costs are.

If You Answered "Yes" to All These Questions ...
... you may be ready to buy a home.

If You Answered "No" to Any of Them ...
... you might need to strengthen those areas first. To strengthen any areas, or to learn more about buying a home, look for homebuyer education classes in your area. These classes are a good source of information and will help prepare you for home ownership.

CASE STUDY

Maya and John are still living in their small one-bedroom apartment in Encino, when their baby girl Vanessa is starting to sit up. They are afraid that when Vanessa starts to crawl, she'd be getting into stuff and they just feel so cramped in their apartment.

Feeling restless and frustrated by their living conditions, Maya and John start looking for a place to buy in the Valley. They have a combined income of $57,000 per year; they have an auto loan payment of $200 per month and a student loan of $250 per month. The couple has $45,000 in their checking and savings accounts.

Help Maya and John find a housing unit they can afford, support your answer using appropriate financial guidelines.

Suppose that they are going to buy the house you suggested; and they are willing and able to put 20% as the down payment, what would be the amount of the mortgage loan? And approximately how much they would need to pay for the closing costs?

Maya and John want to take out a mortgage for 30 years. Assuming they can get a mortgage rate of 4.5 percent. Estimate their monthly PITI expenditures.

CONSUMER RESOURCES:

Checking history of vehicles: http://www.carfax.com
Consumer Reports: http://www.consumerreports.org
Kelley Blue Book: http://www.kbb.com
Leasing information: http://www.leaseguide.com
National Highway Traffic Safety Administration: http://www.nhtsa.gov
Mortgage Bankers Association: http://www.homeloanlearningcenter.com
National Association of Realtors: http://www.realtor.org
U.S. Department of Housing and Urban Development: http://www.hud.gov

CHAPTER 6

CONSUMERS IN THE GLOBAL MARKET

CHAPTER 6 INTRODUCTION

Can you imagine a company that has banks, supermarkets, bookstores, fire brigades, police stations, hospitals, and its own television networks on its campuses; most astonishingly, on just one particular campus there are over 400,000 employees. This is the company that makes your iPhone but no, it is not Apple. It is a company 7,000 miles away in China. Even a company of that size cannot do it all. The manufacture of this small gadget resembles the global market we are living in today: the phone is designed at the Apple headquarters in California; the parts and technologies are from U.S., Japan, Germany, and South Korea, and then it is assembled in China. We are global consumers even we only spend our money locally: 98% of clothing we buy in the U.S. are imported from abroad, 96% of the toys are from foreign countries, and 45% of oil consumed in the U.S. are imported. Globalization certainly brings us more than foreign products, and being a global consumer can have impacts on every facet of our lives.

THE ANCIENT ROAD

An Overview of Globalization

Terry Clark, Monica Hodis, and Paul D'Angelo

INTRODUCTION

The world entered a period of accelerating change in the decades following World War II (WWII). One aspect of this change was the rise and spread of Western Multinational Corporations (MNCs). Primarily in pursuit of markets and profits, MNCs incidentally took production, finance, management and marketing know-how to almost every country on earth. In more recent decades, the invention and worldwide diffusion of electronic media and communication technologies have accelerated the adoption of what had been local or national (mainly Western) tastes in music, food, fashion, and movies across the entire world. Today, nuanced teenage fashion innovations in New York or London spread quickly to Rio and Delhi via MTV. Similarly, the Internet now makes it possible for a professor from Orissa, India, teaching in Saskatoon, Canada, to keep up with the daily news in Bhubaneshwar (capital of Orissa), in her mother tongue (Oriya), by visiting *The Samaja* online (http://www.thesamaja.com/).

A single word points to theses and a host of related changes: globalization. Although there is much disagreement about what globalization is and what exactly it is doing, paradoxically, a statement such as 'globalization is reshaping the lives of the peoples of the world' seems beyond dispute. Over the past 30 years, 'globalization' has gone from being an ethereal 'pie-in-the-sky' concept, to a hotly debated idea, which some people believed had no referent in the real world, to the current widely accepted view that it is something that is revolutionizing and reshaping human life around the world. Today, globalization is accepted by all but a few academic curmudgeons (e.g., 'The evidence is in and it shows that globalization is a myth'[2] (Rugman 2003, p. 409)) as an incontestable reality.

Terry Clark, Monica Hodis, and Paul D'Angelo, "The Ancient Road: An Overview of Globalization," *The SAGE Handbook of International Marketing*, ed. Masaaki Kotabe and Kristiaan Helsen, pp. 15–35. Copyright © 2009 by Sage Publications. Reprinted with permission.

Yet, globalization is a reality we know little about—or rather, one we are only beginning to fathom and to understand.

Before the mid-1980s there was little serious discussion of globalization *per se* in the mainstream academy (notable exceptions include Marx and Engels 1848; McLuhan 1964; Wallerstein 1975). Virtually all of the now burgeoning literature on the subject was published after 1985. One reason for this is that globalization was 'discovered' simultaneously and independently across a variety **[p. 16]** of unrelated disciplines. Contact between these disciplines was infrequent and fragmentary. The result has been that theories of globalization developed in isolation. For example, distinct perspectives on globalization emerged in: philosophy (e.g., Collins 2000); literature (e.g., Brennan 1997; Landow 2006); engineering (Reader 2006); sociology (e.g., Sklair 1991); geography (e.g., Herod, O Tuathail and Roberts 1998); meteorology (e.g., Eddy, Ceschger and Oeschger 1993); labor relations (e.g., Munck 2002); ecology (e.g., Karliner 1997); anthropology (e.g., Lewellen 2002; Edelman 1999); media studies (e.g., Albarran and Chan-Olmsted 1998; Rantanen 2004); music (e.g., Taylor 1997; Baumann and Fujie 2000); psychology (e.g., Sampson 1989; Lewis and Araya 2002); public health (e.g., Barnett and Whiteside 2006; Murray and Lopez 2002), criminology and law enforcement (e.g., Friman and Andreas 1999; Hagedorn 2007); feminism and women's studies (e.g., Eschle 2001); ethics (e.g., Kung 1998); linguistics (e.g., Crystal 1997); education (Burbules 2000; Monkman and Stromquist 2000); higher education (e.g., Currie and Newson 1998); and law (e.g., Shapiro and Brilmayer 1999).

Despite what is now an immense literature, the exact meaning (and even significance) of globalization continues to be the subject of intense debate. A full assessment has been hindered by the fact that dialogue between the various disciplines has been limited, in part because jargons and methodologies differ, but also because scholars naturally tend to focus on those aspects of globalization which are of immediate relevance to their traditional foci. Today, it is increasingly clear that the fragmented views are all pointing to the same phenomenon (Clark and Knowles 2003): globalization. The purpose of this essay is to survey the concept, and specifically to try to understand what it means for International Business (IB) scholars and practitioners. In order to make discussion intelligible, we begin by developing a definition for globalization.

DEFINITION

No consistent, generally accepted or satisfying definition for globalization has emerged from IB. This problem is not limited to IB. In part, the definitional void stems from the fact that the word 'global' has been used in a variety of often contradictory ways (see Clark and Knowles 2003), leading to confusion about the topic and about what any particular author is saying. Indeed, in IB, there has been considerable resistance to embracing a view of globalization that is not strictly trade and/or economics-centric (typical of this perspective are the views of leading IB scholar Alan Rugman (e.g., 2001 and 2003)). The definitional void has been worsened by disciplinary isolation. Scholars naturally want focus on aspects of globalization that have immediate relevance to their own disciplinary interests. However, in doing so, they miss the important fact that globalization is a hugely complex phenomena, with a domain possibly encompassing, or at least touching, all other disciplinary domains.

We begin with the truism that globalization is a phenomena affecting the whole world. In that context, Wallerstein (1975) develops the concept of 'world-system' as a sort of historically evolving planet-wide social system. He offers two examples of such systems—world-empires, and world-economies. For Wallerstein, globalization is simply the dénouement of historical processes, animated primarily by trade, political and military powers. Globalization is what the world-system has evolved into in the modern world. Implicit in Wallerstein's world-system is the idea of 'world subsystems'. A world sub-system is a component of the world-system, relating to a specific and limited set of phenomena, having planet-wide extension. Emerging and/or existing world sub-systems include such things as inflation/interest rates; business cycles; fashion/pop music; technical/professional standards; consumption behaviors; diseases; and media.

Perusal of definitions suggests three common factors in most conceptualizations of globalization: (1) integration of national/regional phenomena into world sub-systems; (2) the process(es) by which this integration occurs; and (3) mechanisms that facilitate integration, by transmitting influence from one location to another. Building on these points, developed by Clark and Knowles (2003), we extend the definition as follows:

DEFINITION OF GLOBALIZATION

The process by which economic, political, cultural, social, and other systems of nations are integrating into world sub-systems is called Globalization:

Although this definition is general, it is not limiting. It embodies the central idea many have been struggling to articulate and model in their own disciplinary contexts, using their own metrics, models, and theories. The definition also conceptualizes globalization as a dynamic process, proceeding in different ways and in varying degrees with different phenomena, and allows for the possibility of having no affect at all. Furthermore, the definition posits two meta-categories of phenomena: world sub-systems and the world system—the presumed dénouement of the globalizing process. This dénouement is, in all probability, hypothetical, occurring if at all, at some indeterminate point in the future. However, the phase plane leading towards that dénouement (partial world and sub-world systems) is of great and tangible interest. Assuming metrics appropriate for a given situation (economic, cultural, social, etc.), the definition also provides a framework for capturing the rate at which globalization is proceeding in particular contexts.

The definition is illustrated in Figures 2.1a, 2.1b and 2.1c. Figure 2.1a represents a stylized autarkic world of impermeable (vertical) boundaries, in which nation-states have absolutely no interactions with each other. In it, all cultural, political, technological, economic, disease systems, etc., are contained strictly within the national system and develop **[p. 18]** idiosyncratically without reference to or benefit from the systems of other nation-states. This represents one end of the globalization continuum.

In Figure 2.1b, boundaries between nation-states now have some degree of permeability (indicated by the dotted portions of the vertical boundaries), allowing the systems within nation-states to influence those of other nations. This influence could be in the way of trade, travel, technology transfer, communication, etc. Such influences may be planned (e.g., technology transfer), or unplanned (e.g., a radio station's footprint extending beyond its intended market, into another country). Note also the emergence of world sub-systems (represented by horizontal dotted lines). These sub-systems represent what happens when national systems interact more broadly and openly, and so meld to become a new and emergent system, common to all nations (e.g., fashion, professional standards, language, etc.). This represents a midpoint in the globalization continuum.

In Figure 2.1c, all boundaries between nation-states are fully permeable, at all levels, allowing for unfettered intermingling of national systems. Note the dominance (over national systems) of the many world subsystems and the emergence of a true world-system. This represents the other end of the globalization continuum.

HISTORY OF AN IDEA

How new is globalization? Answers to this question will be dependent upon how one defines the term. If globalization is defined strictly in terms of trade and economics (e.g., post-WWII international institutions and the rise and spread of Multinational Corporations (MNCs) (Vernon 1973; Rugman 2001)), etc., then the answer is clearly that it is a recent phenomenon. However, nothing could be further from the truth. Indeed, many scholars understand globalization to have its origins in the fifteenth and sixteenth centuries, others argue it is of more ancient lineage, and that it has been operating in different ways, and to different degrees in every age (see, for example, Wallerstein 1975; Braudel 1984; Chanda 2007). This possibility is reflected in the definition developed above, which characterized globalization, neither in terms of technology nor MNC activities (the main drivers of globalization according to some), but rather in terms of processes, which may be ancient and/ or modern, that are integrating world subsystems into world sub-systems. Given that technology *per se* is not the central issue driving globalization (although, it may certainly accelerate it), we are free to seek globalization's roots prior to the twentieth century, and indeed, prior to the industrial revolution.

Our views of globalization are often weighted heavily by events subsequent to WWII. For example, the justly influential *Sovereignty at Bay* (Vernon, 1973), paints a picture of the rise and seemingly inexorable spread of US MNCs throughout the world, and of the often unintended changes they brought with them. In this way, it is tempting to see globalization as beginning in 1945 and co-evolving with rising US economic power. However, this view is historically myopic, and simply inaccurate. Even if globalization has accelerated since WWII (which it surely has), it has been developing for a very long time. There is much evidence to support this view. For example, Chanda (2007) explains globalization in terms of the ancient (and modern) activities of business people (traders); religious missionaries (preachers); explorers (adventurers); and soldiers (warriors). His argument is that these four classes of human beings/human activities unwittingly became agents in the grand historical process of world integration—globalization. Chanda's chronology provides some compelling illustrations. For example:

We can extend Chanda's point by considering how, from ancient times, migration, cartography, linguistic trends, religion and economics have all either reflected, or been agents in the ancient globalizing trend:

To sum up the discussion in this section, we conclude that globalization is clearly not a recent phenomenon. To ignore this fact would perpetuate IB's disciplinary isolation, and encourage an idiosyncratic view of the subject. Acknowledgment of globalization's ancient lineage makes richer, wider, and deeper theorizing possible. Moreover, it **[p. 18]** throws open a wide door for data gathering, and for the examination of the forces behind the process. Readers interested in a fuller discussion of this point should peruse the classic works by Wallerstein (2001) and Polanyi (1947), the enlightening essays by Kysucan (2001) and Holub (2001), and Chanda's (2007) interesting book.

HISTORY OF A WORD

Although, as we have shown, the process of globalization is ancient, our awareness of it is not. Indeed, the term 'globalization' itself is of relatively recent origin. In this section, we provide a brief background on the use of this humble word which is now used to characterize our age.

Human beings seem always to have had an appetite for labeling times—those past, and those in which they live,—'stone age', 'age of discovery', 'age of reason', 'silver age', the 'enlightenment', etc. More recently, the 1950s were dubbed the 'atomic age', the 1960s the 'industrial society', the 1970s 'late capitalism', the 1980s the 'risk society', and the 1990s the 'postmodern society'. The grand successor to these (and all such) epithets is the term 'globalization'. Whatever meaning is implied by this word 'globalization', and whatever controversy surrounds it, it has become the label *nonpareil* for the world in which we live today.

'Globalization' derives from 'globe' and 'global', geometric terms used to describe spheres. Use of 'global' to refer specifically to the earth is over 400 years old (Waters 1995). By extension, and in common usage, the term was also used in reference to things related to, influencing, or covering the world, taken as a whole (Elden 2005). However, the term was not used in reference to travel until the 1890s, and in reference to trade until the 1950s. Probably the first use of the term in English, in the way it is used today, was in a 1959 *Economist* article reporting an increase in Italy's 'globalized quota' for imports of cars (Waters 1995). Shortly afterwards, the 1961 Merriam-Webster dictionary included definitions of 'globalism' and 'globalization' (ibid.). The entry traced uses of 'global' back to 1640, and 'globalization' to 1951. The Oxford English Dictionary's first example of the word's use, from the October 1962 *Spectator*, notes that: 'Globalisation[4] is, indeed, a staggering concept'.

But the word (or at least the thing it was to represent) was not limited to English. Similar concepts also emerged outside the English-speaking world. In the German-speaking world the term 'weltanschauung',[5] introduced as a neologism by Kant in the eighteenth century, gradually evolved into the notion of an all-encompassing idea of the universe and of man's relation to it. More recently, around the time of their appearance in English language publications, the French words 'mondialization' and 'globalization', were used in *Le Monde* (Worthington 2001). The term 'mondialisation' was explicitly and extensively discussed in the French journal *Arguments* in the 1950s (Elden 2006). Although 'mondialization' and 'globalization' are clearly related, they are not identical. For example, as Axelos explains:

> ... *globalization* is a kind of mondialization without the world ... Globalization names a process which universalizes technology, economy, culture. But it remains empty. The world as an *opening* is missing. The world is not the physical and historical totality, it is not the more or less empirical ensemble of theoretical and practical ensembles. It deploys itself. (Kostas Axelos in Elden 2005, p. 3)[6]

Abstract and vague though it is, this discussion clearly argues for the adoption of a world-embracing gestalt, because humanity was entering a planetary (global) era. Viewed from the vantage point of 2007, the discussion certainly reflects, at the least, a kind of proto-globalization and presages the notion of a global society and of globalization, as we understand the terms today.

Marshal McLuhan was the first to articulate the modern idea of globalization in his discussions of a 'global village', opening the way to the current usage of the terms global **[p. 21]** and globalization: '... we have extended our central nervous system itself in a global embrace, abolishing both space and time as far as our planet is concerned' (McLuhan 1964, p. 3).

McLuhan's insight was almost prophetic of things to come—of the time (through which we are now living) when technology and communications were to revolutionize human life on the planet. Long before the Internet, McLuhan understood that media was in some sense integrating the humanity, creating a global community not unlike a small village. Interestingly, he saw communication, not trade nor technology *per se* as the key driver.

Although McLuhan articulated the concept with uncanny clarity in the 1960s, globalization was not to become academically significant until around the mid-1980s (Robertson 1992). Despite a slow start, the globalization literature has, by some accounts, emerged at a faster rate than the process itself! (Guillen 2001).

'Globalization' entered the vocabulary of business practitioners and academics via Levitt's classic 1983 *HBR* article 'Globalization of Markets'. This article sets out with manifesto-like cadence to articulate the world Levitt saw emerging. And, although Marx and Engels used quite different vocabularies, the similarities between the worlds envisaged by the *Communist Manifesto* and Ted Levitt are startling. Levitt argued that:

> 'A powerful force drives the world towards a converging commonality ... a new commercial reality—the emergence of global markets for standardized consumer Products ... Gone are accustomed differences in national or regional preferences' (p. 92)

Because consumer preferences were being homogenized, global corporations were encouraged to bring standardized products at lower prices to markets worldwide. Cosmopolitanism was becoming '... the property and defining characteristics of all sectors everywhere in the world' (Levitt 1983, p. 101); different cultural preferences, national tastes, standards, and business institutions were seen now as vestiges of a past that was being falsely perpetuated by misguided corporations that erroneously customized their international offering.

Levitt uses the words 'globe', 'global', and 'globalization' over 50 times throughout his account. While his views on globalization are now viewed as somewhat crude, and have either been discredited or modified considerably, his 1983 account remains seminal, both for what he tried to describe, and for the vocabulary he brought to the task, and into the lives of IB practitioners and scholars.

MEASURING GLOBALIZATION

Any idea that purports to be as extensive, as all-encompassing and as (potentially) world-changing as globalization, could never hope to remain a 'mere' concept for very long. The stakes are simply too high. While the academic pioneers of globalization theory struggled to give empirical expression to what they were describing, they also felt the need for tangible ammunition on the polemical front. Similarly, national and international policy advocates, feeling an obligation to respond to what they believed was a momentous historical phenomena, needed something more than narrative arguments to convince skeptics. Hence, there have been numerous attempts to develop quantitative measures of globalization. Interestingly, none of these efforts to quantify globalization does so *in toto*. Rather, they all quantify globalization at either level of the nation-state or at the level of the organization (MNC). We briefly describe and evaluate two measures that take a nation-state perspective, and one that takes an MNC-perspective.

The Swiss Institute for Business Cycle Research (the Konjunktur for schungsstelle, der ETH Zürich, or more simply KOF), developed a globalization index based on an assessment of cross-border economic, social and political activities in 122 countries. Their longitudinal data set covers the period **[p. 22]** 1970–2005, and attempts to capture economic flows and restrictions, information flows and personal contacts across national boundaries, as well as cultural proximity between countries. The index is developed by applying a series of nested weightings (determined using principle components analysis), to the various data sets. For example, economic activities are weighted 36%, social activities 38%, and political activities 26%. Each of these general categories is broken down into sub-areas, each of which receives a weighting within the category. For example, 'social activities' is broken down into 'data on personal contact' (29%), 'data on information flows', (35%) and 'data on cultural proximity' (37%).

Finally, these subcategories are broken down into specific, weighted and measurable items. For example, 'data on cultural proximity' is broken down into the number of McDonald's restaurants per capita (40%), the number of IKEA stores per capita (40%), and trade in books as a percentage of GDP (20%). All in all, the index uses 25 specific empirical measures. These are combined using the weights (as shown above), into a single globalization index for each country. A sampling of these is shown in Table 2.1.

Management consultancy firm A. T. Kearney, in collaboration with *Foreign Policy* magazine, also developed a widely influential metric of globalization. The A. T. Kearny/ *Foreign Policy* globalization index (hereafter the ATK/FP index) is quite similar to the KOF index in that it identifies conceptual areas of global integration, and breaks them down in various ways to arrive at specific empirical measures. These measures are weighted and combined to build up the numerical indices for the general categories. The four components of globalization the ATK/FP envisages are: (1) Economic integration (unbundled into trade and FDI inflows and outflows); (2) Cross-border personal contacts (unbundled into cross-border travel and tourism, telephone traffic, remittances and personal transfers; (3) Technological connectivity (unbundled into the number of Internet users, Internet hosts, and secure servers); and (4) Political engagement (unbundled into the country's membership in representative international organizations, contributions to UN peace-keeping, ratification of certain multilateral treaties, and governmental transfer payments and receipts). Unlike the KOF index, which assigns weights to the components using a statistical technique, the ATK/FP index assigns component weightings somewhat arbitrarily (e.g., triple weighting on FDI and double weighting). However, in other respects, the ATK/FP index is more sophisticated in that the index is normalized, adjusted for country/economy size, and more amenable for longitudinal comparisons. A sampling of the ATK/FP index is shown in Table 2.2.

An alternative perspective to measuring globalization from the perspective of nation-states can be found in UNCTAD's [p. 23] 'Transnationality Index' (TNI). Although ostensibly a measure of how internationalized MNCs are, the TNI can also be construed as reflecting organizational responses to globalization (or, perhaps, reflecting the degree to which MNCs are driving globalization). As such, it represents an interesting supplement to the KOF and ATK/FP globalization indices. TNI is calculated by averaging a firm's ratios of: (1) foreign assets to total assets; (2) foreign sales to total sales; and (3) foreign employment to total employment (UNCTAD 2005). The resulting index reflects each firm's degree of engagement in world trade. Put another way, it suggests the extent of the firm's response to globalization. As such, it provides insight lacking in the more general indices described above. A sampling of the TNI is shown in Table 2.3.

Alternatively, the TNI may be interpreted as providing insight into one of the vehicles of globalization. For example, by aggregating firms by industry, it is possible to identify [p. 24] which sectors of the world economy are the most integrated, or most globalized (Ietto-Grillies and Seccombe-Hett 1997). Table 2.4 provides a sampling of industry TNIs.

One of the problems with many definitions of globalization is that while they help us to imagine, classify and describe a large-scale phenomena, which many believe is transforming the world, they are so general that they don't easily lend themselves to empirical examination. On the other hand, the quantitative indices that have been developed (including those mentioned above), leave one wondering what to do with statements such as 'Belgium has a globalization index of 92.09, while Burundi has a globalization index of 22.41' (KOF 2008 Globalization Index). All economic indices are abstractions of 'life on the ground', of what real people are doing in and with their lives. As such, perhaps, at the margin, viewed collectively, the measures of globalization outlined above may be interpreted as connective nerves into the living heart of globalization. However, our views of what globalization is might well change, suggesting that what we believe is indicative that globalization will change too. Moreover, the technologies driving communication, travel, etc. today could change in unimaginable ways (as they have in the past), shifting the dynamic, speed, content, and even the locus of globalization. Thus, a strong caveat is suggested in the use of all current quantitative globalization indices: none of them measures globalization *per se*. What they do measure are variables and vectors, believed to be significantly indicative of the historic process we call globalization, as it is progressing at the present time, in the context of present political, cultural technological regimes. Globalization indices (those above, and others) are used in three ways: (1) in the popular press, to illustrate stories on globalization (e.g., Chen 2007); (2) by NGOs as polemical ammunition in a variety of policy debates (e.g., Gutierrez 2007); and (3) by economic and business academic researchers in combination with other quantitative variables in pursuit of a variety of research questions (e.g., Baily and Solow 2001).

A less grandiose and perhaps more useful and tractable approach to gaining empirical insight into globalization is suggested by Clark and Knowles (2003), in the form of four questions: 'What are the pertinent integrating mechanisms [of globalization]?'; 'In which direction is [globalization's integrating] influence flowing?'; 'What is the strength of the [various integrating mechanisms'] influence?' 'Which factors inhibit globalization?' (p. 367). These questions suggest a way out of the 'grand-index' trap. They also open up novel ways of thinking about globalization. Perhaps more importantly, they imply a multidisciplinary agenda for globalization studies in IB.

PARADOXES OF GLOBALIZATION

A paradox is a statement or proposition, contrary to received opinion, or seemingly opposed to common sense: yet it is true. In this context, there are many unexamined beliefs surrounding globalization, which when unbundled and considered in the cold light of reason, are in fact not true. Put another way, there are several globalization paradoxes which are worth examining. In this section, we look at five of these: the philosophical, the logical, the economic, the Americanization, and the emotional paradoxes.

PHILOSOPHICAL PARADOX

For many, globalization is seen as the invention of Western corporations and of American Business Schools: MBAs are its evangelists. Anti-globalization protests in Madrid in 1994, in London, Seattle and elsewhere in 1999, and at the G-8 meeting in Genoa in 2001, were fueled in large measure by a somewhat misguided and popularized understanding of anti-globalization thinkers John Zerzan and Arundhati Roy. This perspective understands globalization to be a new and dangerous idea, foisted on the world by multinational corporations in pursuit of profit. The scenario goes further to pit grass-roots and local interests against 'evil' global corporations.

The paradox is that Karl Marx and Friedrich Engels were the first to describe globalization—and they did so in 1848! It should be noted that while Marx, the economist, and Marx, the political scientist, have largely been discredited, Marx, the sociologist, remains relevant (e.g., Tushman and Nelson 1990; Clegg, Hardy, Lawrence and Nord 2006). It is in this context that the remarkable picture of globalization painted by Marx should be seen. Moreover, as mentioned above, the Communist Manifesto bears some striking resemblances to Levitt's 1983 description of globalization. Consider the following excerpts (arcane words such as *bourgeoisie, proletarian,* etc. have been replaced by more modern terms, to highlight the remarkable picture Marx and Engels paint:

> Modern industry has established the world market ... This market has given an immense [boost to the] development [of] ... communication ... [which] ... in turn ... [further emphasizes] the extension of [Western corporate] industry ... From http://www.anu.edu.au/polsci/marx/classics/manifesto.html
>
> The need of a constantly expanding market for its products [pushes corporations] ... over the entire surface of the globe ... [they] ... must nestle everywhere, settle everywhere, establish connections everywhere (ibid.)
>
> [Multinational Corporations have] ... through ... [their] exploitation of the world market, given a cosmopolitan character to production and consumption in every country ... old-established national industries have been destroyed or are daily being destroyed. They are dislodged by new [global] industries ... [which draw] ... raw material ... from the remotest [parts of the earth] ... whose products are consumed ... in every [part] ... of the globe. In place of the old wants ... we find new wants, requiring for their satisfaction the products of distant lands ... (ibid.)
>
> National differences and antagonism ... are daily ... vanishing, owing to the development of ... [a world business class] ... to free ... [trade] ... to the world market, to uniformity in the [methods] ... of production and in the conditions of life ... (ibid.)

Note in particular how similar this last quote is to Levitt (1983):

> A powerful force drives the world towards a converging commonality ... a new commercial reality—the emergence of global markets for standardized consumer products ... Gone are accustomed differences in national or regional preferences (p. 92).

At the very least, we can say that as an exercise in descriptive imagination, the *Communist Manifesto* is remarkable. Re-reading it today, one is struck by an amazing portrayal of the world we recognize around us, circa 2009, and of what we now call globalization.

LOGICAL PARADOX

A second paradox has to do with what we expect from globalization. A central tenet of virtually all globalization literature is that world markets, cultures and governmental institutions are increasingly becoming integrated. Indeed, this thought is central to the definition developed in this article. A naïve interpretation of this fact is that nations are becoming less important as globalization proceeds. One version of this naïve view, sometimes referred to as 'hyperglobalization' (Held *et al.* 1999), is captured exquisitely in the titles of Kenichi Ohmae's two highly influential books—*Borderless World* (1990), and *The End of the Nation State* (1996). These (and many other) books make the argument that nations and their associated structures, are being trumped and **[p. 26]** transcended by the advance of multinational enterprise and economic globalization.

The paradox is that, if anything, the opposite is happening. At the very time when globalization is moving, full steam ahead, nationalism and related phenomena are increasing. There are many indicators of this. For example, the 'mere' fact that the number of nation-states has increased sharply since WWII, rising from around 104 in 1945 to over 214 today, is not insignificant. Far from the world becoming more and more borderless, it is, at least in this very practical way, becoming encumbered with more and more borders, more and more nation-states. Moreover, nationalism is also stronger throughout the world today than at any time since the 1930s. Reflecting on this, prominent globalization scholar Castells (1998) observes that the '... age of globalization ... [is] also the age of nationalist resurgence ...' (p. 27). Paradoxically, at the very time the hyper-globalizationalists are anticipating a one world economy, the number of aspirant 'nationalist' movements (e.g., for the Kurds and in Scotland, East Timor, and Chechnya, etc.) pushing for an independent existence is increasing alarmingly, leading political scientist Ernest Gelner to argue that the '... number ... of potential nations is probably much, *much* larger than that of possible viable states' (Gellner 1983, p. 2).

ECONOMIC PARADOX

Leading pro-globalization arguments make a strong case that globalization is simply the industrial revolution, going out to the rest of the world—a growth- and wealth-engendering mechanism that rationalizes economic activity everywhere. One result is that infrastructural blank spots around the globe—roads, communications, human capital, etc. are filling in, leading to vastly increased industrial efficiency everywhere. In light of these arguments, one might be forgiven for assuming that the gap between the haves and the have-nots in the world is closing.

The paradox is that, in many cases, the gap between the rich and the poor is increasingly widening. Consider the following samples of remarks:

> [Globalization] ... has generated anxieties about inequality ... [and] shifting power ... (World Bank 2002, p. 1).
>
> One of the most disturbing global trends of the past two decades is that countries with around 2 billion people are in danger of becoming marginal to the world economy. Incomes in [certain developing] ... countries are falling, poverty has been rising, and they participate less in trade today than they did 20 years ago (ibid., p. x).
>
> The process that has come to be called 'globalization' is exposing a deep fault line between groups who have the skills and mobility to flourish in global markets and those who either don't have these advantages or perceive the expansion of unregulated markets as inimical to social stability and deeply held norms (Rodrik 1997, p. 2).
>
> ... the inequality trends which globalization produced prior to WWI were at least partly responsible for the interwar retreat from globalization ... (Williamson 1996, p. i).
>
> [in the context of globalization] ... in both the most advanced and the least advanced countries the rich have gotten richer and the poor have gotten poorer. This is a great paradox ... (Luttwak 1999, p. 61).

This widening gap is as perplexing as it is disturbing. While economic theory suggests, and in fact persuades, that such gaps should be short-lived, their emergence is alarming, and may in fact be fuelling anti-globalization arguments. While such views are myopic, the economic paradox is disturbing.

AMERICANIZATION PARADOX

Ritzer (2004) developed an interesting theory explaining why globalization is so often taken to be an American phenomenon thrust upon the world. According to Ritzer, globalization's primary drivers are the market and consumption activities of capitalism. With capitalism as the main driver Ritzer goes on to argue that McDonaldization is the effective means for globalization's spread. Ritzer defines McDonaldization as '... the process by which the principles of the fast-food restaurant [**p. 27**] are ... [dominating] more and more sectors of ... the world' (p. 1). McDonalization is not primarily about the fast food industry. Rather, it reflects a particular type of economic rationalization that has swept all sectors of the US economy, and is now proceeding to do the same thing all over the world—in other words, globalization.

Implied in Ritzer's argument is the notion that globalization has taken a particular form and tone. To understand this better, imagine that a capitalist Fiji, or India, or Chile, and not the USA had been the dominant economy in the modern world. Given an energetic and expansive capitalism, the resulting globalization would surely have had a distinctively Fijian, Indian or Chilean character to it. However, it is the USA, and not these other nations, that has enjoyed economic and cultural hegemony since WWII. As a result, globalization has, thus far, had a distinctly American character. Indeed, since WWII, American media, firms, their products and symbols have gained a ubiquitous presence across the globe—hence, globalization is sometimes referred to as the Americanization of the world. This is mistaking the first mover for the process itself. The paradox is that American media, firms, their products and symbols are getting stiff competition from all over the world.

The explanation is that US firms, products, symbols, etc. enjoyed a first mover's advantage after WWII. That is, they had the first opportunity to give post-WWII globalization its complexion. However, as globalization proceeds and more and more nations climb aboard the global bandwagon, that advantage is simply not sustainable. How could it be otherwise when globalization is taking modern methods of organization, production and communication to every corner of the planet? For example, many US industries, including highly influential cultural industries are experiencing increasing competition. Europeans are turning away from American TV programming in favor of European programming. Movies produced in Britain, Hong Kong, and elsewhere are increasingly hitting a global nerve. When the Mumbai movie industry turns its attention to producing films for global markets—watch out Americanization! This is globalization's Americanization paradox.

EMOTIONAL PARADOX

Clark and Knowles (2003) argue that globalization makes a strange bedfellow, in the sense that it polarizes people into those who are *for*, and those who are *against* it, and that it does so in paradoxical ways. In the IB literature, globalization is usually portrayed as generally beneficial. However, serious and sophisticated critiques of globalization do exist. In the context of a wider consideration of all views, an examination of the political distribution of arguments, pro- and con-globalization, is very enlightening. One might be forgiven for assuming that those who are for or against globalization come from the same political perspective. Yet, not all who are against globalization are anti-business or politically left of center, nor are all those who are for globalization pro-business or politically right of center. There are groups on both the right and left who are pro-globalization *and* groups on the right and left who are contra-globalization (the entire argument here derives from Clark and Knowles 2003).

A closer look reveals that globalization makes for some strange bedfellows. Not surprisingly, most MNCs and most IB literature is implicitly right of center and proglobalization. More surprising however is where Marxists fall—pro-globalization. Indeed, Marxists were among the first to hold positive views of globalization (re-read *sans* political content, the *Communist Manifesto*, and Bukharin's (1973) *Imperialism and the World Economy*, both of which portray a remarkable modern view of globalization). Compare this with the moderate left-of-center pro-globalization views held by such institutions as the World Bank.

However, those with anti-globalization views also form an unexpectedly mixed group. **[p. 28]** For example, right-of-center nationalists such as Ross Perot (in the USA), Sir James Goldsmith (in the UK), and Jean-Marie Le Pen (in France), shared an anti-globalization stance with left-of-center union organizers and ecologists.

Clearly, opinions on globalization are not as simple as they may appear at first glance: important, relevant and complex counter-perspectives exist on all sides of the issue. Clark and Knowles (2003) sum up the matter of globalization's emotional paradox in this way:

> The dominant opinion in IB is only one *opinion* on the subject. Such an opinion is held on the basis of values, political conviction, and taste, rather than on an indisputable analysis of incontrovertible facts ... IB scholars do not have to agree with the counter-perspectives to benefit from some of the serious scholarship they provide. Even if one disagrees with all counter-perspectives, the fact that important decision makers hold those views and develop policy consistent with them suggests, at the very least, that there will be variables of interest to IB scholars emanating from them (p. 364).

THE FUTURE OF GLOBALIZATION

Globalization is the process by which economic, political, cultural, social, and other relevant systems of nations are integrating into world sub-systems. It is a complex process that has been at work, in various ways, and to different degrees, since ancient times. Oddly, it is also a phenomenon that has gone largely unnoticed (and unnamed) until fairly recently. Reflecting this fact, a number of accounts of globalization begin with the rise and spread of American MNCs immediately after WWII. Only in the past two decades (or so) has globalization *per se* become of interest to the IB, or any academic community.

Much of the literature implicitly assumes globalization represents a sort of perpetual revolution. Serious reflection suggests that is improbable. We are in what might be called globalization's 'phase plane'. The changes wrought in this phase plane have been so consuming to contemporary observers that little effort has gone into looking beyond what we are presently going through, into imagining what the steady-state outcomes might look like. However, we may now be within shouting distance of globalization's climax, its dénouement. At least, if we have defined our subject adequately, it is now possible to imagine what its end-state might look like.

Like all transitions, globalization's phase plain implies a 'from what', and a 'to what'. The 'from what' is history, and, since WWII, we have increasingly characterized that history in terms of the globalizing process—at a minimum, the commercial/economic/social/cultural integration the world has experienced since 1945. The 'to what' (25 years out and beyond) is, as yet, unknown. In this final section, we explore the likely end-state of the ancient historical process we call globalization. Our speculations are based on four heroic assumptions: (1) no worldwide conflict (WWIII) occurs; (2) no new and devastating diseases emerge; (3) the tendency towards democracy continues around the world; and (4) technology continues evolving along the current trajectory (electronics, communication, etc.). These are heroic assumptions, because they have never held over long periods in the past, and it is improbable they will hold in the future.

Nevertheless, in the short-to mid-range time horizon (#25 years), they may hold up well enough for us to support some reasonable speculations. We foresee three likely 'steady-state' features of the world after globalization: (1) the re-emergence of the political as the world's key organizing principle; (2) the reversal of some cultural flows; and (3) a middle class world.

RE-EMERGENCE OF THE POLITICAL AS THE KEY ORGANIZING PRINCIPLE

The *Communist Manifesto* describes a world increasingly dominated by economic **[p. 29]** and decreasingly influenced by political interests. Less ideological characterizations of the world Marx and Engels imagined would simply argue the virtues of markets. Ted Levitt, probably put it best, in his seminal 1983 article (eerily reminiscent of the *Communist Manifesto*), when he argued that:

> A powerful force drives the world towards a converging commonality ... a new commercial reality—the emergence of global markets for standardized consumer products ... Gone are accustomed differences in national or regional preferences (p. 92).

All sides of the current globalization debate seem to concede, gladly or unhappily, that free trade, markets, marketing, the pursuit of profit, etc., have been major factors in reshaping the world (i.e., globalization) since 1945. Those who endorse the changes (e.g., Bhagwati 2003) see the economic side of globalization as taking the industrial revolution (i.e., higher standards of living, etc.) to the rest of the world. Those who are unhappy with globalization (e.g., Klein 2002, 2007; Danaher 1997; Danaher and Burbach 2000),[7] see it essentially as toxic, devastating to human lives, and fundamentally lacking in democratic consent.

In the 1960s, MNCs were often portrayed as exploiters of developing nations (e.g., Baran 1973). By the 1980s, the wealth and job creation power of MNCs began to be apparent (Bauer 1984), and a sort of bidding war began as national (and regional) governments attempted to attract and/or keep MNCs in their territory. For their part, some MNCs were able to extract concessions in exchange for their job-creating presence (Narula and Dunning 2000). In the process, the relative strength of governments declined vis-à-vis the MNCs.[8] The situation has been facilitated by the integration of the world economy in the technical sense—trade arrangements, currencies, inflation, interest rates, etc. Such technical integration has made it necessary for governments to coordinate economic policy. The result was a *de facto* erosion of national governmental power, and the growth of corporate influence and power.

The current hegemonic dominance of MNCs and global markets is untenable in the long run. It is untenable, not because globalization's more radical critics are correct, but because global firms are ill-equipped to address some of the larger common issues facing humanity—global pollution, intellectual property protection, disease, and warming, use of the high seas, Antarctica, etc. As Kuttner (1997) puts it, society is logically prior to markets. Without a counterbalancing civil/political force, global markets would likely produce global company towns. However, in a converging world, in which there are differing views of the place of the market in society, the hegemonic dominance of global markets and global companies will not likely continue as it has, because they cannot, independently, provide the stability (laws, property rights) needed for their own existence. Only governments can do that. Just as early articulations of environmentalists' concerns seemed at first radical (e.g., Carson 1962), only to be made mainstream by the 1990s (recall George Bush senior's campaign pledge to become the environmentalist president), so current radical antiglobalization arguments will become domesticated, non-controversial, and main stream over the next decade or so, as globalization brings more and more nations into its sweep [this seems to be exactly the point Kagan (2008) is making]. Thus, we expect the emergence of international, national, regional and other significant governance regimes to emerge to counterbalance the current dominance of global markets.

REVERSAL OF CULTURE FLOWS

Since the end of WWII, the USA has enjoyed a significant economic, cultural, technological and military hegemony over the rest of the world. One reason for this dominance was the USA's first mover advantage after WWII—the USA was the only significant economy not materially devastated by the war. [**p. 30**] At the war's end, America's productive capacity, geared up to make tanks, ships and airplanes, simply switched over to produce autos, washing machines and toasters. In 1945, when the fighting stopped, there was a world of burgeoning demand, and only one country ready to meet it—the USA. For a generation, US MNCs went out into the world, with virtually no foreign competition (Vernon 1973). One unintended consequence of this was that US culture went along with the MNCs. The result was an effective cultural hegemony in American expressive products (movies, books, TV shows, music, etc.). We referred to this as the 'Americanization Paradox' above. A generation came to maturity under the influence of this US cultural dominance.

However, the world did recover from WWII, and by the early 1970s, US commercial hegemony began to erode as serious competitors entered the fray (particularly, but not limited to, German and Japanese auto manufacturers). One interpretation of this is that after a hiatus caused by WWII, the process we call globalization kicked back into life. In short order, France, Italy, Britain, the Netherlands, Korea, etc. followed, and began vying for market share in an increasingly open trade environment. By the early 1990s, India, China, Brazil, and many other nations made a showing in global markets, first simply as attractive manufacturing locations, then as legitimate competitors in world trade.

Although the USA is likely to continue as an economic and cultural leader, it is unlikely it can continue the dominance it enjoyed 1945–1975. In a globalizing world, in which free trade is the order of the day, it is inevitable that other nations vie for, and win, a share of global markets. Just as US cultural hegemony was an unintended consequence of its emergence as a first mover after WWII, so an unintended consequence of China, India and other nations becoming serious players in global markets, is that US cultural hegemony will be eroded as the expressive products of those other nations become available. Although the USA may have invented the modern movie and music industries, globalization has spread industry savvy worldwide. Diffusion of such savvy can only reasonably lead to many reversals of culture flows:

> Over the next century, disruptive innovations won't be coming from countries like the United States. They'll also be emerging from dynamic, hungry, rising economies that offer plenty of room for risk taking, flights of fancy and cross border synthesis (Caryl 2007, p. 45)

Moreover, since the current dominant global language is English, there will be an advantage to countries outside of the West that employ English as their working language. India, for example, has a domestic market of over a billion people. Indian film makers churn out more film products each year than does Hollywood. Moreover, Indian film makers are as sophisticated and as technically astute as their Hollywood colleagues, in every way. When Bollywood turns its immense resources more fully toward larger world markets, two consequences will emerge: (1) they will begin to produce film products suitably tailored to wider tastes; and (2) they will produce products with distinctly Indian values embedded in them. Multiply this sort of change across the developing world, wherever and whenever local expressive products can be suitably refocused toward world markets, and we begin to understand the potential for unusual and historically unprecedented patterns of cultural influence.

MIDDLE CLASS WORLD

Perhaps the most amazing outcome of globalization to emerge over the next 25 years will be a substantially middle class world. By 'substantially middle class world', we mean that most people on the planet will [p. 31] have left the drudgery of subsistence living behind them to become discerning consumers, with appetites for the same commercial accoutrements and life of ease and satiability enjoyed by most in the West. If our heroic assumptions hold, that outcome is certain.

Globalization, that great and ancient integration of the world, means, among other things, that technological know-how travels, eventually, to the ends of the earth. This dispersion of know-how has accelerated since the end of WWII, when free trade emerged as the regime of choice around the world. That openness meant, of course, the availability of every type of Western consumer product, with a consequent impact on tastes around the world. It also meant the grandstanding of Western wealth-producing capital goods, technological savvy and managerial know-how, everywhere on the planet. This potent combination of taste for Western goods, and the ability to make them, is transforming production and consumption everywhere. Idiosyncratic, inefficient, local capital goods and methods are being swept away in favor of global best practices. Increasingly, tastes, and expectations of what one may hope for in life, are molded, everywhere in the world, in the same way, by the same influences.

The largest growth rates for most industries are no longer found in the West. Rather, they are found in the developing world. The emergent demand for consumer goods in India, China, and elsewhere is gigantic. As tastes for the good life mature, and as global firms compete to supply that good life—urban and rural infrastructure (electricity, water, power, roads, sewers, etc.), TVs, DVDs, Internet, mobile phones, automobiles, fashionable clothes, magazines, music and food snacks—a middle class existence will begin to take shape everywhere on earth. Signs of the middle class explosion are already evident in India, where '... since 1985, more than 400 m ... have risen out of relative poverty ... and another 300 m will follow over the next two decades if the economy continues to grow ...' (Ram-Prasad 2007). In 2003, China's middle class had risen to around 1.9% of China's 1.3 billion people (i.e., 250 million). The proportion of middle class is expected to rise to 40% by 2020.[9]

CONCLUSION

Too much energy has been wasted in debate over whether or not globalization exists, on when it started, and on whether we should foster it or stop it. Globalization is not a human invention; rather, it is an unintended consequence of human life and human behavior here on earth. It cannot be stopped—at least not by any deliberate human effort. Certainly unintentional human actions—wars, depressions, disease, etc. might do that. The reality seems to be, that no matter what we call it, globalization is simply part of the natural evolution of humanity. At the margin, we may be able to influence and manage some of its effects. The re-emergence of the political, outlined above, reflects one way this will occur. However, it is unlikely we will be able to eliminate all negative consequences of the process. No change comes without trade-offs. And, arguably, never in the history of mankind has there been such a sweeping all-pervasive change as the phase of globalization we are currently moving through.

As an historically complex phenomenon, a fuller understanding of globalization will emerge only from multiple perspectives, across multiple disciplines. There is, perhaps, no discipline better positioned to lead this intellectual expedition than IB. Yet, because of a pervasive intellectual myopia (see Clark and Knowles 2003; Clark, Knowles and Hodis 2004) there is perhaps no discipline currently more ill-suited for the task. Let us hope we do not cede ownership of such an important topic to others.

NOTES

1. Much of the material in this section is an adaptation and extension of Clark and Knowles (2003) and Clark, Knowles and Hodis (2004).
2. In answer to Rugman, and others with similar views, Chanda has written '... the economic definition [of globalization] leaves other questions unanswered. How, for example, did the coffee bean, grown first in Ethiopia, end up in our cups after a journey through Java and Columbia? How did the name of Bodhisattva *Avalokiteswar*, translated into Chinese as *Guanyin* and into Japanese as *Kwanon*, inspire the Japanese brand name for a camera?' (2007, p. xi).
3. About 200 million people (3% of the world's population) were international migrants in 2005. Between 1995 and 2000, around 2.5 million migrants per year moved from less to more developed nations (Population Reference Bureau 2007).
4. *Globalisation* is the British variant of the word *globalization*.
5. Note related words *weltwirtschaft* (global economy) and *weltethos* (global ethic).
6. In translation from *Des Demons—Atelier en directe de la Pensee d'Edgar Morin*, August 2000, Sao Paulo.
7. Suggestively titled *Corporations Are Gonna Get Your Mama* (1997) and *Globalize This!* (2000).
8. The suggestively titled *Sovereignty at Bay* (Vernon 1973) and *Twilight of Sovereignty* (Wriston 1992), are representative of the literature taking this view.
9. A widely reported figure coming from a report of the Chinese Academy of Social Sciences (see http://www.chinadaily.com.cn/english/doc/2004-03/30/content_319105.htm)

Terry Clark, Monica Hodis and Paul D' Angelo

REFERENCES

Albarran, Alan B. and Chan-Olmsted, Sylvia M. (1998) Global Media Economics: Commercialization, Concentration and Integration of World Media Markets. Ames: Iowa State University Press.

Baily, M. N. Solow, R. M. 'International productivity comparisons built from the firm level' Journal of Economic Perspective vol. 15 no. (3)(Summer) pp. 151–172. (2001)

Baran, Paul A. (1973) The Political Economy of Growth. London: Penguin Books.

Barnett, T. and Whiteside, A. (2006) AIDS in the Twenty-First Century: Disease and Globalization. New York: Palgrave Macmillan.

Bauer, Peter. T. (1984) Reality and Rhetoric: Studies in the Economics of Development. Cambridge: Harvard University Press.

Baumann, M. P. Fujie, L. 'Local musical traditions in the globalization process' The World of Music vol. 42 no. (3) pp. 121–144. (2000)

Bhagwati, J. (2003) In Defense of Globalization. New York: Oxford University Press.

Braudel, F. (1984) The Perspective of the World. New York: Harper and Row.

Brennan, T. (1997) At Home in the World: Cosmopolitanism Now. Cambridge: Harvard University Press.

Burbules, N. (2000) Globalization and Education. London: Routledge Falmer.

Burkharin, N. (1973) Imperialism and World Economy, Monthly Review Press New york.

Carson, R. (1962) Silent Spring. Boston: Houghton Mifflin.

Caryl, C. 'Why Apple Isn't Japanese' Newsweek vol. 10 December, pp. 42–45. (2007)

Castells, M. (1998) End of the Millennium. London: Blackwell.

Chanda, N. (2007) Bound Together. New Haven: Yale University Press.

Chen, Louis 'In creativity, size doesn't matter' Taipei Times, 26 Aug pp. 8. (2007),

Clark, T. Knowles, L. 'Global myopia: globalization theory in international business' Journal of International Management vol. 9 no. (4) pp. 361–372. (2003) http://dx.doi.org/10.1016/j.intman.2003.08.007

Clark, T., Knowles, L. and Hodis, M. (2004) 'Global dialogue: a response to the responders in the special globalization issue of JIM', 19(4): pp. 511–514.

Clegg, S., ed., Hardy, C., ed., Lawrence, T., ed. and Nord, W. R. (eds) (2006), SAGE Handbook of Organization Studies. London: Sage Publications. http://dx.doi.org/10.4135/9781848608030

Collins, R. (2000) The Sociology of Philosophies: A Global Theory of Intellectual Change. Cambridge: The Belknap Press of Harvard University Press.

Crystal, David (1997) English As A Global Language. Cambridge: Cambridge University Press.

Currie, J., ed. and Newson, J. (eds) (1998) Universities and Globalization: Critical Perspectives. London: Sage Publications.

Danaher, K. (ed.) (1997) Corporations Are Gonna Get Your Mama: Globalization and the Downsizing of the American Dream. Monroe: Common Courage Press.

Danaher, K., ed. and Burbach, R. (eds) (2000) Globalize This! The Battle Against the World Trade Organization and Corporate Rule. Monroe: Common Courage Press.

Dornbusch, R. (1980) Open Economy Macroeconomics. New York: Basic Books.

Eddy, J. A., ed., Ceschger, H., ed. and Oeschger, H. (eds) (1993) Global Changes in the Perspective of the Past, the Dahlem Workshop on Global Changes in the Perspective of the Past. Hoboken: John Wiley & Son Ltd.

Edelman, Mark (1999) Peasants Against Globalization: Rural Social Movements in Costa Rica. Stanford: Stanford University Press.

Elden, S. 'Mondialisation without the world: interview with Kostas Axelos' Radical Philosophy vol. 130 pp. 25–28. (2005a)

Elden, S. 'Missing the point: Globalization, deterritorialization and the space of the World' Transactions of the Institute of British Geographers vol. 30 no. (1) pp. 8–19. (2005b) http://dx.doi.org/10.1111/j.1475-5661.2005.00148.x

Elden, S. Introducing Kostas Axelos and "the World" Environment and Planning D: Society and Space vol. 24 no. (5) pp. 639–642. (2006) http://dx.doi.org/10.1068/dtrans1a

Eschle, C. (2001) Global Democracy, Social Movements and Feminism. Boulder: Westview Press.

Friman, R. H. and Andreas, P. (1999) Illicit Global Economy and State Power. Boulder: Rowan & Littlefield Publishers.

Gellner, E. (1983) Nations and Nationalism. Oxford: Blackwell.

Guillen, M. F. 'Is globalization civilizing, destructive or feeble? A critique of six key debates in the social-science literature' Annual Review of Sociology vol. 27 no. (1) pp. 235–260. (2001) http://dx.doi.org/10.1146/annurev.soc.27.L235

Gutierrez, L. T. (ed) (2007) Solidarity, Sustainability and Non-Violence (E-Newsletter),

Vol. 3, No. 6 (June).

Hagedorn, John M. (2007) Gangs in the Global City. Champaign: University of Illinois Press.

Held, D., McGrew, A., Goldblatt, D. and Perraton, J. (1999) Global Transformations: Politics, Economics, and Culture. Stanford: Stanford University Press.

Herod, A., O Tuathail, G. and Roberts, S. M. (1998) An Unruly World? Globalization, Governance, and Geography. New York: Routledge.

Holub, Margaret (2001) Globalization and the Maccabees. (http://www.mcjc.org/mjoldart/MJAMH039.htm)

Ietto-Grillies, G. and Seccombe-Hett, T. (1997) 'What so internationalization indices measure?' Research Working Papers in International Business. Centre for International Business Studies, London: South Bank University, pp. 6–97. (http://www.lsbu.ac.uk/cibs/pdf/6-97.pdf)

Karliner, J. (1997) The Corporate Planet: Ecology and Politics in the Age of Globalization. San Francisco: Sierra Club Books.

Kagan, R. (2008), The Return of History, Alfred A. Knopf.

Klein, N. (2002) No Logo. New York: Picador.

Klein, N. (2007) The Shock Doctrine: The Rise of Disaster Capitalism. New York: Metropolitan Books.

Koslowski, R. (2005) International Migration and the Globalization of Domestic Politics. New York: Routledge.

Kung, H. (1998) A Global Ethic for Global Politics and Economics. New York: Oxford University Press.

Kuttner, R. (1999) Everything For Sale: University of Chicago Press.

Landow, G. P. (2006) Hypertext 3.0: Critical Theory and New Media in an Era of Globalization. Baltimore: The Johns Hopkins University Press.

Levitt, T. 'The globalization of markets' Harvard Business Review vol. 61 no. (3) pp. 92–102. (1983)

Lewellen, Ted C. (2002) Anthropology of Globalization. Westport: Greenwood Publishing Group.

Lewis, G. and Araya, R. (2002) 'Globalization and Mental Health', in N. Sartorius, ed., W. Gaebel, ed., J. J. Lopez-Ibor, ed., and M. Maj (eds), Psychiatry in Society. Chichester: Wiley, pp. pp. 57–78. http://dx.doi.org/10.1002/0470846488.ch3

Lopez, A., ed., Mathers, C., ed., Ezzati, M., ed., Jamison, D., ed. and C. Murray (Editors) (2006), Global Burden of Disease and Risk Factors, Oxford University Press, NY. http://dx.doi.org/10.1596/978-0-8213-6262-4

Luttwak, E. (1999) Turbo-Capitalism: Winners and Losers in the Global Economy. New York: HarperCollins Publishers Inc.

Marx, K. and Engel, F. (1848) The Manifesto of The Communist Party. (http://www.gutenberg.org/etext/61)

McKibbin, W. and Sachs, J. (1991) Global Linkages: Macroeconomic Interdependence and Cooperation in the World Economy. Washington, DC: The Brookings Institution.

McLuhan, M. (1964) Understanding Media: The Extensions of Man. New York: McGraw-Hill.

Mitchell, W. C. (1927) Business Cycles the Problem and Its Setting. New York: National Bureau of Economic Research.

Michael, L. Richard R. Nelson "Introduction: Technology, Organizations, and Innovation" Administrative Science Quarterly Vol. 35 No. 1, Special Issue: Technology, Organizations, and Innovation: March, pp. pp. 1–8. (1990),

Monkman, N. P. and Stromquist, K. (2000) Globalization and Education. Lanham: Rowman & Littlefield Publishers.

Munck, R. 'Globalization and democracy: A new "great transformation"?' Annals of the American Academy of Political and Social Science vol. 581 no. (1) pp. 10–21. (2002) http://dx.doi.org/10.1177/0002716202058001003

Murray, C. J. L., ed. and Lopez, A. D. (eds) (1996) The Global Burden of Disease. Cambridge: Harvard University Press.

Murray, C. J. L. Lopez, A. D. 'Industrial development, globalization and multinational enterprises: New realities for developing countries' Oxford Development Studies vol. 28 no. (2) pp. 141–167. (2000)

Narula, R. and Dunning, J. H. (1990) Borderless World. New York: Harper Collins Publishers.

Ohmae, K. (1996) The End of the Nation State: The Rise of Regional Economies. New York: Free Press Paperbacks.

Ostler, N. (2006) Empires of the Word: A Language History of the World. New York: Harper Perennial.

Papastergiadis, N. (2000) The Turbulence of Migration: Globalization, Deterritorialization and Hybridity. Cambridge: Polity Press.

Polanyi, K. (1947) The Great Transformation. Boston: Beacon Press.

Population Reference Bureau Population Bulletin. Vol 62, No. 3 (September). (2007)

Ram-Prasad, C. 'India's middle class failure' Prospect Magazine vol. 138(September) http://www.prospect-magazine.co.uk/pdfarticle.php?id=9776 (2007)

Rantanen, T. (2004) The Media and Globalization. London: Sage Publications. http://dx.doi.org/10.4135/9781446221198

Reader, J. (2006) Globalization, Engineering and Creativity. San Francisco: Morgan and Claypool Publishers.

Ritzer, G. (2004) The Globalization of Nothing. Thousand Oaks: Pine Forge.

Robertson, R. (1992) Globalization: Social Theory and Global Culture. London: Sage Publications.

Rodrik, D. (1997) Has Globalization Gone too Far? Washington, DC: Institute for International Economics.

Rugman, A. M. (2001) The End of Globalization. New York: AMACOM/American Management Association.

Rugman, A. M. 'Regional strategy and the demise of globalization' Journal of International Management vol. 9 no. (4) pp. 409–417. (2003) http://dx.doi.org/10.1016/ j.intman.2003.08.004

Sampson, E. E. 'The challenge of globalization for psychology: Globalization and psychology's theory of the person' American Psychologist vol. 44 no. (6) pp. 914–921. (1989) http://dx.doi.org/10.1037/0003-066X.44.6.914

Schumpeter, J. A. (1939) Business Cycles: A Theoretical, Historical, and Statistical Analysis of the Capitalist Process. New York: McGraw-Hill.

Shapiro, I. and Brilmayer, L. (1999) Global Justice. New York: New York University Press.

Sklair, L. (1991) Sociology of the Global System. Baltimore: Johns Hopkins University Press.

Taylor, P. M. (1997) Global Communications, International Affairs and the Media Since 1945. London: Routledge.

UNCTAD (2005) World Investment Report: Transnational Corporations and the Internationalization of R&D. New York: United Nations.

Vernon, R. (1973) Sovereignty at Bay: The Multinational Spread of U. S. Enterprises. London: Penguin Books.

Wallertsein, I. M. (1975) Modern World-System I: Capitalist Agriculture and the Origins of European World-Economy in the 16th Century. Burlington: Academic Press.

Wallertsein, I. M. 'America and the World: The Twin Towers as Metaphor' Social Science Research Council (2001) http://www.ssrc.org/sept11/essays/wallerstein.htm

Waters, M. (1995) Globalization. London: Routledge.

Williamson, J. (1996) 'Globalization and inequality then and now: the late 19th and late 20th centuries compared', National Bureau of Economic Research, Working Paper Series No. 5491, March.

Worthington, G. 'Globalisation: perceptions and threats to national government in Australia' Politics and Public (2001).

Administration Group, Parliamentary Library of the Parliament of Australia, Research Paper 27. (http://www.aph.gov.au/library/pubs/rp/2000-01/01rp27.htm)

World Bank, Washington, DC (2002) Globalization Growth, and Poverty, Building an Inclusive World Economy. New York: Oxford University Press (http://goingglobal2006.vtt.fi/pdf/wir05overviewfull.pdf)

Wriston, W. B. (1992) Twilight of Sovereignty. New York: Scribner Book Company.

THE U.S. CONTENT OF "MADE IN CHINA"

Galina Hale and Bart Hobijn

G oods and services from China accounted for only 2.7% of U.S. personal consumption expenditures in 2010, of which less than half reflected the actual costs of Chinese imports. The rest went to U.S. businesses and workers transporting, selling, and marketing goods carrying the "Made in China" label. Although the fraction is higher when the imported content of goods made in the United States is considered, Chinese imports still make up only a small share of total U.S. consumer spending. This suggests that Chinese inflation will have little direct effect on U.S. consumer prices.

The United States is running a record trade deficit with China. This is no surprise, given the wide array of items in stores labeled "Made in China." This *Economic Letter* examines what fraction of U.S. consumer spending goes for Chinese goods and what part of that fraction reflects the actual cost of imports from China. We perform a similar exercise to determine the foreign and domestic content of all U.S. imports.

In our analysis, we combine data from several sources: Census Bureau 2011 U.S. International Trade Data; the Bureau of Labor Statistics 2010 input-output matrix; and personal consumption expenditures (PCE) by category from the U.S. national accounts of the Commerce Department's Bureau of Economic Analysis. We use the combined data to answer three questions:

- What fraction of U.S. consumer spending goes for goods labeled "Made in China" and what fraction is spent on goods "Made in the USA"?
- What part of the cost of goods "Made in China" is actually due to the cost of these imports and what part reflects the value added by U.S. transportation, wholesale, and retail activities? That is, what is the U.S. content of "Made in China"?

- What part of U.S. consumer spending can be traced to the cost of goods imported from China, taking into account not only goods sold directly to consumers, but also goods used as inputs in intermediate stages of production in the United States?

Share of Spending on "Made in China"

Although globalization is widely recognized these days, the U.S. economy actually remains relatively closed. The vast majority of goods and services sold in the United States is produced here. In 2010, imports were about 16% of U.S. GDP. Imports from China amounted to 2.5% of GDP.

Table 1 shows our calculations of the import content of U.S. household consumption of goods and services. A total of 88.5% of U.S. consumer spending is on items made in the United States. This is largely because services, which make up about two-thirds of spending, are mainly produced locally. The market share of foreign goods is highest in durables, which include cars and electronics. Two-thirds of U.S. durables consumption goes for goods labeled "Made in the USA," while the other third goes for goods made abroad.

Chinese goods account for 2.7% of U.S. PCE, about one-quarter of the 11.5% foreign share. Chinese imported goods consist mainly of furniture and household equipment; other durables; and clothing and shoes. In the clothing and shoes category, 35.6% of U.S. consumer purchases in 2010 was of items with the "Made in China" label.

Local Content of "Made in China"

Obviously, if a pair of sneakers made in China costs $70 in the United States, not all of that retail price goes to the Chinese manufacturer. In fact, the bulk of the retail price pays for transportation of the sneakers in the United States, rent for the store where they are sold, profits for shareholders of the U.S. retailer, and the cost of marketing the sneakers. These costs include the salaries, wages, and benefits paid to the U.S. workers and managers who staff these operations.

Table 1 shows that, of the 11.5% of U.S. consumer spending that goes for goods and services produced abroad, 7.3% reflects the cost of imports. The remaining 4.2% goes for U.S. transportation, wholesale, and retail activities. Thus, 36% of the price U.S. consumers pay for imported goods actually goes to U.S. companies and workers.

This U.S. fraction is much higher for imports from China. Whereas goods labeled "Made in China" make up 2.7% of U.S. consumer spending, only 1.2% actually reflects the cost of the imported goods. Thus, on average, of every dollar spent on an item labeled "Made in China," 55 cents go for services produced in the United States. In other words, the U.S. content of "Made in China" is about 55%. The fact that the U.S. content of Chinese goods is much higher than for imports as a whole is mainly due to higher retail and wholesale margins on consumer electronics and clothing than on most other goods and services.

Total Import Content of U.S. PCE

Not all goods and services imported into the United States are directly sold to households. Many are used in the production of goods and services in the United States. Hence, part of the 88.5% of spending on goods and services labeled "Made in the USA" pays for imported intermediate goods and

Table 1: Import content of U.S. personal consumption expenditures by category.

| | | SHARE SPENT ON | | IMPORT CONTENT | | | |
| | | | | DIRECTLY SOLD TO FINAL DEMAND | | TOTAL | |
	EXPENDITURE SHARE	"MADE IN USA"	"MADE IN CHINA"	TOTAL	CHINESE GOODS	TOTAL	CHINESE GOODS
Total	100.0	88.5	2.7	7.3	1.2	13.9	1.9
Less food and energy	86.1	88.0	3.1	7.7	1.4	13.0	2.0
Durables	9.9	66.6	12.0	18.7	6.2	26.3	7.3
Motor vehicles	3.4	74.9	1.2	17.5	0.6	27.4	1.9
Furniture/household equip.	4.7	59.6	20.0	21.4	10.6	27.8	11.6
Other durables	1.8	69.0	11.8	14.2	5.3	20.5	6.2
Nondurables	23.2	76.2	6.4	12.1	2.6	22.1	3.3
Food	8.0	90.8	0.4	5.2	0.2	13.9	1.1
Clothing/shoes	3.4	24.9	35.6	29.5	13.8	33.6	14.7
Gasoline/fuel oil/other energy goods	3.6	88.4	0.1	7.4	0.0	34.1	0.5
Other nondurables	8.4	77.7	3.1	13.8	1.4	20.1	2.0
Services	66.9	96.0	0.0	4.0	0.0	9.2	0.6
Housing	16.6	100.0	0.0	0.0	0.0	2.5	0.4
Household operations	7.2	99.7	0.0	0.3	0.0	10.6	0.6
Transportation	1.6	90.4	0.0	9.6	0.0	20.8	0.4
Medical care	18.4	99.3	0.0	0.7	0.0	6.0	0.6
Recreation	8.2	99.6	0.0	0.3	0.0	6.6	0.8
Other services	14.9	84.3	0.0	15.7	0.0	20.2	0.5

Source: Authors' calculations based on 2008 input/output matrix from Bureau of Labor Statistics (2010) and 2010 trade statistics, from Census Bureau (2011), and national accounts data.

services. To properly account for the share of imports in U.S. consumer spending, it's necessary to take into account the contribution of these imported intermediate inputs. We use input-output tables to compute the contribution of imports to U.S. production of final goods and services. Combining the imported share of U.S.-produced goods and services with imported goods and services directly sold to consumers yields the total import content of PCE.

Table 1 also shows total import content as a fraction of total PCE and its subcategories. When total import content is considered, 13.9% of U.S. consumer spending can be traced to the cost of imported goods and services. This is substantially higher than the 7.3%, which includes only final imported goods and services and leaves out imported intermediates. Imported oil, which makes up a large part of the production costs of the "gasoline, fuel oil, and other energy goods" and "transportation" categories, is the main contributor to this 6.6 percentage point difference.

The total share of PCE that goes for goods and services imported from China is 1.9%. This is 0.7 percentage point more than the share of Chinese-produced final goods and services in PCE. This difference is mainly due to the use of intermediate goods imported from China in the U.S. production of services.

Figure 1 plots the total and Chinese import content of U.S. PCE over the past decade. The import content of PCE has been relatively constant at between 11.7% and 14.2%. Import content peaked in 2008 at 14.2%, which was probably due to the spike in oil prices at the time. The share of imports in PCE is slightly lower than in GDP as a whole because the import content of investment goods turns out to be twice as high as that of consumer goods and services.

The fraction of import content attributable to Chinese imports has doubled over the past decade. In 2000, Chinese goods accounted for 0.9% of the content of PCE. In 2010, Chinese goods accounted for 1.9%. The fact that the overall import content of U.S. consumer goods has remained relatively constant while the Chinese share has doubled indicates that Chinese gains have come, in large part, at the expense of other exporting nations.

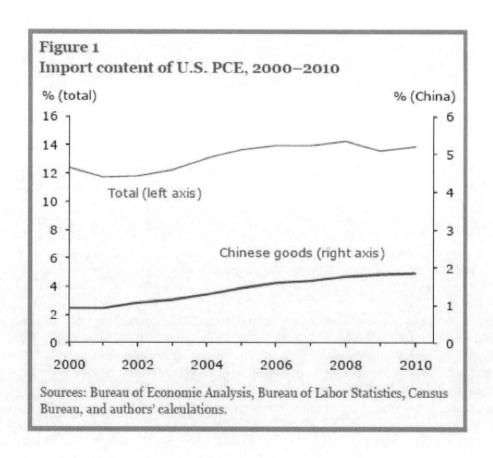

Figure 1
Import content of U.S. PCE, 2000–2010

Sources: Bureau of Economic Analysis, Bureau of Labor Statistics, Census Bureau, and authors' calculations.

Broader Implications

The import content of U.S. PCE attributable to imports from China is useful in understanding where revenue generated by sales to U.S. households flows. It is also important because it affects to what extent price increases for Chinese goods are likely to pass through to U.S. consumer prices.

China's 2011 inflation rate is close to 5%. If Chinese exporters were to pass through all their domestic inflation to the prices of goods they sell in the United States, the PCE price index (PCEPI) would only increase by 1.9% of this 5%, reflecting the Chinese share of U.S. consumer goods and services. That would equal a 0.1 percentage point increase in the PCEPI. The inflationary effects would be highest in the industries in which the share of Chinese imports is highest—clothing and shoes, and electronics. In fact, recent data show accelerating price increases for these goods compared with other goods.

However, it does not seem that so far Chinese exporters are fully passing through their domestic inflation. In May 2011, prices of Chinese imports only increased 2.8% from May 2010. This is partly because a large share of Chinese production costs consists of imports from other countries. Xing and Detert (2010) demonstrate this by examining the production costs of an iPhone. In 2009, it cost about $179 in China to produce an iPhone, which sold in the United States for about $500. Thus, $179 of the U.S. retail cost consisted of Chinese imported content. However, only $6.50 was actually due to assembly costs in China. The other $172.50 reflected costs of parts produced in other countries, including $10.75 for parts made in the United States.

Conclusion

Figure 2 shows the share of U.S. PCE based on where goods were produced, taking into account intermediate goods production, and the domestic and foreign content of imports. Of the 2.7% of

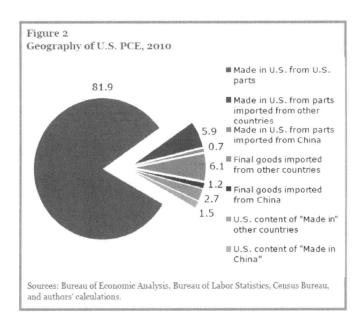

Figure 2
Geography of U.S. PCE, 2010

81.9

5.9
0.7
6.1
1.2
2.7
1.5

■ Made in U.S. from U.S. parts
■ Made in U.S. from parts imported from other countries
■ Made in U.S. from parts imported from China
■ Final goods imported from other countries
■ Final goods imported from China
■ U.S. content of "Made in" other countries
■ U.S. content of "Made in China"

Sources: Bureau of Economic Analysis, Bureau of Labor Statistics, Census Bureau, and authors' calculations.

U.S. consumer purchases going to goods labeled "Made in China," only 1.2% actually represents China-produced content. If we take into account imported intermediate goods, about 13.9% of U.S. consumer spending is attributable to imports, including 1.9% imported from China.

Since the share of PCE attributable to imports from China is less than 2% and some of this can be traced to production in other countries, it is unlikely that recent increases in labor costs and inflation in China will generate broad-based inflationary pressures in the United States.

Galina Hale is a senior economist in the Economic Research Department of the Federal Reserve Bank of San Francisco.

Bart Hobijn is a senior research advisor in the Economic Research Department of the Federal Reserve Bank of San Francisco.

References

Bureau of Labor Statistics. 2010. "Inter-industry relationships (Input/Output matrix)." http://www.bls.gov/emp/ep data input output matrix.htm

U.S. Census Bureau. 2011. "U.S. International Trade Data." http://www.census.gov/foreign-trade/statistics/country/

Xing, Yuqing, and Neal Detert. 2010. "How the iPhone Widens the United States Trade Deficit with the People's Republic of China." Asian Development Bank Institute Working Paper 257. http://adbi.org/working-paper/2010/12/14/4236.iphone.widens.us.trade.deficit.prc/

CONSUMER TOPIC 6.1: SOCIAL MEDIA AND GLOBALIZATION

Friend Me: Which Factors Influence Top Global Brands Participation in Social Network Sites

Theo Araujo and Peter Neijens

The Amsterdam School of Communication Research/ASCoR, University of Amsterdam, Amsterdam, The Netherlands

ABSTRACT

Purpose—This study focuses on how brands participate in social network sites (SNSs) and investigates both the different strategies they adopt and the factors that influence these strategies.

Design/methodology/approach—The activities of top brands in SNSs were investigated through a content analysis of brand web sites in three countries, measuring two primary dimensions: presence in SNSs and level of engagement which the brand hoped to establish with stakeholders. The study then built logistic regression models to understand which factors drive brands to adopt and use SNSs, using insights from previous studies related to internet innovation adoption cycles.

Findings—The study confirmed that SNS adoption follows a general path of Internet innovation adoption by brands. Industry markets exert influence, with technology and consumer intensive brands being more likely than all other industry segments to be present in SNSs and to participate at higher engagement levels, while brands targeting younger audiences also engage at higher levels than brands targeting generic audiences. The country in which the brand operates plays a significant role in a brand's likelihood of adopting SNSs: web sites in the USA are more likely to use SNSs than other countries, even after controlling for factors such as pre-existing web operations or the headquarters being in the same country. It was also found that top brands operate in a global world, as shown by their preference for SNSs with global coverage compared to local SNS, even when the penetration rates of these local SNSs were higher.

Theo Araujo and Peter Neijens, "Friend Me: Which Factors Influence Top Global Brands Participation in Social Network Sites," Internet Research, vol. 22, issue 5, pp. 626–640. Copyright © 2012 by Emerald Group Publishing Limited. Reprinted with permission.

Originality/value—The paper advances research on SNS adoption by brands from an organizational standpoint, at a time when the majority of the top global brands actively promote such services.

Keywords Social networking sites, Marketing strategy, Brands, Internet, Brand communication

Paper type Research paper

INTRODUCTION

The sharp increase in the popularity of social network sites (SNSs) has turned services such as Facebook and Twitter into attractive spaces for both consumers and brands. Used by over 70 percent of the global online population (comScore, 2010), SNSs are used not only for entertainment, but also as places where consumers discuss brand experiences and preferences (Needham, 2008; Jansen and Zhang, 2009; Acar and Polonsky, 2008; Dunne *et al.*, 2010)[1]. SNSs are not, however, only used by consumers: Coca-Cola, for example, has over 36 million users on its Facebook page and actively promotes its activities on its brand web site[2]. This study focusses on how brands participate in SNSs and investigates the different strategies they adopt and the factors influencing these strategies.

Recent trade studies propose that brands have several reasons to adopt SNSs (Bernoff and Li, 2008; Edelman and Salsberg, 2010; Kaplan and Haenlein, 2010; Zeisser, 2010). First, SNSs are popular web sites (second only to search engines): Facebook, the largest SNS, is used by 44 percent of the online population, with over 800 million users[3]. Second, establishing a presence on SNSs has little upfront cost: pages in Facebook or Twitter are free. Third, consumers trust brand pages on SNSs, with about 20 percent online American consumers considering brand's Facebook pages "influential" or "very influential" in their purchase decision process[4].

These reasons are, however, insufficient to explain why certain brands adopt SNSs while others do not, or why some brands engage actively, asking users to publish their own content on the brand pages, while others restrict their content to advertisements or press releases. Earlier research has largely focussed on case studies (e.g. Sicilia and Palazón, 2008; Syed-Ahmad and Murphy, 2010) or on how to best use SNSs (Palmer and Koenig-Lewis, 2009). Peters and Salazar (2010) have also provided an initial analysis of why companies adopt an SNS strategy, concluding that global brands were more likely to use SNSs than local brands, with 17 percent of the top brands using SNSs in 2009, and Waters and Lemanski (2011) has found that non-profit organizations are significantly more likely to use social media in general in 2010 (including SNSs) than the corporations on the Fortune 500 ranking (58.2 percent of non-profit organizations used social media in comparison to 22.2 percent of the corporations).

Despite this, no overall understanding of the mechanisms and strategies adopted by brands has been developed to date; this is especially important now that SNSs are so widely used. This study aims to fill this gap by providing a comprehensive overview of brand strategies in SNSs, and by identifying factors influencing such activities. This is a pressing subject in communication research not only due to the increasing numbers of consumers and brands that are interacting via SNSs, but also because this interaction could potentially accelerate the ongoing disruption of the traditional roles of advertiser, media, and consumer.

USAGE OF SNSS AT DIFFERENT LEVELS

Boyd and Ellison (2008) characterize SNSs as services where users can construct public or semi-public profiles, present a list of other users with whom they share a connection, and view lists of connections made by these "friends" and by others. The profile is considered the "backbone" of the SNS; this is an individual user's unique page, typically displaying "descriptors such as age, location, interests, and an 'about me' section," and also multimedia content (Boyd and Ellison, 2008, p. 213). In more recent versions of Facebook, profiles also display cultural preferences, including web sites and brands liked by the user.

Like individuals, brands can also create profiles or pages in SNSs. Their use of SNSs may be analyzed from two perspectives: first, whether the brand uses SNSs or not (SNS presence), and second, the level of engagement promised when interacting with consumers. SNS presence may be described as the creation of an official brand space (e.g. a profile or a page) within the SNS. This space can be used to post-brand content such as links to the brand web site, text, images, videos, and interactive applications aimed at consumers. Consumers can then establish relationships by adding the brands to their own profiles. The consumer-brand relationship in SNSs is often public or semi-public, which means that other users who are friends with the consumer can see such a relationship.

Level of engagement within SNSs may be defined as how a brand decides to interact with consumers within the SNS space. Although SNSs have different privacy options, the communication made by brands in these services is inherently public, except when messaging a user privately. The brand must therefore decide how this communication will take place, its limits, and its content—including whether the brand will allow or solicit public feedback, or simply use the SNS page to display official brand content.

FACTORS INFLUENCING HOW BRANDS USE SNSS

SNSs provide brands with a new set of requirements and possibilities as opposed to the brand web site. First, SNSs are an external environment where a balance is needed between the control over brand messaging and consumers' resentment of corporate intrusion into what they perceive as their space (Palmer and Koenig-Lewis, 2009). Second, since users are in control of the SNS environment, they may post negative or damaging information about the brand (Bernoff and Li, 2008; Mei *et al.*, 2010). Third, consumers expect interaction with brands in SNSs to be "trustworthy, open, interesting, relevant, and engaging with the target audience" (Palmer and Koenig-Lewis, 2009, p. 167). These new requirements may be seen as a new innovation adoption cycle within internet development, and this study, therefore, draws a parallel between the recent adoption of SNSs by brands and the deployment of online commercial web sites (ca. 2000), and additional internet technologies ever since.

Earlier studies on adoption of innovations have indicated that the market in which a brand operates influences its deployment of new technologies, particularly in the case of internet. When analyzing differences in usage of more advanced features on brand web sites, Perry and Bodkin (2000) have proposed two reasons why companies operating in different markets would behave differently when adopting internet technologies: different expectations when it comes to the customer base being comfortable with technology and the management of the company being more or less aware and comfortable in using and deploying the technology itself. Between market differences were also found, for example, in the early adoption of corporate blogging (Cho and Huh, 2010) and modes of online advertising and electronic word-of-mouth (Golan and Zaidner, 2008). Another aspect brought forward by Perry *et al.* (2003) was the difference in business environments across markets, which would influence the level of interaction required with customers. Companies operating in the technology and consumer markets, in particular, would be more likely to adopt internet due to their "competitive business environment and needing to solicit feedback to improve products and services" (Perry *et al.*, 2003, p. 224).

Although these studies have produced mixed results and measured different dimensions, the general assumption is that brands in different markets have different incentives to seek an active connection with their customers, and also operate with different technology comfort levels both from their customers as well as from their own team. This leads to *H1*:

> *H1.* The market in which the brand operates influences SNS presence as well as the level of SNS engagement; in particular, brands operating in information technology and consumer markets will show higher SNS adoption.

Moving one step further, studies on internet innovation adoption such as the work by Doherty and Ellis-Chadwick (2003) have found that the demographics of a brand or company target market influences the decisions that the brand or company will take when it comes to the innovation adoption. The age of the target customer base, in particular, has been found as a significant predictor of internet technology adoption by companies, considering the different usages that different age groups make of internet. Doherty and Ellis-Chadwick (2003) found that the age of the target user had a significant influence on an organization's use of e-commerce: the lower the average age of the target user, the greater the likelihood of the organization using e-commerce. It is expected that brands would behave similarly now with SNSs—considering 73 percent of American teenagers used SNSs in 2008 vs 47 percent of online adults (Lenhart *et al.*, 2010). This leads to the second hypothesis:

> *H2.* Brands targeting younger segments of the population will show higher SNS presence and engagement levels than those targeting older segments.

Furthermore SNS use cross borders. One could argue that Facebook is a global SNS, since 75 percent of its users are outside the USA[5], but this does not mean that all its users communicate in the same language. Facebook is available in over 70 languages and earlier literature on SNSs (Herring *et al.*, 2007) has shown that users organize themselves within language networks. Considering that research on brand communication as well as internet adoption has discussed the impact of country on the strategies and decisions of global brands, this study also proposes a set of hypotheses related to the impact of country context on the decision to use SNSs.

The first country-level hypothesis is related to strategy differences between a brand's home market—where the company is headquartered—vs. other markets. As indicated by Palmer and Koenig-Lewis (2009), participation in SNSs presents brands with a new set of consumer requirements, including the need to update the content of the brand profile. This is further reinforced by Booth and Matic (2011, p. 190), who state that "practitioners must listen and act strategically and almost immediately" within social media. Brands need, therefore, to consider who will update their

SNS profiles in each country or language. It is expected that home markets, where companies have more available resources, will have higher levels of SNS presence and engagement:

H3. SNS presence will be stronger, and levels of engagement higher, in a brand's home market than in other markets.

Brands, however, do not start globalizing their internet activities with SNSs: teams may already be set up in countries other than the home market to engage with consumers in other online contexts. We propose that running sales activities through branded online stores or offering online support would provide a pool of resources for adopting SNSs in a given country, which leads to *H4:*

H4. Availability of online support or online sales activities in a country will positively influence brand SNS usage and levels of engagement in that country.

In our study, we compared brand activities in three different markets to understand how much the decision to participate in SNSs is dependent on the context of the target country. To allow for a better geographical coverage and in line with earlier studies that compared internet technology adoption across markets (e.g. Okazaki, 2004), three markets were selected based on their different economic, linguistic, geographic, and cultural aspects: the USA, the Netherlands, and Brazil[6]. We expect that global brands will show higher levels of SNS use in the USA and the Netherlands given the internet penetration rates[7] in these countries, which are for the Netherlands: 90 percent, the USA: 78 percent, and Brazil: 39 percent. Earlier studies into country differences have drawn on Hofstede's (1983) cultural dimensions to explore how the specific cultural context of a country influences organizational decisions, as well as brand decisions on internet strategies (e.g. Kampf, 2007; Okazaki, 2004; Roberts and Ko, 2001; Sinkovics and Hossinger, 2007). Okazaki (2004) found that the USA has more reciprocal communication on web sites compared to Japan and Spain, and Roberts and Ko (2001) indicate that research has shown that some cultures have a more direct mode of communication. This is particularly true when cultures are highly individualistic such as the USA and the Netherlands. These considerations lead to the following hypothesis:

H5. The target country will influence a brand's SNS use and levels of engagement; brands will show higher levels of SNS use in the USA and the Netherlands when compared to Brazil.

METHOD

Sample

This study employed content analysis to determine SNS presence and levels of engagement displayed by the top global brands. Two rankings of top global brands were combined to ensure a more comprehensive coverage[8], yielding a total of 132 brands for analysis. The unit of analysis was the brand web site homepage (when available) for each of the three countries. The brand was considered to have a web site for a given country when it was in the native language of the country and/or contained references to the country in its URL, header or footer. Of the 132 top global brands analyzed, 124 had web sites in the USA, 88 in Brazil, and 87 in the Netherlands. In total, 299 web sites were analyzed: 129 brands had a presence in at least one of the three countries, and 72 brands were present in all three.

Dependent Variables

The first dependent variable—SNS presence—was defined as the availability of links to SNSs on the brand web site homepage. An entry was considered as linking to an SNS if the target web site met the criteria established by Boyd and Ellison (2008). The presence of at least one link to an SNS on the brand web site homepage was used to determine that SNSs were adopted for that country.

The second dependent variable—SNS engagement level—was measured by analyzing each individual entry linking to an SNS from brand web site homepages. Due to its exploratory nature and the lack of literature directly on the subject, this study created a classification based on an initial review of a subsample, measuring different levels of interactivity according to how the SNS was linked (see Table I). While some brands simply displayed the logo of the SNS linking to their profile, without further call to action, other brands alluded to increasingly higher levels of engagement. These higher levels of engagement ranged from inviting the user to display the brand in their own profile or sharing content from the brand with their friends on the SNS (Share/Like), following the brand or its updates in the SNS in a one-way communication (Follow Us), joining or participating in a conversation or a community implying two-way interaction (Community) or inviting the user to contribute with content to the brand's profile, such as adding photos or sharing stories (Participate). When different levels of engagement were displayed, the highest level was used for analysis.

Four coders participated in the content analysis between April 28 and May 10, 2011. Two coders analyzed the web sites that each brand had for each country, with 20 percent of the sample reviewed by both coders to measure intercoder reliability. Intercoder reliability, calculated using Cohen's κ, was above 0.68 for SNS presence (0.68 for the Netherlands, 0.77 for Brazil, and 0.89 for the USA) and above

LEVEL	DEFINITION
Just the logo	Only the logo (or name) of the SNS is displayed on the brand web site, without any specific suggestion of interactivity or call to action
Share/Like	The brand web site allows the consumer to share content using the consumer's SNS profile. When clicking on Share or Like, the consumer's profile will display the brand content to the consumer's friends on the SNS
Follow Us	The SNS link on the brand web site invites the consumer to subscribe to news or updates about the brand, implying one-way communication from the brand towards the consumer
Community	The SNS link invites the consumer to be part of the brand community, suggesting two-way communication and interaction between the brand and the consumer
Participate	The brand web site explicitly asks the consumer to post content to the brand's SNS page, or to co-create content

0.48 for SNS engagement levels (0.48 for Brazil and the Netherlands, and 0.64 for the USA—where all the entries were coded by at least one coder, and the first author), values considered fair to good.

Independent Variables

The following variables were used in the models to test the hypotheses:

- *Market:* brand characteristics were used to classify each brand according to the primary market in which they operate, following the Global Industry Classification Standard[9]. Brands were assigned to the following markets: consumer discretionary (automobiles, durables and apparel, services, media, and retailing), consumer staples (food, beverage and tobacco, household and personal products), energy, financials (banks, insurance, real estate), industrials (commercial and professional services, capital goods, transportation), information technology (software, hardware), and telecommunications.
- *Younger target audience:* the brand web sites were rated on whether they targeted younger audiences or general ones according to the products they displayed, the language used, and the overall design. A dummy variable was created, where 0 was used for general audiences and 1 for younger target audiences.
- *Home market:* the headquarters of the company owning the brand was used to determine the brand's home market.
- *Web operations in target country:* availability of links to either online e-mail or chat support, or an online shop on the country web site, was used to determine whether the brand had web operations in that country. With online shops, only stores operated by the company were considered.
- *Country:* the country (USA, the Netherlands, and Brazil) was determined by the web site homepage. When a brand's main domain (.com) displayed a global homepage, inviting the user to select a country, coders selected the appropriate country version of the homepage before performing the analysis.

Organization size, measured as the total annual revenue of the company owning the brand[10], was used as a control variable considering innovation adoption theory posits that organization size may facilitate innovation, as indicated by Hurley and Hult (1998). Such a measure, however, has found mixed support in empirical studies of internet technology adoption (e.g. Marston, 2003; Papastathopoulou and Avlonitis, 2009), and therefore the study considered relevant to control for its potential impacts on the activities of top global brands.

RESULTS

The review of the web sites of 129 top global brands with activities in at least one of the three countries showed that 64 percent of the brands had adopted SNSs in at least one of the three countries. American homepages showed the highest level of adoption, with 56 percent of the brands having at least one SNS entry, followed by Brazil with 45 percent, and the Netherlands with 32 percent (see Table II). USA also had the highest number of SNS entries on homepages, with an average of 1.4, while the Netherlands displayed the lowest number, with an average of 0.8.

Table II: SNS presence and number of entries by brand/country

Market	BRAZIL		THE NETHERLANDS		USA		OVERALL	
	SNS PRESENCE %	AVERAGE ENTRIES (SD)	SNS PRESENCE %	AVERAGE ENTRIES (SD)	SNS PRESENCE %	AVERAGE ENTRIES (SD)	SNS PRESENCE %	AVERAGE ENTRIES (SD)[a]
Consumer discretionary	42	0.85 (1.22)	31	0.81 (1.38)	59	1.27 (1.23)	67	1.01 (1.28)
Consumer staples	58	1.38 (1.49)	23	0.36 (0.79)	78	1.78 (1.48)	84	1.26 (1.44)
Energy	50	1.5 (2.12)	0	–	33	1.33 (2.31)	50	1 (1.73)
Financials	14	0.36 (0.93)	0	–	21	0.71 (1.49)	28	0.48 (1.21)
Industrials	0	–	0	–	50	1.5 (1.73)	50	0.5 (1.17)
IT	65	1.82 (1.59)	65	1.82 (1.67)	59	1.76 (1.64)	76	1.80 (1.60)
Telecom	100	0 (1)	100	2.5 (0.71)	67	1.67 (1.53)	80	1.83 (1.17)
Young target	69	1.69 (1.54)	26	0.58 (1.21)	91	2.14 (1.32)	91	1.49 (1.46)
Same country[b]	100	2.5 (0.71)	0	–	54	1.44 (1.53)	53	1.41 (1.52)
Web operations[b]	46	1.08 (1.38)	32	0.79 (1.32)	55	1.38 (1.47)	46	1.13 (1.42)
Total	45	1.08 (1.39)	32	0.80 (1.34)	56	1.37 (1.47)	64	1.12 (1.43)

Notes: [a]SNS presence overall numbers calculated using brands across three countries (i.e. if a brand had presence in at least one country, it was considered as SNS present), except for same country and web operations. Number of SNS Entries calculated with three countries combined (results of each brand in each country considered). SD in parentheses; [b]the same country variable measured whether the brand had their headquarters in the same country of the web site (e.g. Philips being headquartered in the Netherlands, or Google in the USA) and web operations measured whether the brand had either online support or online sales activities in the web site of the country evaluated

SNSs with global coverage were most frequently used by the brands. Facebook was referred to by 41 percent of the brands at least once (USA: 67 percent, Brazil: 33 percent, the Netherlands: 23 percent), while Twitter was shown by 35 percent of the brands (USA: 56 percent, Brazil: 31 percent, the Netherlands: 19 percent). Local SNSs—services with a high penetration rate in just a few countries—were barely used. Orkut, which reached 78 percent of Brazilian internet users[11] (Facebook usage in the country was just 24 percent), was only used by 7 percent of the Brazilian brand web sites. Similar results were found for Hyves, used by 64 percent of the Dutch internet population[12] (Facebook usage: 31 percent), was only used by 8 percent of the Dutch brand web sites.

The most commonly used level of engagement was one-way communication—Follow Us, followed by two-way communication—Community (see Table III). The most intense level of engagement—Participation—was almost non-existent on brand web site homepages. Exceptions came from information technology and consumer staples. For example, Kleenex asked users to tell their story about a loved one on the brand's Facebook page.

Explaining SNS Presence

The influence of each potential factor on the dependent variables was analyzed using logistic regression models. Using a logistic model was considered beneficial for the analysis not only due to its rigor, but also because it allows investigating the influence of any one potential factor on the likelihood of a brand being present in an SNS. First, each potential factor was analyzed separately with each of the dependent variables, in order to confirm the hypotheses individually. Then, a full model containing

Table III: Highest SNS engagement level by brand

	NONE %	JUST THE LOGO %	SHARE/ LIKE %	FOLLOW US %	COMMUNITY %	PARTICIPATE %
Market						
Consumer discretionary	36	12	5	24	21	2
Consumer staples	16	6	16	25	28	9
Energy	50		–	50		
Financials	72	8	–	16	4	
Industrials	50	25	–	25		
IT	24	18	6	29	18	6
Telecom	20			40	40	
Young target	9	5	23	23	36	5
Same country	34	5	5	25	14	4
Web operations	54	9	6	21	10	1
Brazil	55	11	9	20	5	0
The Netherlands	68	7	1	16	7	1
USA	44	8	6	23	16	3
Total	36	10	6	25	19	3

Notes: All numbers calculated using highest level of engagement from brands across three countries, except for same country—measuring the activity of the brand in the country where it is headquartered—and web operations—on whether the brand has online sales or support activities—in the country being evaluated

Table IV: SNS presence—coefficients and odds ratios from logistic regression

	BIVARIATE ESTIMATES COEFFICIENT (ODDS RATIO)	FULL MODEL COEFFICIENT (ODDS RATIO)
Market		
Consumer discretionary	0.02 (1.02)	1.18 (3.25)
Consumer staples	0.56 (1.75)*	1.47 (4.37)
Energy	−0.78 (0.46)	−0.19 (0.83)
Financials	−1.79 (0.17)*	−0.39 (0.68)
IT	0.81 (2.26)*	2.24 (9.42)**
Telecom	1.79 (6.02)	3.17 (23.79)*
Industrials[a]	−1.51 (0.22)	–
Young target	0.86 (2.35)**	0.92 (2.51)*
Size	−0.001 (0.99)	−0.001 (1)
Same country	0.39 (1.47)	−0.19 (0.83)
Web operations	0.57 (1.76)	0.39 (1.47)
Country		
USA	0.66 (1.93)**	1.35 (3.87)**
Brazil	−0.04 (0.96)	0.67 (1.96)*
The Netherlands[a]	−0.75 (0.47)**	–
χ^2		60.96**

Notes: [a]Base category; *$p < 0.05$; **$p < 0.01$

all potential factors was created to understand which effects remained significant when all variables were controlled for.

The outcome of the logistic regression models partially supports *H1*. As shown in Table IV, brands from the information technology market—such as IBM, Microsoft, and HP—and telecommunication services—such as Vodafone or T-Mobile—have significantly higher odds-ratios for SNS presence than other sectors. However, contrary to this hypothesis, the consumer discretionary and consumer staples markets do not display significant relationships with SNS presence in the full model.

The results indicate a statistically significant relationship between brands targeting younger audiences, like Sprite or MTV, and SNS presence, thus supporting *H2*. Further inspection of the data also indicates that younger target audience may contribute to the loss of statistical significance from consumer staples on the full model: a relatively high number of brands with young target audiences are included in this segment (47 percent of the brands have a young target focus) and we found a high correlation between both independent variables ($\phi = 0.43$, $p < 0.001$).

The hypotheses related to brand headquarters being present in the same country (*H3*) and the brand having internet operations in the country (*H4*) were rejected. Finally, the country where the brand operates did show a statistically significant influence on the dependent variable: the odds ratios for SNS presence of brands operating in the USA or in Brazil were significantly higher than those operating in the Netherlands (base category for country), which is not fully consistent with *H5*.

Explaining Levels of SNS Engagement

SNS Engagement was also analyzed, first by estimating the bivariate relationships of each potential factor and the dependent variable, and then using a full model with all factors combined. A multinomial model was built, since the dependent variable failed to meet the proportional odds assumption of the ordered logistic regression model.

The outcome of the multinomial logistic regression supports the first hypothesis, as shown in Table V. Consumer markets (consumer staples and consumer discretionary), technology-related markets (information technology and telecommunication services), and financial services display significant relationships with SNS engagement at the community level, with brands such as American Express, Coca-Cola, or Starbucks inviting the user to participate in their online communities and join the discussion. The only sectors that had significant relationship at the highest SNS engagement level—Participate—were consumer staples and information technology. Likewise, brands targeting younger audiences show statistically significant influence particularly at the Share/Like and the community levels, providing full support for *H2*. The country in which the brand operates has a statistically significant influence on SNS engagement, thus confirming *H5*. Brands operating in the USA are more likely to have higher engagement levels than those in Brazil and the Netherlands, which implies that *H5* has to be (partly) rejected.

Finally, web operations and the brand headquarters being in the same country do not have any significant influence on the dependent variable (neither in the specific model nor in the full model); thus both *H3* and *H4* are rejected.

DISCUSSION

The aim of this study was to provide an overview of top global brand activities in SNSs, and to identify the factors that influence such activity across countries. A review of the SNS presence and levels of engagement of the top global brands was performed in three different countries, and potential factors drawn from literature on internet innovation were analyzed to determine their influence.

One important finding is that the markets in which top global brands operate continue to exert an influence on the adoption of internet innovations. SNS presence was significantly higher for information technology and telecommunication brands. Information technology and consumer staples brands were also more likely to engage with consumers at higher levels. Previous studies have found similar patterns, with different markets having different internet innovation adoption strategies (Perry and Bodkin, 2000; Cho and Huh, 2010; Perry *et al.*, 2003; Golan and Zaidner, 2008); our study thus reinforces these findings.

Another important finding was the significant influence that the age of a brand's target market had on decisions related to SNSs. Top global brands targeting younger audiences were more likely to display SNSs prominently on their homepages, and were also more likely to use SNSs to ask consumers to share brand content, or to engage with a brand community. This is in line with earlier findings related to adoption of e-commerce (Doherty and Ellis-Chadwick, 2003). It would be interesting to further study what additional characteristics (beyond markets and target group) make a brand more likely to engage in SNS activities and why.

Table V: SNS engagement levels—coefficients from logistic regression

	JUST THE LOGO		SHARE/LIKE		FOLLOW US		COMMUNITY		PARTICIPATE	
	BIVARIATE ESTIMATES	FULL MODEL	BIVARIATE ESTIMATES	FULL MODEL	BIVARIATE ESTIMATES	FULL MODEL	BIVARIATE ESTIMATES	FULL MODEL	BIVARIATE ESTIMATES	FULL MODEL
Market										
Consumer discretionary	−0.12	0.18	−0.41	16.7	0.07	1.19	0.15	22.1**	−0.69	21.25
Consumer staples	−0.38	0.09	2.11**	17.53	0.4	1.48	0.48	22.23**	1.73	22.98**
Energy	−33.5	−34.09	−33.5	−17.04	0.08	0	−33.5	−12.32	−33.5	−14.48
Financials	−1.34	−0.98	−45.92	−16.79	−1.49**	−0.17	−2.22*	2.04**	−44.92	−12.37
IT	1.71**	1.77	−0.69	17.42	0.73	2.06	0.63	23.14**	0.63	22.37**
Telecom	−42.5	−36.89	−41.5	−19.14	1.71	2.97	2.88*	25.35	−4.5	−15.38
Industrials	−0.5		−3.7		−1.36		−3.7		−3.7	
Young target	−0.58	−0.16	3**	2.81**	0.52	0.7	1.06*	1.21*	0.52	−0.38
Revenue	0	0	0	0	0	0	0	0	0	0
Same country	−0.38	−1.01	0.23	−0.36	0.48	0.15	0.63	−0.48	1.73	0.59
Web operations	0.5	0.38	–	18.63	1.36	1.14	−0.08	−0.55	−1.34	−2.38
Brazil	0.39	0.8	0.86	2.74*	0.02	0.59	−1.01	0.14	−34.4	−32.27
The Netherlands	−0.65		−2.15*		−0.63		−0.83		−0.83	
USA	0.2	1.39*	0.41	2.81*	0.53	0.94*	1.36**	2.12**	2.05	2.08

Notes: No entry is the base outcome; *p<0.05; **p<0.01

Finally, this study has also shown how decisions over SNS use vary from country to country. Top global brands are still much more likely to adopt internet innovations—in this case the use of SNSs—in the USA, even after other country-related factors have been controlled. The findings also indicate that brands prefer global SNSs—such as Facebook or Twitter—to local SNSs, even in countries where the global SNSs do not have the highest market share. Top global brands seem to prefer to operate in a global world, disregarding local SNSs no matter how large they are in a given country. Neither the internet penetration figures, nor the expectations based on cultural differences (Hofstede, 1983; Kampf, 2007; Okazaki, 2004; Roberts and Ko, 2001; Sinkovics and Hossinger, 2007) could explain the differences between the countries included in this study. Further research is necessary to understand these differences.

Although this study identified a number of factors influencing brands' decisions related to SNSs, certain limitations must be considered when interpreting the results. First, SNSs are still growing rapidly, both in terms of numbers of users and in brands using them. For example, Peters and Salazar (2010) reported that 17 percent of the top global brands used SNSs in 2009, whereas our study found that this number had increased to 64 percent by 2011. This rapid growth indicates the need to continue researching how brands use SNS in the coming years. Second, this study focussed on the brand web site as the unit of analysis, and as an indicator of the importance that a brand attributes to SNSs. The results of this study, therefore, only address SNS activities that are communicated on the brands' web sites and the study did not investigate whether the brand fulfills the promise of interactivity in the SNS environment. Such a limitation calls for further research inside SNSs to identify activities that brands perform but may not necessarily promote or announce on the brand web site itself. Third, this study focussed on how top global brands operate across different markets. Future studies should focus on the different behaviors between local and global brands, as well as differences among small and larger brands. Finally, the independent variables identified in this study were collected from publicly available data and provide a macro-level understanding of the factors influencing SNS adoption by brands. Additional research on the micro-level factors influencing SNS presence and level of engagement—with data coming from interviews or surveys with decision makers inside the organizations—would also help provide a more comprehensive view.

This study, despite these limitations, fulfilled its objectives by advancing academic discussion on the brand use of SNSs—and by demonstrating how SNS usage has so far followed an innovation cycle similar to that seen in early internet adoption, with common factors influencing the adoption and implementation of the new medium. The role played by the country context was reinforced by the results of this study, as was the fact that this new technology is currently focussed on younger target audiences, and on businesses in the technology and consumer intensive sectors. Furthermore, while SNSs offer several opportunities for brands to interact in innovative ways with consumers directly, few brands prominently display or promote more advanced types of interaction, calling for further research not only on why such types of interaction are not more frequently used, but also on the consumer expectations when interacting with brands on SNSs. Brands and practitioners should also be aware that considerable opportunities exist for differentiation from competitors by adopting and promoting more innovative ways of interaction with consumers, considering that a majority of the brands simply links to or promotes SNSs as a resource to follow news about the company. Overall, not only does this study provide a general set of results for SNS usage and engagement levels from top global brands across three countries—a welcome addition to case studies or experimental research in the area—, but it also reinforces the importance of SNSs for brand communication research, which should also take into consideration the increasingly larger—and more global—usage that brands make of SNSs as part of their communication strategies.

NOTES

1. http://advertising.microsoft.com/research/young-adults-revealed (accessed June 19, 2011).
2. www.coca-cola.com and www.facebook.com/cocacola (accessed December 1, 2011).
3. www.facebook.com/press/info.php?statistics (accessed December 1, 2011).
4. http://blog.compete.com/2011/06/23/facebook-pages-attract-online-shoppers-to-retailer-sales-and-promotions/ (accessed June 29, 2011).
5. www.facebook.com/press/info.phpFstatistics (accessed December 1, 2011).
6. A comparison in several of the dimensions of Hofstede's index show large differences: for individualism, the USA scores 91, the Netherlands 80, and Brazil 38; for masculinity, the US scores 62, Brazil 49, and the Netherlands 14; for uncertainty avoidance, Brazil scores 76, the Netherlands 53, and the USA 46; finally, for long-term orientation, Brazil scores 65, the Netherlands 44, and the USA 29. www.geert-hofstede.com/hofstede_dimensions.php (accessed July 8, 2011).
7. 2010 World Bank Data.
8. Interbrands and Brandz 100 top global brands, 2010.
9. Industry classification guidelines developed by Standard & Poor's and MSCI Barra. www.standardandpoors.com/indices/gics/en/us (accessed June 24, 2011).
10. Financial data gathered from financial reports to the US Securities and Exchange Commission (SEC), or similar reports for non-US brands. Only one brand belonged to a non-publicly listed company (Subway), and in that case data were collected from trade publications.
11. www.comscore.com/ Press_Events/Press_ Releases/2010/10/Orkut_ Continues_to_Lead_ Brazil_s_Social_ Networking_ Market_Facebook_ Audience_Grows_Fivefold (accessed June 24, 2011).
12. www.comscore.com/Press_Events/Press_Releases/2011/4/The_Netherlands_Ranks_number_one_ Worldwide_in_Penetration_ for_Twitter_and_ LinkedIn (accessed June 24, 2011).

REFERENCES

Acar, A. and Polonsky, M. (2008), "Online social networks and insights into marketing communications", *Journal of Internet Commerce*, Vol. 6 No. 4, pp. 55–72.

Bernoff, J. and Li, C. (2008), "Harnessing the power of the oh-so-social web", *MIT Sloan Management Review*, Vol. 49 No. 3, pp. 36–42.

Booth, N. and Matic, J.A. (2011), "Mapping and leveraging influencers in social media to shape corporate brand perceptions", *Corporate Communications: An International Journal*, Vol. 16 No. 3, pp. 184–91.

Boyd, D.M. and Ellison, N.B. (2008), "Social network sites: definition, history, and scholarship", *Journal of Computer-Mediated Communication*, Vol. 13 No. 1, pp. 210–30.

Cho, S. and Huh, J. (2010), "Content analysis of corporate blogs as a relationship management tool", *Corporate Communications: An International Journal*, Vol. 15 No. 1, pp. 30–48.

comScore (2010), "comScore data passport second half 2010", available at: www.comscore.com/ Press_Events/Presentations_Whitepapers/2010/comScore_Data_Passport_-_Second_Half_2010 (accessed June 19, 2011).

Doherty, N.F. and Ellis-Chadwick, F.E. (2003), "The relationship between retailers' targeting and e-commerce strategies: an empirical analysis", *Internet Research*, Vol. 13 No. 3, pp. 170–82.

Dunne, A., Lawlor, M.-A. and Rowley, J. (2010), "Young people's use of online social networking sites—a uses and gratifications perspective", *Journal of Research in Interactive Marketing*, Vol. 4 No. 1, pp. 46–58.

Edelman, D. and Salsberg, B. (2010), "Beyond paidmedia: marketing's new vocabulary", *McKinsey Quarterly*, pp. 1–8, available at: www.mckinseyquarterly.com/Beyond_paid_ media_Marketings_new_vocabulary_2697 (accessed June 19, 2011).

Golan, G.J. and Zaidner, L. (2008), "Creative strategies in viral advertising: an application of Taylor's six-segment message strategy wheel", *Journal of Computer-Mediated Communication*, Vol. 13 No. 4, pp. 959–72.

Herring, S., Paolillo, J.C., Ramos-Vielba, I., Kouper, I., Wright, E., Stoerger, S., Scheidt, L.A. and Clark, B. (2007), "Language networks on live journal", *2007 40th Annual Hawaii International Conference on System Sciences (HICSS'07), p.79.*

Hofstede, G. (1983), "The cultural relativity of organizational practices and theories", *Journal of International Business Studies*, Vol. 14 No. 2, pp. 75–89.

Hurley, R.F. and Hult, G.T.M. (1998), "Innovation, market orientation, and organizational learning: an integration and empirical examination", *The Journal of Marketing*, Vol. 62 No. 3, pp. 42–54.

Jansen, B.J. and Zhang, M. (2009), "Twitter power: tweets as electronic word of mouth", *Journal of the American Society for Information Science*, Vol. 60 No. 11, pp. 2169–88.

Kampf, C. (2007), "Corporate social responsibility: Walmart, Maersk and the cultural bounds of representation in corporate web sites", *Corporate Communications: An International Journal*, Vol. 12 No. 1, pp. 41–57.

Kaplan, A.M. and Haenlein, M. (2010), "Users of the world, unite! The challenges and opportunities of social media", *Business Horizons*, Vol. 53 No. 1, pp. 59–68.

Lenhart, A., Purcell, K., Smith, A. and Zickuhr, K. (2010), "Social media & mobile internet use among teens and young adults", Pew Internet & American Life Project, available at: www.pewInternet.org/Reports/2010/Social-Media-and-Young-Adults.aspx (accessed June 19, 2011).

Marston, C. (2003), "Financial reporting on the internet by leading Japanese companies", *Corporate Communications: An International Journal*, Vol. 8 No. 1, pp. 23–34.

Mei, J.S.A., Bansal, N. and Pang, A. (2010), "New media: a new medium in escalating crises?", *Corporate Communications: An International Journal*, Vol. 15 No. 2, pp. 143–55.

Needham, A. (2008), "Word of mouth, youth and their brands", *Young Consumers*, Vol. 9 No. 1, pp. 60–2.

Okazaki, S. (2004), "Do multinationals standardise or localise? The cross-cultural dimensionality of product-based web sites", *Internet Research*, Vol. 14 No. 1, pp. 81–94.

Palmer, A. and Koenig-Lewis, N. (2009), "An experiential, social network-based approach to direct marketing", *Direct Marketing*, Vol. 3 No. 3, pp. 162–76.

Papastathopoulou, P. and Avlonitis, G.J. (2009), "Classifying enterprises on the basis of WWW use: a behavioral approach", *Internet Research*, Vol. 19 No. 3, pp. 332–47.

Perry, D.C., Taylor, M. and Doerfel, M.L. (2003), "Internet-based communication in crisis management", *Management Communication Quarterly*, Vol. 17 No. 2, pp. 206–32.

Perry, M. and Bodkin, C. (2000), "Content analysis of 100 company web sites", *Corporate Communications: An International Journal*, Vol. 5 No. 2, pp. 87–97.

Peters, A. and Salazar, D. (2010), "Globalization in marketing: an empirical analysis of business adoption and use of social network sites", Paper No. 570, AMCIS 2010 Proceedings, Lima, Peru, August 12–15.

Roberts, M.S. and Ko, H. (2001), "Global interactive advertising: defining what we mean and using what we have learned", *Journal of Interactive Advertising*, Vol. 1 No. 2, pp. 18–27.

Sicilia, M. and Palazón, M. (2008), "Brand communities on the Internet: a case study of Coca-Cola's Spanish virtual community", *Corporate Communications: An International Journal*, Vol. 13 No. 3, pp. 255–70.

Sinkovics, R.R. and Hossinger, M. (2007), "Cultural adaptation in cross border e-commerce: a study of German companies", *Journal of Electronic Commerce Research*, Vol. 8 No. 4, pp. 221–35.

Syed-Ahmad, S.F. and Murphy, J. (2010), "Social networking as a marketing tool: the case of a small Australian company", *Journal of Hospitality Marketing & Management*, Vol. 19 No. 7, pp. 700–16.

Waters, R.D. and Lemanski, J.L. (2011), "Revisiting strategic communication's past to understand the present", *Corporate Communications: An International Journal*, Vol. 16 No. 2, pp. 150–69.

Zeisser, M. (2010), "Unlocking the elusive potential of social networks", *McKinsey Quarterly*, June, pp. 1–3, available at: www.mckinseyquarterly.com/Unlocking_the_elusive_potential_of_social_networks_2623 (accessed June 19, 2011).

ABOUT THE AUTHORS

Theo Araujo is a Doctoral student in Communication Science at the University of Amsterdam, with an MBA in Marketing and a Bachelor degree in Journalism. His research interests include social network sites, corporate communication and media and advertising. Theo Araujo is the corresponding author and can be contacted at: Theo.TrostlideAraujoCosta@student.uva.nl

Peter Neijens is Chair of Persuasive Communication in the Amsterdam School of Communication Research at the University of Amsterdam. He is Dean of the Graduate School of Communication and Acting Director of The Amsterdam School of Communication Research. His research interests include media and advertising, public opinion, and persuasion processes.

CASE STUDY

Maya walks into Target knowing full well the consequences of coming. She came to buy only a few things, the necessities only, she told herself but she found herself wandering to the toys and kids areas. She puts in a few things in her basket and before she knows it, it's bulging everywhere and she can barely get through the aisles. So much for the necessities, she thinks.

She goes home and starts to unload the things from her car when she takes out a toy she notices it's made in China. Then she notices that the shoes for her daughter are also made in China. And she asks herself, why everything is made somewhere else. She looks at all of the labels she has bought and not one thing was made in U.S.A.

John comes home and rests at the couch.

"Honey, why is everything made in other countries?" Maya asks.

"Because we cannot afford for things to be made here, it's too expensive." John says changing the channel on the TV (which is made in Japan).

"What do you mean?" Maya persists.

"It would cost the producer too much money to make things here, the market is more profitable for the producer to get it made, say in China and have it shipped here." John says.

"But how is that helping our country?" Maya asks.

Help John answer Maya's question, how is that helping the U.S.?

Also, discuss the following questions:

In what ways can outsourcing production benefit the U.S. economy; in what ways can it hurt the economy?

Can we bring the productions and jobs back to the U.S.?

What gains and losses can consumers get from globalization?

CONSUMER RESOURCES

Consumers International: http://www.consumersinternational.org
Global Trade Watch: http://www.citizen.org/trade
International Economics Study Center: http://www.internationalecon.com
International Standards Organization: http://www.iso.org
Transparency International: http://www.transparency.org
United National Development Programme: http://www.undp.org

CHAPTER 7

SUSTAINABILITY AND CONSUMERS

CHAPTER 7 INTRODUCTION

There are many recommendations from educators and activists on how to become a 'green' consumer, such as 'four ways to be a green consumer,' 'five ways to practice eco-friendly shopping,' and 'seven steps to become a green consumer,' etc. We are encouraged to buy organic and local food, minimize fuel and energy consumption, switch to natural fiber for clothing, use the 'energy star' appliances, and ditch the bottled water. All of these are advocated as opportunities to 'make a difference' via our sustainable consumption choices. But can we do it alone to make a difference and save the planet?

SUSTAINABLE CONSUMPTION

Doris Fuchs and Frederike Boll

INTRODUCTION

The notion of sustainable consumption approaches environmental problems through the lens of consumption decisions. Thereby, it aims to highlight the underlying and most fundamental causes of environmental problems and to attribute responsibility where it is due. Specifically, a large share of the environmental degradation arising from production processes in developing countries then has to be linked to consumption decisions made in industrialized countries. At the same time, sustainable consumption pinpoints the question of social justice in the use of the world's ecological resources and highlights the enormous asymmetries existing there.

Consumption patterns and levels can therefore no longer be seen as an individual or national problem; they have become a global political issue. Additional links to global politics arise because various aspects of the global political economy, such as the politics of trade and finance, impact consumption patterns and levels and their environmental (and social) implications (Fuchs and Lorek 2002). Not surprisingly, sustainable consumption has been explicitly present on the global political agenda, in the form of *Agenda 21*, since the Earth Summit in Rio in 1992 (UN 1992).

This chapter explores the concept of sustainable consumption and delineates the task faced by sustainable consumption governance. It then identifies relevant political actors in global sustainable consumption governance, traces current affairs, discusses obstacles to progress in this field, and explores policy implications. Finally, it briefly introduces current lines of enquiry and research fields in the area of sustainable consumption.

WHAT IS CONSUMPTION AND WHY STUDY IT?

The *International Encyclopedia of the Social Sciences* (Eglitis 2008: 105) defines consumption as "the personal expenditure of individuals and families that involves the selection, usage, and disposal or reuse of goods and services." In other words, consumption entails all phases of our dealing with goods (and services to some extent): purchase, use, and disposal. As sociologists and psychologists will tell us, such consumption can take place for a variety of purposes. Food and water as well as the need for shelter and some way to stay warm are all requisites for survival. In today's developed societies, however, the purpose of consumption goes beyond this necessary fulfillment of fundamental needs. We consume to entertain ourselves, to increase our happiness (even though we sometimes achieve the opposite), to define our identity, and/or to express status.

But why is consumption a topic in environmental politics and policy? The answer to this question becomes highly obvious if we consider the resource use associated with our consumption. Western society spends huge amounts of resources and creates huge amounts of pollution with its consumption patterns and levels. In fact, this consumer society may be identified as the main villain when identifying causes of the absence of sustainability in development.

It is more convenient to attribute responsibility for environmental degradation to production methods and processes, of course. After all, one can argue that the consumer has little information or influence on the environmental degradation caused at that stage. Moreover, the number of companies involved may still be large, but it is certainly smaller than the number of consumers and thus easier to reach and regulate. Likewise, environmental degradation caused by a production plant is much more visible and concentrated, and can be targeted more directly. Finally, and perhaps most fundamentally, it is politically much more acceptable to regulate production than to constrain consumption, as long as we view consumer choice as part of our freedom in the pursuit of happiness and as long as economic growth, which in turn is supposed to depend on consumption, remains the primary and unassailable political goal.

Yet, a focus on production is insufficient for a range of reasons. For example, it does not include the environmental degradation caused during the use and final disposal of a product. Most importantly, a focus that is limited to production hides the ultimate driving forces behind environmental degradation. Thereby, it fails to attribute responsibility where it is due. Simultaneously, it obscures a substantial share of potential strategies for intervention and change.

The question of responsibility is also one of the starting points of the focus on sustainable consumption in the scientific and political community. It originally arose in the context of debates on the main causes of environmental problems in the world today. At international conferences, developed countries tended to be concerned about population growth in developing countries, while developing countries pointed out the environmental degradation caused by consumption levels and patterns in developed countries. Thus, consumption also has a moral and an ethical side. Indeed, the sustainable consumption debate gained considerable momentum when environmental activists and scholars started to highlight that in his or her lifetime a single American will consume the same amount of environmental resources as a large number of Indians (Durning 1992). Even in today's political debates, we run into these questions of justice again and again. The Chinese can not only easily challenge demands to reduce their greenhouse gas emissions by juxtaposing their per capita emissions with those of the developed countries; they can also challenge such demands on the basis that a large share of the emissions is caused by production for Western consumers.

THE CONCEPT OF SUSTAINABLE CONSUMPTION

Without sustainable consumption, sustainable development is impossible. As pointed out above, unsustainable consumption patterns and levels, especially in industrialized countries, are currently driving a large share of environmental degradation in the world (Haake and Jolivet 2001). But what is sustainable consumption? The Oslo Roundtable defined it as

> the use of services and related products which respond to basic needs and bring a better quality of life while minimizing the use of natural resources and toxic materials as well as the emissions of waste and pollutants over the life cycle of the service or product so as not to jeopardize the needs of further generations.
>
> (Ministry of the Environment Norway 1994)

It is important, however, to differentiate between strong and weak sustainable consumption. Weak sustainable consumption can result from increases in the efficiency of production and consumption, which are typically reached via technological improvements. In this case, improvements in the sustainability of consumption result from a reduction in resource consumption per consumption unit due to improvements in production processes or, for example, an efficiency-friendly design. Many times, such improvements are win–win scenarios.

Weak sustainable consumption can be seen as the necessary condition to achieve sustainable development. However, existing limits to the Earth's resources and to its capacity to serve as a sink for pollutants mean that improvements in the efficiency of consumption will not suffice for achieving sustainable development. As research on the so-called rebound effect has documented, achievements based on efficiency alone are almost always overcompensated by a growth in consumption volumes (Greening *et al.* 2000).

In consequence, changes in patterns and reductions in levels in industrialized countries—i.e. strong sustainable consumption—need to be pursued if we want to achieve sustainability. Strong sustainable consumption can then be defined as a sufficient condition for sustainable development. It requires changes in infrastructures and choices as well as a questioning of the levels and drivers of consumption. The necessary steps for achieving strong sustainable consumption are of course, politically speaking, highly controversial. Yet there are those issues that take center stage when approaching sustainable development from the perspective of sustainable consumption rather than sustainable production.

Not surprisingly, the concepts of strong and weak sustainable consumption were introduced into the scientific debate in the context of analyses of the promises and pitfalls of sustainable consumption governance (Fuchs and Lorek 2005). These analyses started from the observation that a considerable amount of activity was taking place under the heading of sustainable consumption in global governance, while little substantial progress was being achieved. In consequence, scholars delineated the specific objectives of the various activities and demonstrated the narrowness of their focus on efficiency questions. They subsequently explained the almost complete absence of strong sustainable consumption governance by assessing the interests and relative influence of the various state and non-state actors involved in this policy field (see below). Thus, the distinction between strong and weak sustainable consumption serves as a useful analytical tool for differentiating between the pursuit of marginal improvements and substantial (and thus politically costly) changes in the sustainability of consumption as derived from changes in patterns and levels.

Beyond the fundamental distinction between strong and weak sustainable consumption governance, a number of alternative or supplementary conceptual distinctions for sustainable consumption exist in the literature (Charkiewicz *et al.* 2001; Cohen and Murphy 2001; Princen *et al.* 2002). Philosophical and sociological approaches, for instance, emphasize differentiations between motivations, allowing for an enhanced understanding of the meaning of consumption today. Princen (1999), for instance, develops categories such as *misconsumption* and *overconsumption* to pinpoint the problematic aspects of the consumption behavior of today's consumer class. A similar perspective shows up in the four consumption categories identified by UNEP. The *Consumption Opportunities* report (UNEP 2001) differentiates between efficient consumption, different consumption, conscious consumption, and appropriate consumption, associating the first with dematerialization and the latter three with the optimization of consumption.

THE TASK

In order to pursue sustainable consumption, one needs first to understand the causes and drivers of consumption decisions and the consumption areas causing a particular burden for the environment and society. In industrialized countries, consumption generally goes far beyond attempts to satisfy people's needs for food and shelter. Rather, decisions are influenced by aspects such as convenience, identity setting, signaling of status, distraction, participation, and/or creativeness. Political measures to improve the sustainability of consumption need to take these aspects into account if they want to be successful.

Moreover, consumers make their decisions in specific socio-economic, political, and cultural contexts. They act rarely as fully autonomous individuals, but rather within constraints set by their professional and social environment (Georg 1999; Schor 1999). These constraints include factors such as time and money, but also expectations or traditions. In fact, the individualization of the responsibility for sustainable consumption frequently advocated by politicians and business has to be viewed very critically (Princen *et al.* 2002). In consequence, political steps to improve the sustainability of consumption should take not just (and maybe not even primarily) the individual consumer into account but also the consumption environment.

Furthermore, such political strategies need to target the consumption clusters associated with the largest environmental and social burdens. Research has identified food, mobility, and housing as three major areas of concern here (Lorek and Spangenberg 2001). First, the increasing quantity of meat consumption, greenhouse production, and pesticide use, the introduction of genetically modified organisms (GMOs), and the dominance of long-distance transport are known for the detriment they cause to sustainability. Second, distances travelled by car (as well as urban planning practices that lead to a growing need to use cars), the fuel efficiency of the car fleet, and, most importantly, the dramatic rise in miles travelled by air transport are all areas of primary concern. Third, the growing size of homes and associated heating and cooling needs, as well as the destruction of open space, cause major challenges to sustainable development.

Finally, a particular challenge to sustainable consumption politics and policy arises from the context of globalization (Fuchs and Lorek 2002; Haake and Jolivet 2001). Consumption patterns and levels are a moving target and are influenced by transnational interactions in trade, finance, information, and technology. The extent and breadth of the influence of globalization means that it has the potential to undermine any sustainable consumption policy which ignores this context. Given the further existence of a significant free-rider problem, sustainable consumption cannot be pursued at the national level alone but has to be an objective of global governance.

THE GLOBAL POLITICS OF SUSTAINABLE CONSUMPTION[1]

Sustainable consumption explicitly appeared on the global governance agenda when the United Nations Conference on Environment and Development (UNCED) called for the adoption of sustainable consumption patterns in *Agenda 21* (UN 1992: Chapter 4). Since then, various actors, notably international governmental organizations (IGOs), have addressed the issue of sustainable consumption. Their goals have lacked ambition, however, and any progress has yet to be achieved. In particular, the politically controversial issue of strong sustainable consumption vanished from the agenda. Global sustainable consumption governance has to date concentrated almost exclusively on questions of efficiency (and even here we find more rhetoric than action). The earliest "global" meetings on sustainable consumption, in particular the Oslo meeting in 1994, adopted a much broader approach. It explicitly noted that a focus on eco-efficiency would not provide a sufficiently comprehensive framework for identifying, understanding, and changing unsustainable consumption patterns. In the following years, however, IGOs systematically reduced the focus and ambitions of sustainable consumption governance, and this more comprehensive understanding disappeared from the political agendas.

Actors in global sustainable consumption governance
The Commission on Sustainable Development and the Division on Sustainable Development

The Commission on Sustainable Development (CSD) has been among the most active participants in the sustainable consumption arena. Its work has drawn on the technical and organizational resources of the Division for Sustainable Development (DSD), which, in turn, is part of the United Nations Department for Economic and Social Affairs (UNDESA). The CSD adopted an International Work Program on Changing Consumption and Production Patterns in 1995 and conducted and commissioned work on a range of aspects, such as consumption trends and impacts and relevant policy measures (UNDESA 1995). It fostered especially the development of sustainable consumption indicators and the revision of the UN *Guidelines on Consumer Protection* (UNDESA 2003).

In parallel, the DSD decided to make changing consumption and production patterns part of its multiyear program, collaborating, for instance, with the International Institute for Sustainable Development (IISD). Based on this cooperation, the IISD developed and maintained a website from 1997 to 2000 covering definitions and concepts of sustainable consumption, key resources on the topic, and a compendium of policy instruments for changing consumption and production patterns.

The work of the CSD and DSD on sustainable consumption trends, indicators, and policy measures was important. It provided sustainable consumption with increased visibility on the global governance agenda. Yet both institutions failed in broadly fostering the implementation of Chapter 4 of *Agenda 21*, as they did not manage to move beyond the debate and indicator stage. Moreover, they neglected strong sustainable consumption as a governance goal. Questions regarding fundamental changes in consumption patterns and reductions in consumption levels were raised only in the context of discussions at the CSD of "common but differentiated responsibilities" and did not find their way into official reports and documents.

UNEP

UNEP's Sustainable Consumption Program is housed in the Production and Consumption Unit of the Division of Technology, Industry, and Economics (DTIE). The program started in 1998 with the intention of developing demand-side-oriented activities to complement the DTIE's supply-side-oriented ones. Its stated goal has been to understand the forces driving global consumption patterns, to develop appropriate activities for business and other stakeholders, and to look for potential advances for business, governments, and NGOs. In addition, the DTIE has conducted a "global consumer survey" to gain a better understanding of consumer wants. Finally, it has investigated consumption trends and indicators in a variety of fields. Overall, then, UNEP has addressed a substantial range of topics related to sustainable consumption. Yet its work up to 2001 focused almost exclusively on increasing the eco-efficiency of consumption, with a particular interest in innovations for business.

Interestingly, UNEP's report *Consumption Opportunities* (UNEP 2001) explicitly addressed the politically sensitive topic of overconsumption. However, UNEP did not pursue the ambitious goals of the report further, but instead initiated a Sustainable Consumption Opportunities for Europe (SCOPE) process, with a regional emphasis on Central and Eastern Europe (thus avoiding the most critical overconsuming countries), and little attention has been paid to these politically sensitive questions.

Finally, in 2002, UNEP issued a *Global Status Report* (UNEP 2002), identifying six strategic areas in which it perceives the greatest need for further work on sustainable consumption, such as clarifying the various meanings of the term "consumption," developing better feedback indicators to measure consumption pressures and quality of life, and supporting and enhancing localized campaigns to transform trends in the consumption of certain resources or goods and services. In addition, UNEP quickly picked up the idea of a 10-Year Framework of Programmes following the World Summit on Sustainable Development (WSSD) in Johannesburg in 2002 (see below), an idea that had originally been promoted by the European Union. Thus at that stage UNEP's plans and activities again appeared broad and promising. However, it has yet to demonstrate its willingness and ability to move beyond its former intentional and explicit exclusion of the strong sustainable consumption perspective.

The Organization for Economic Cooperation and Development

The OECD is another important actor that has worked substantially on sustainable consumption. Acknowledging that the OECD countries are home to 19 percent of the world's population but consume 80 percent of the world's resources, the organization started to address the subject in 1995 with an integrated work program, Environmental Impacts of Production and Consumption. Its focus has been on resource efficiency and the link between technological change and the environment, through which the program aimed to explore mutually supportive relationships between environmental improvements and economic growth. The core activities were similar to those of the CSD and included the development of a conceptual framework and indicators as well as analyses of trends in and policy options for OECD countries.

The OECD explicitly concentrated on important sectors and consumption clusters, specifically tourism, food, energy and water consumption, and waste generation (OECD 2002). In addition, it conducted and commissioned reports on policy instruments, information and consumer decision-making, and participatory decision-making with respect to sustainable consumption. Yet, the framework for its consumption work was clearly set in line with the OECD's traditional focus on economic growth. Thus, in the end it failed to go beyond the aim of improving eco-efficiency and the mutual pursuit of economic growth and environmental quality.

In 2008, the OECD started to approach (sustainable) consumption from a different angle by analyzing the distributional effects of environmental policies. The jury is still out on whether this shift in perspective will allow it to play a more noteworthy role in sustainable consumption governance.

The European Union

In 2001, the European Council adopted a Sustainable Development Strategy (EU SDS), revised in 2006, which made sustainable consumption and production one of the key objectives and priorities at the European level. In response to the WSSD in Johannesburg, the European Council strengthened its position in 2003 by stressing again its leading role in promoting and supporting sustainable consumption and production. Several European stakeholder meetings took place involving representatives of governments, the private sector, civil society, and NGOs. However, these meetings turned out to be "discussion platforms" rather than "working platforms."

The *Monitoring Report* of the EU SDS (Eurostat 2007), besides stressing the importance of weak sustainable consumption in the form of eco-efficiency, mentioned that sustainable development can only be achieved by changing patterns of consumption and production, which is part of strong sustainable consumption governance. Additionally, the report underscores the importance of decoupling environmental degradation and economic growth as well as of successful national initiatives which are part of the sustainable development strategy. The impression arises that the European Union is trying to put real effort into fulfilling its goal of having a leading role in shaping policies for sustainable global consumption.

In 2008, the Sustainable Consumption and Production and Sustainable Industrial Policy Action Plan was presented by the EU and defined concrete actions such as eco-design requirements for more products, reinforced energy, and environmental labeling, and supported resource efficiency, eco-innovation, and enhancing the environmental potential of industry. However, the action plan, in comparison with the monitoring report, again focuses solely on weak sustainable consumption and mentions only eco-efficiency and innovations as the major driving forces to achieve sustainable consumption and production. Thereby, it strengthens these aspects in the work of the European Environmental Agency but docs not allow it to go further. In addition, mandatory commitments are still very rare. For example, EU labeling of environmentally friendly products is still voluntary.

Thus, the EU in some respects has taken a number of initiatives and actions to meet its leading role in promoting sustainable consumption and production by starting to stimulate and foster these processes. However, it has yet to address consistently and support strong sustainable consumption and the associated, necessary mandatory commitments.

National governments

National governments and NGOs, as well as researchers and research networks, have also been active in the area of sustainable consumption. Except for perhaps national governments, these actors clearly are not in the same privileged position as IGOs when it comes to the forging of global agreements. Nevertheless, efforts by individual governments to promote national sustainable consumption dialogues and measures can prepare the ground for global sustainable consumption governance. Particularly noteworthy have been the efforts of the Norwegian and Danish governments, which have not only sponsored a substantial amount of research on the topic of sustainable consumption but also pursued specific initiatives to foster global and national sustainable consumption governance. The Norwegian government has been particularly active with respect to the global agenda. It hosted sustainable consumption workshops in 1994 and 1995 and pushed for a broad understanding of requirements and potentials for sustainable consumption governance. It has also collaborated with Norwegian research centers in promoting sustainable consumption ideas at the national level. The Danish government took the lead in the preparation of the WSSD and initiated the development of the 10-Year Framework of Programmes under its EU presidency. However, these efforts have to date failed to address and endorse policy measures for fostering strong sustainable consumption systematically.

Only a few countries accepted the challenge to develop an explicit sustainable consumption and production (SCP) action plan, and they did so with very different approaches and different levels of ambition. For example, while the SCP program of the UK emphasizes the role of business in advancing its agenda, Sweden counts on the involvement of consumers and Finland on R&D and stakeholders. In any case, the popularity of weak instruments (i.e. informational tools) is evident throughout. All SCP programs give very scarce attention to the possibilities of governmental regulation in the context of sustainable consumption and production. The political difficulties involved with this topic were most evident in Sweden, where a change in government led the program to be canceled immediately.

NGOs

NGOs have played a strong and active role in the global campaign to promote sustainable production and consumption. Throughout the many program cycles of the CSD, NGOs working on production and consumption patterns regularly coordinated their advocacy and education efforts, and eventually Organized themselves into the International Coalition for Sustainable Production and Consumption (ICSPAC).

Many of these NGOs ask politically sensitive questions regarding consumption patterns and levels. Moreover, they contribute to the development of strong sustainable consumption governance by promoting the diffusion of alternative lifestyles and values. A mapping of the North American civil society movement revealed how many NGOs and other civil society groups are contributing their share to make sustainable consumption possible, or at least to address the structural unsustainability of current consumption patterns. Voluntary simplicity and "right to know" groups, local money and social investment groups, eco-labeling, and fair trade initiatives all are trying to make a difference—but have so far failed to develop a larger potential via collaborative action. After the Marrakech Process (see below) was launched, NGOs created an online discussion forum to evaluate current developments of the international governmental community and to help promote their ideas of principles, practices, and policies concerning sustainable production and consumption. While NGOs clearly aim to increase their strength via transnational coalitions and coordination activities, their influence at the global level has thus far proven to be limited.

Academia

Scholars have also contributed much to the understanding of sustainable consumption. Importantly, current research addresses a whole range of sustainable consumption issues, including controversial questions of overconsumption and the need for changes in levels and patterns. Most notably in Europe, assessments of the willingness and ability of people to reduce their consumption have been the focus of numerous research efforts and collaborations. Unfortunately, few of the critical ideas raised by this research reach the official global sustainable consumption discourse. Some national and international agencies have assumed the role of a "translator" between politics and science in this respect; however, the results of such efforts have to date been rather poor. To improve this situation, the Sustainable Consumption Research Exchange (SCORE) network was established, which has tried to contribute knowledge and momentum to the 10-Year Framework of Programmes on the basis of a collaborative effort of scientists and NGO activists. Its success remains to be seen.

Business

The International Chamber of Commerce and the World Business Council for Sustainable Development issued a report dealing with the topic of sustainable consumption (WBCSD 2002). The report gave consumers the key role in shaping markets, thus placing responsibility firmly on the demand side rather than on the supply side. It identified increasing eco-efficiency as business's contribution to sustainable consumption, but clearly avoided any discussion of the role of business in driving and reducing overconsumption. The only additional responsibility the report attributed to business was to inform consumers about the social and environmental effects of their choices and to offer them appropriate options. A later report again analyzed sustainable consumption facts and trends from a business perspective and identified roles for consumers, businesses, NGOs, and governments (WBCSD 2008). Not surprisingly, according to this report, little responsibility for fundamental change rests with the business community.

The state of affairs

The central outcome of the last global summit on sustainable development, the WSSD in 2002, was the call for governments to "*encourage* and *promote* the development of a 10-year framework of programmes in support of regional and national initiatives to accelerate the shift towards sustainable consumption and production" (UN/WSSD 2002; emphasis added). This specification is vague and does not mention aspects of strong sustainable consumption. However, even this outcome has to be seen as a positive result in some respects. It was achieved only after long and controversial discussions about the inclusion of the issue of sustainable consumption in the plan of implementation (Barber 2003). Moreover, here the aspect of life-cycle analysis has been included in an approved UN document for the first time.

In 2003, the first major conference after Johannesburg, held in Marrakech, Morocco, launched the "Marrakech Process." This process is meant to support the elaboration and implementation of the 10-Year Framework of Programmes (10YFP). The goals of the Marrakech Process are divided into four areas: providing assistance to countries to develop sustainability; strengthening them to "green" their economies; developing sustainable business models; and encouraging consumers to make more sustainable consumption choices. A range of activities is taking place in the context of the Marrakech Process. UNEP and UNDESA are the leading agencies, and they decided that sustainable production and consumption would continue to appear as a cross-cutting issue in the CSD's 2004–17 Multi-Year Program of Work and that the 2010–11 cycle would additionally highlight the 10YFP as a thematic cluster. Several international and regional meetings have been held around the world since 2003 to foster the Marrakech Process. Nevertheless, these meetings have so far failed to provide substantial changes and served merely as platforms for the exchange of knowledge.

The Marrakech Process has shown major weaknesses already. There was much controversy over the architecture of an institution which could lead it, so it took five years to create an advisory committee, which was supposed to initiate and to develop the first official draft of the 10YFP. The framework draft considered as global objectives decoupling economic growth from environmental degradation, promoting more sustainable lifestyles, cities, and societies, and supporting regional and national sustainable consumption and production initiatives.

Could this be the beginning of a shift toward strong consumption governance? In the draft, the initiatives to promote sustainable consumption are voluntary rather than prescriptive. Every country can decide whether it will support the strategy of strong or weak sustainable consumption. Yet, in respect to the emerging world, especially to China and India, one can see that the increasing hunger for resources and energy should encourage the international community to find mandatory global (including the industrialized, developing, and emerging world) regulations to stop environmental degradation.

The framework draft will be continually enhanced until the year 2011 and will finally be discussed at the nineteenth session of the UN Commission on Sustainable Development. There is still a chance of a conceptual shift toward strong sustainable consumption, a starting point for real change. However, an evaluation of the progress that the Marrakech Process has made in the last five years does not inspire confidence. Unfortunately, past experience makes it difficult to believe in a successful transition to (strong) global sustainable consumption governance.

From the beginning, NGOs criticized the fact that the 10YFP was developed as part of the Johannesburg Plan of Implementation. Implementation was already requested in 2002, and the weak wording of the documents did not indicate any substantial progress. If such progress is to be achieved, the 10YFP has to forward a binding commitment to develop national policy frameworks on sustainable production and consumption. It also has to enable the development of legal frameworks and multilateral agreements to ensure that the actions taken indeed lead to sustainability in practice.

COPYRIGHTED MATERIAL — DO NOT DUPLICATE, DISTRIBUTE, OR POST

Obstacles to progress

In sum, weak sustainable consumption has received some attention, while strong sustainable consumption is almost entirely absent from global governance (Fuchs and Lorek 2005). Strong sustainable consumption exists only in marginal sectors of society and research or as a symbolic reminder in official documents. The activities of IGOs, in particular, have avoided strong sustainable consumption issues. How can this development be explained if strong sustainable consumption is after all a fundamental precondition for sustainable development? The answer to this question lies in the "weakness" of IGOs and the alignment of consumer and business interests against strong measures.

IGOs initially took on the issue of sustainable consumption as such but started to restrict their focus during the early phases of issue definition on account of its political sensitivity. They shied away from a more ambitious approach because strong measures would be highly unpopular with consumers in industrialized countries, with business, and, as a consequence, with governments. Contrary to frequent claims of the increasing environmental activism of consumers and the growth of corporate citizenship—which the more optimistic sustainable consumption literature cites as a source of much hope—the prospects for support for such strategies from consumers and business are rather weak.

As consumers are also voters, their opposition would reduce the inclination of governments to agree to appropriate international policy measures. Some scholars and practitioners proclaim a new awareness and interest among people in the environmental and social effects of consumption. Similarly, surveys tend to report a high ratio of consumers concerned about the impacts of their behavior. Yet environmental, social, or sustainability values are competing with a multitude of criteria in their influence on consumption decisions in real life (Jackson 2004; RØpke 1999). In the sum of global communications, "sustainability" messages are overpowered by opposing ones (Fuchs and Lorek 2002). In fact, there is ample evidence that sustainability criteria often rank low compared with competing aims. This is the case even when the question is just one of consuming a different product. When it comes to consuming less, the hurdle is even higher (Jackson 2005). In other words, while there is some indication of a willingness to move toward green consumption, there is little evidence of a fundamental change toward reducing consumption for sustainability objectives. Rather, consumption is proclaimed more than ever to be an individual right, allowing the expression of self, the pursuit of one's legitimate professional and social goals, and the opportunity to exercise freedom of choice.

Similar opposition to (strong) sustainable consumption governance exists in the business community. Most business actors tend to reject the notion that they carry any responsibility with respect to consumption levels. According to representatives of the business sector, the latter's role is to promote eco-efficiency. Some optimistic scholars and activists point out that business opposition to strong sustainable consumption governance does not necessarily have to be the case. They argue that business may earn its profits through, for instance, the selling of fewer but more expensive products with a higher profit margin. However, the ability of products to achieve distinction on the basis of quality irrespective of price is limited, as only a share of products can be marketed accordingly. Moreover, the globalized economy is characterized to a large extent by a high level of competition in mass markets and cheap products and correspondingly high pressures for externalization of social and environmental costs. Likewise, corporate social responsibility and related measures often proclaimed to signal the ethical turn in business conduct tend to perform badly when it comes to actual improvements. More importantly, these measures are unlikely to contribute to

COPYRIGHTED MATERIAL — DO NOT DUPLICATE, DISTRIBUTE, OR POST improvements in strong sustainable consumption. The only area in which business may be interested in fostering strong sustainable consumption is in the area of eco-efficient services—i.e. the purchase of a service instead of the ownership of a good—which actually involve a reduction in consumption levels (Michaelis 2003). However, eco-efficient services only provide an option in certain areas and are frequently not accepted by consumers.

Given this lack of consumer and business support for strong sustainable consumption governance, then, one should not expect too much activity in this respect on the part of governments or of IGOs, who in turn depend on their member governments. In addition, governments and IGOs themselves are still attached to the growth discourse and tend to want to foster consumption in order to encourage growth. Accordingly, they may sign up to continued efforts to increase eco-efficiency, but will not agree to or pass policies that seriously transform consumption patterns or reduce consumption levels.

Policy implications

What will the future of global sustainable consumption governance look like? Our analysis of developments to date has shown that some efforts to improve the efficiency of consumption exist. Thus, we can expect, for instance, policy proposals promoting efficient technologies for consumer products. However, a rather significant number of scholars argue that sustainable consumption can only be achieved if consumers in industrialized countries shift patterns and reduce levels. As our analysis has shown, hardly any progress has been made on these issues as a result of constraints imposed by the global political and economic setting. Moreover, the potential for future strong sustainable consumption efforts is limited. The alignment of consumer and business interests against such measures means that both IGOs and national governments (of industrialized countries) will continue to frame sustainability in terms of improvements in efficiency. In consequence, we should expect few policy proposals addressing consumption levels.

In this situation, political rather than policy recommendations are needed. The question is not how to design policies allowing further or maybe faster progress in sustainable consumption governance. The question has to be how a new area of governance can be opened up. For this, one of two developments would have to take place. First, the strengthening of relevant IGOs would potentially provide them with sufficient leeway to address strong sustainable consumption issues, even if they are controversial with consumers, business, and therefore governments. Such a strengthening could take place in the form of a change in institutional structure and competencies. The expansion of UNEP to a global environmental organization with broad expertise, sanctioning, and enforcement capacities similar to the WTO, which has repeatedly been discussed, would be one possibility in this context.

The strength of IGOs, however, is not just a function of their institutional structures and formal sanctioning and enforcement capacities; it is also a function of the willingness and ability of the individuals in the organization to provide leadership. While global governance scholars are correct in questioning exaggerated accounts of a general acquisition of "new" political capacities by IGOs, even those without such capacities can play important political roles. History has shown IGOs and/or the individuals leading them as effective agenda-setters and farsighted promoters of crucial policy initiatives. In fact, IGOs sometimes seek to justify their existence precisely by forcefully pursuing new societal visions and goals. The current lack of activities by IGOs on strong sustainable consumption governance, then, is not just a function of their lack of formal competencies, but also a question of ideational leadership. Therefore, a smaller but related institutional change, for example, could be the relocating of UNEP's sustainable consumption work away from the DTIE, with its traditional focus on industry, and its location higher up in the organizational hierarchy.

The second development that could potentially foster strong sustainable consumption governance is the adoption of new political strategies by relevant NGOs. Given the current alignment of interests against strong sustainable consumption, improved coalition-building of NGOs with academia and developing countries would be needed to provide some basis for political effectiveness. Moreover, such coalitions should make the question of organizational venues in IGOs (the relevance of which the above discussion demonstrated) part of their strategy. Clearly, coalitions between NGOs, academia, and developing countries would still face the problem of limited capacities. The strong sustainable consumption message would still have to compete with extensive advertising and consumption-inducing communication through the mass media. Moreover, NGOs and, increasingly, academic research do depend on public and financial support. Therefore, even some environmental NGOs and scholars convinced of the need to reduce consumption levels shy away from such a discussion. Despite all of these obstacles, however, such coalitions are likely to remain the only potentially significant driving force for strong sustainable consumption governance.

CURRENT RESEARCH DEVELOPMENTS

The research field of sustainable consumption and production has gained increasing attention over recent decades. It took some time to establish a firm link between consumption and sustainable development. But since the early 1990s sustainable consumption issues have acquired visibility and acceptance in environmental research. Concerns about unsustainable production processes were broadened to include those pertaining to misconsumption and overconsumption as well as the long-distance effects of what had been seen as local activities of societies.

One reason the field of sustainable consumption research is so vibrant and interesting at this point is the truly interdisciplinary nature of the topic. Such research receives contributions from a wide variety of disciplines, including political science, economics, sociology, anthropology, psychology, philosophy, and cultural studies, and focuses on a broad range of topics. Thus scholars are still trying to gain a better understanding of the determinants of consumer behavior. To this end, they try to identify different types of consumers and lifestyles in order to develop targeted strategies to reduce and change their patterns of consumption.

A second focus today is on the gap between knowledge/values on the one hand and action on the other (Lebel *et al.* 2006). Surveys show that most people believe that they can change environmental degradation by consuming less or in a different way. Moreover, they tend to report that their consumption decisions are influenced significantly by environmental criteria. However, there is a wide gap between this reported environmental consciousness and action as expressed in actual consumption decisions.

In addition, it is not only the consumer who is in charge of sustainable development. Put differently, consumption decisions are made under socio-economic, political, and temporal constraints (Røpke 1999). The structural contexts of the consumer environment strongly influence the characteristics of the available options for such decisions (Fuchs and Lorek 2002). In order to not overestimate the individual's responsibility and ability for change, sustainable consumption research has to take an integrated perspective and link consumer decisions to their societal environment as well as develop a joint production–consumption strategy.

Furthermore, sustainable consumption research is taking up the long-neglected question of the social dimension of sustainability. Retail food standards, for example, have the potential to improve environmental conditions as well as food safety in industrialized countries while threatening rural incomes in developing countries (Fuchs and Kalfagianni 2010). In consequence, research also has to pursue an integrated perspective.

Finally, of course, the question of how to improve the sustainability of consumption remains. Scholars thus continue to try to derive strategies against the background of the size of the task faced. After all, the objective is to change consumption levels and patterns of entire societies in the structural context of a system in which more tends to be viewed as better. Accordingly, scholars explore the potential of alliances between different political and societal actors as well as the availability of alternative models and lighthouse projects and their diffusion.

CONCLUSION

Sixteen years after the World Summit in Rio, progression toward the political pursuit of sustainable consumption is far from satisfactory. This chapter has highlighted more political weaknesses and obstacles than progress, and the future of sustainable consumption governance is still bleak. Meanwhile the pressure to achieve sustainable development through sustainable consumption and production is mounting because of climate change, environmental degradation, and continuing worldwide poverty.

Many reports, meetings, and/or frameworks were initiated and many actors are involved in the process, so there is hope that a change in sustainable consumption and production pplicy can be achieved. As mentioned above, IGOs could play a leading role in this context. They would have to push a global solution by overcoming national interests and by strengthening their power in global politics to achieve improvements. This, in turn, requires leadership.

As it applies to nearly every policy field, it is important that the approach of sustainable consumption governance is a global and integrated one, which is linked not only to environmental policy but also to economic and/or social policy. Moreover, it has to be an approach that makes strong sustainable consumption governance a central focus. Weak sustainable consumption governance found its way onto the international and national political agendas, but strong sustainable consumption governance is still neglected by most political actors. Without this, however, the international community will not be able to fulfill its responsibility for sustainable development.

NOTE

1. For a detailed discussion of the role of the various actors, see Fuchs and Lorek (2005).

RECOMMENDED READING

Dauvergne, P. (2008) *The Shadows of Consumption: Consequences for the Global Environment*, Cambridge, MA: MIT Press.

Jackson, T. (2006) *The Earthscan Reader in Sustainable Consumption*, London: Earthscan.

Princen, T. (2005) *The Logic of Sufficiency*, Cambridge, MA: MIT Press.

Worldwatch (2004) *State of the world 2004: Special Focus: The Consumer Society*, Washington, DC: Worldwatch Institute.

REFERENCES

Barber, J. (2003) "Production, consumption and the World Summit on Sustainable Development," *Environment, Development and Sustainability*, 5: 63–93.

Charkiewicz, E., Bennekom, S., and Young, A. (2001) *Transitions to Sustainable Production and Consumption: Concepts, Policies, and Actions*, The Hague: Tools for Transition.

Cohen, M. J., and Murphy, J. (2001) *Exploring Sustainable Consumption: Environmental Policy and the Social Sciences*, Oxford: Pergamon Press.

Durning, A. (1992) *How Much is Enough?* Washington, DC: Worldwatch Institute.

Eglitis, D. S. (2008) "Consumption," in *International Encyclopedia of the Social Sciences*, 2nd ed., Detroit: Thomson Gale.

Eurostat (2007) *Measuring Progress towards a More Sustainable Europe: Monitoring Report of the EU Sustainable Development Strategy*, Luxembourg: European Commission.

Fuchs, D., and Lorek, S. (2002) "Sustainable consumption governance in a globalizing world," *Global Environmental Politics*, 2(1): 19–45.

— (2005) "Sustainable consumption governance: a history of promises and failures," *Journal of Consumer Policy*, 28(3): 261–88.

Fuchs, D., and Kalfagianni, A. (2010) "Private food governance and implications for social sustainability and democratic legitimacy," in P. Utting and J. C. Marques (eds). *Business, Social Policy and Corporate Political Influence in Developing Countries*, New York: Palgrave Macmillan, pp. 225–47.

Georg, S. (1999) "The social shaping of household consumption," *Ecological Economics*, 28: 455–6.

Greening, L. A., Green, D. L., and Difiglio, C. (2000) "Energy efficiency and consumption—the rebound effect: a survey," *Energy Policy*, 28: 389–401.

Haake, J., and Jolivet, P. (2001) "The link between production and consumption for sustainable development," *International Journal of Sustainable Development*, 4(1) [special issue].

Jackson, T. (2004) *Motivating Sustainable Consumption: A Review of Evidence on Consumer Behaviour and Behavioural Change,* Guildford: University of Surrey, Centre for Environmental Strategy.

— (2005) "Live better by consuming less? Is there a 'double dividend' in sustainable consumption?," *Journal of Industrial Ecology,* 9(1): 19–36.

Lebel, L., Fuchs, D., Garden, P., Giap, D., *et al.* (2006) *Linking Knowledge and Action for Sustainable Production and Consumption Systems,* USER Working Paper WP-2006-09, Chiang Mai: Unit for Social and Environmental Research.

Lorek, S., and Spangenberg, J. H. (2001) "Indicators for environmentally sustainable household consumption," *International Journal of Sustainable Development,* 4: 101–20.

Michaelis, L. (2003) "The role of business in sustainable consumption," *Journal of Cleaner Production,* 11(8): 915–21.

Ministry of the Environment Norway (1995) *Report of the Oslo Ministerial Roundtable,* Oslo: Ministry of the Environment Norway.

OECD (2002) *Towards Sustainable Household Consumption? Trends and Policies in OECD Countries,* Paris: Organization for Economic Cooperation and Development.

Princen, T. (1999) "Consumption and environment: some conceptual issues," *Ecological Economics,* 31: 347–63.

Princen, T., Maniates, M., and Conca, K. (eds) (2002) *Confronting Consumption,* Cambridge, MA: MIT Press.

Røpke, I. (1999) "The dynamics of willingness to consume," *Ecological Economics,* 28: 399–420.

Schor, J. (1999) *The Overspent American: Why We Want What We Don't Need,* New York: Harper.

UN (1992) *Earth Summit: Agenda 21: The United Nations Programme of Action from Rio,* New York: United Nations.

UNDESA (1995) *International Work Programme on Changing Consumption and Production Patterns,* New York: United Nations.

— (2003) *United Nations Guidelines for Consumer Protection (as Expanded in 1999),* New York: United Nations.

UNEP (2001) *Consumption Opportunities: Strategies for Change,* Paris: United Nations.

— (2002) *A Global Status Report,* Paris: United Nations Environmental Programme.

UN/WSSD (2002) *Plan of Implementation,* New York: United Nations.

WBCSD (2002) *Sustainable Production and Consumption: A Business Perspective,* Geneva: World Business Council for Sustainable Development.

— (2008) *Sustainable Consumption Facts and Trends from a Business Perspective,* Geneva: World Business Council for Sustainable Development.

CONSUMER TOPIC 7.1: CAN WE SAVE THE PLANET?

Can Sustainable Consumers and Producers Save the Planet?

Mohan Munasinghe

Household consumption drives modern economies, but unsustainable consumption, production, and resource exploitation have led to multiple crises that threaten the future survival of humanity. Climate change is now considered the ultimate threat multiplier that will exacerbate the formidable problems of development we already face—such as poverty, hunger, illness, water and energy scarcities, and conflict.

The world is facing economic, social, and environmental risks, best characterized by a "bubble" metaphor based on greed and false expectations, whereby a few enjoy immediate gains and the vast, unsuspecting majority will pay huge future costs. These threats may interact catastrophically unless they are addressed urgently and in an integrated fashion.

ECONOMIC, SOCIAL, AND ENVIRONMENTAL BUBBLES

First, the ongoing economic recession was caused by the collapse of a greed-driven asset bubble that inflated financial values well beyond the true value of underlying economic resources. These "toxic" assets are estimated at about $100 trillion (twice the annual global gross domestic product [GDP]).

Second, a social bubble based on poverty and inequity is developing despite economic growth; billions of poor people are excluded from access to productive resources and basic necessities, such as food, water, and energy. Currently, 1.2 billion people in the top 20th percentile of the world's population by income consume almost 85% of global output, or 60 times more than the poorest 20th

Mohan Munasinghe, "Can Sustainable Consumers and Producers Save the Planet?" *Journal of Industrial Ecology* (Special Issue: Sustainable Consumption and Production), vol. 14, issue 1, pp. 4–6. Copyright © 2010 by John Wiley & Sons, Inc. Reprinted with permission.

percentile. Poverty is being exacerbated by the economic recession, worsening unemployment, and reduced access to survival needs.

Finally, humankind faces the bubble of environmental harm and resource shortages, due to myopic economic activities that severely degrade natural assets (air, land, and water) on which human well-being ultimately depends. Climate change is just one grim global manifestation of this threat, and, ironically, the worst impacts will fall on the poor, who are not responsible for the problem.

Unfortunately, human responses to these issues are uncoordinated and inadequate. Governments have quickly found more than $4 trillion dollars for stimulus packages to revive shaky economies. Meanwhile, only about $100 billion per year is devoted to alleviating poverty, and far less is directed to combating climate change. The recession is further dampening enthusiasm to address the more serious long-term poverty and climate issues.

Clearly, world leaders lost a major opportunity to allocate a much larger share of the stimulus packages to green investments, sustainable livelihoods, education and health, and safety nets for the poor, instead of mainly propping up banks and promoting unsustainable consumption. We should now seek to recoup the momentum for longer-term change by promoting sustainable consumption.

KEY ROLE OF SUSTAINABLE CONSUMPTION AND PRODUCTION

Anthropogenic carbon emissions exemplify modern resource overexploitation. The consumption of 1.2 billion richer humans accounts for some 75% of total emissions. Instead of viewing these consumers as part of the problem, we should persuade them to contribute to the solution. A recent report (Munasinghe et al. 2009) shows how to mobilize the power of sustainable consumers and producers.

Making consumption patterns more sustainable will reduce carbon emissions significantly (e.g., using energy-saving light bulbs, washing laundry at lower temperatures, eating less meat, planting trees, or using fuel efficient cars). Such actions not only save money but are also faster and more achievable than many so-called big technology solutions. Furthermore, families who purchase low-carbon products and services can stimulate innovation in businesses while encouraging politicians to take radical steps toward a lower carbon world. Many existing "best" practice examples can be replicated widely, and innovative businesses are already developing the future "next" practice products and services.

A "virtuous cycle" of mutually supportive sustainable consumption and production can cut across national boundaries and interests. It will complement the traditional top-down emphasis on action by governments that lack political will to take bold steps. Finally, the rich must not only help the many billions of poor to emerge from poverty but also set a better example that will encourage the latter to seek more sustainable consumption paths.

A Sustainable Consumption Institute launch meeting in October 2009, including political leaders, business leaders from the Consumer Goods Forum (an organization representing companies with an annual turnover that collectively approaches $1 trillion), and top academics, endorsed the report's findings. They pledged to overcome barriers faced by consumers, including the availability and affordability of low-carbon products, lack of information, and a sense of hopelessness. This was a welcome contrast to the continuing reluctance of world leaders to boldly address climate change issues at the Copenhagen summit.

SUSTAINOMICS

The sustainomics framework (Munasinghe 2009), originally proposed at the 1992 Rio Earth Summit, provides four core principles that underpin this novel approach to addressing climate change and sustainable development problems together.

- First, making development more sustainable (MDMS) becomes the main goal. This is a step-by-step method that empowers people to take immediate action. It is practical because many unsustainable activities are easy to recognize and eliminate. The sustainable consumption—production path epitomizes this approach.
- Second, the three key dimensions of the sustainable development triangle (economic, social, and environmental) must be given balanced treatment. Consumers need simplified and relevant information on these three aspects to make sustainable choices, through pricing, advertising, labeling, and the media.
- Third, our thinking should transcend traditional boundaries. It is essential to replace unsustainable values, such as greed, with sound moral principles, especially among the young. People must be made aware that problems such as climate change span the whole planet, play out over centuries, and concern every human being on earth. Stakeholders need to work together to meet the common threat—more than ever, government needs the support of civil society and business. Transdisciplinary analysis will help producers find innovative solutions that cut across conventional disciplines. SCP requires such a revolution in thinking and behavior.
- Finally, full life cycle analysis that uses integrated tools is required. In particular, producers need to reexamine the entire value chain, from raw material extraction to consumer end use and disposal, from the economic, social, and environmental perspectives. This will help identify weak areas where innovation can improve production sustainability, reform pricing, and yield accurate labeling information (e.g., carbon footprint). The principles of industrial ecology would help to minimize both resource inputs and waste outputs.

CONCLUDING IDEAS

Ordinary citizens and businesses are often ahead of political leaders in terms of willingness to address climate change and sustainable development issues. Given the many existing best practice examples, we do not need to wait for new technologies, laws, or infrastructure. Consumers can be encouraged to behave more sustainably without lowering their quality of life.

All human beings are stakeholders when it comes to sustainable development and climate change. Consumers and producers can and must strive to make development more sustainable—economically, socially, and environmentally. By acting together now, we will make the planet a better and safer place for our children and grandchildren.

REFERENCES

Munasinghe, M. 2009. *Sustainable development in practice: Sustainomics framework and applications.* Cambridge, UK: Cambridge University Press.

Munasinghe, M., P. Dasgupta, D. Southerton, A. Bows, and A. McMeekin. 2009. *Consumers, business and climate change.* Manchester, UK: Sustainable Consumption Institute, University of Manchester. www.sci.manchester.ac.uk/. Accessed December 2009.

ABOUT THE AUTHOR

Mohan Munasinghe is director general of the Sustainable Consumption Institute at the University of Manchester, in Manchester, United Kingdom; chairman of the Munasinghe Institute of Development (MIND), in Colombo, Sri Lanka; and co-winner of the 2007 Nobel Prize for Peace (vice chair, IPCC-AR4).

CASE STUDY

Did you know the primary cause of increases in Earth's temperature, how much of the water on Earth is considered fresh water, and what percentage of energy from gasoline in most conventional engines is used to move your car down the road? You are probably interested in being 'green;' but do you really know what 'green' means in your life? Do you know how your personal choices are adding up to your sustainable footprint? There is a multinational and longitudinal study about environmentally sustainable consumption. Take the following quiz and survey to assess your knowledge and your choices, also to learn what behaviors people are adopting globally that have a positive impact on environmental sustainability:

http://environment.nationalgeographic.com/environment/greendex/knowledge-quiz/
http://environment.nationalgeographic.com/environment/greendex/calculator/

CONSUMER RESOURCES:

Consumer Reports Greenchoices: http://www.greenerchoices.org/
Fair Trade Federation: http://www.fairtradefederation.org/
International Institute for Sustainable Development: http://www.iisd.org
Organic Consumers Association: http://www.organicconsumers.org
United Nations Environment Programme: http://www.unep.org
United States Environmental Protection Agency: http://www.epa.gov

CONSUMER RIGHTS: ISSUES AND CHALLENGES

The anthology *Consumer Rights: Issues and Challenges* contains cutting-edge research and critical reviews dealing with consumer economics. The material shows how an understanding of basic economics concepts and analytical tools can help consumers make sound financial decisions.

The reader is organized around issues confronting typical American consumers, such as advertising practices to beware of, tips for resolving consumer complaints, car loans vs. car leases, budgeting, and earning and maintaining a good credit score. Later chapters provide a different perspective on consumer choice by addressing topics such as consumers and sustainability, and globalization vs. localization.

For each topic students will learn about the macro-level research, as well as current research on consumers' decisions. A series of case studies tracing the life of a couple trying to appropriately allocate their financial resources and make economics decisions provides real-world examples of consumer choices and analysis of those choices.

Knowledgeable and practical, *Consumer Rights* is appropriate for upper level undergraduate courses in family and consumer sciences. It can also be used in general education courses focusing on becoming an informed consumer.

Yi Cai earned both his M.S. and his Ph.D. in housing and consumer economics from the University of Georgia. He is an associate professor of family and consumer sciences in the College of Health and Human Development at California State University, Northridge. Dr. Cai's teaching interests include consumer rights, consumer economics, family economics, and family financial issues. His primary research interests center on consumer behavior and financial literacy, specifically consumer on-line decision-making and behavior, financial risk tolerance, and the international perspective on financial planning and education.

cognella®
academic publishing

www.cognella.com   800-200-3908